Math to Know

A Mathematics Handbook

Mary C. Cavanagh

GReaT SouRCe

EDUCATION GROUP
A Houghton Mifflin Company

About the author Mary C. Cavanagh is currently the project coordinator for Math, Science, and Beyond at the Solana Beach School District in Solana Beach, CA.

Acknowledgments We gratefully acknowledge the following teachers and supervisors who helped make *Math to Know* a reality.

Senior Consultant:

Dr. Marsha W. Lilly
Secondary Mathematics Coordinator
Alief ISD
Alief, TX

C. Milton Burnett, Ed.D.
Administrator of Instruction
Peabody Public Schools
Peabody, MA

Lucile Demanski
Teacher
Warren Consolidated Schools
Warren, MI

Carole Halka
Mathematics Curriculum Specialist
Broward County School District
Ft. Lauderdale, FL

Marilyn LeRud
Retired Elementary Teacher
Tucson Unified School District
Tucson, AZ

Lance Menster
Math Specialist
Kennedy Elementary, Alief ISD
Houston, TX

Sharon Fields Simpson
Elementary Mathematics
  Curriculum Support Teacher
Cherry Creek Schools
Englewood, CO

Roberta M. Treinavicz
Instructional Resource Specialist
Hancock School
Brockton, MA

Writing: Fred Warshaw, Ann Petroni-McMullen, Kane Publishing Services, Inc.
Editorial: Carol DeBold, Justine Dunn; Arlene Grodkiewicz, Kane Publishing Services, Inc.;
    Edward Manfre, Susan Rogalski
Design Management: Richard Spencer
Production Management: Sandra Easton
Design and Production: Bill SMITH STUDIO
Marketing: Lisa Bingen
Illustration credits: see page 483

Printed in the United States of America.

International Standard Book Number -13: 978-0-669-53597-6 (hardcover)
International Standard Book Number -10: 0-669-53597-4 (hardcover)
2 3 4 5 6 7 8 9 0 RRDC 10 09 08 07

International Standard Book Number -13: 978-0-669-53596-9 (softcover)
International Standard Book Number -10: 0-669-53596-6 (softcover)
2 3 4 5 6 7 8 9 0 RRDC 10 09 08 07

Table of Contents

iv

Computing with Whole Numbers and Decimals

Fractions

Algebraic Thinking

Graphing, Statistics, and Probability

Geometry

Measurement

Problem Solving

Almanac 401

Yellow Pages

Index 474

How This Book Is Organized

Math to Know is a resource book. That means you're not expected to read it from cover to cover. Instead, you'll want to keep it handy for those times when you're not sure about a math topic and need a place to look up definitions, explanations, and rules.

This color tells you what major section of the book you're in. This page is from Computing with Whole Numbers and Decimals.

Each sub-section has its own table of contents.

Often you will find more than one way to get an answer.

These page numbers tell you where in the handbook you can go to get more help.

topic

sub-topic

example

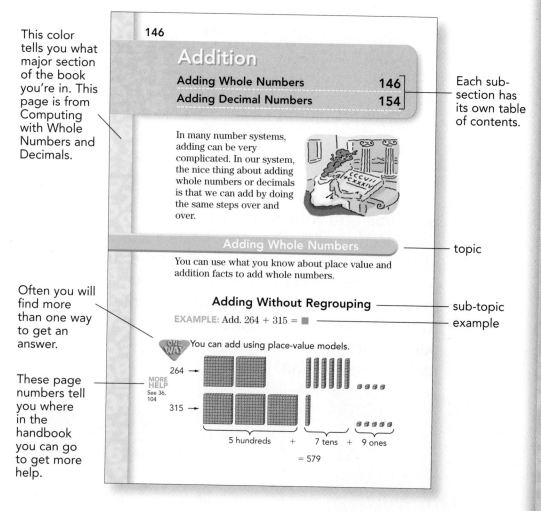

146

Addition

In many number systems, adding can be very complicated. In our system, the nice thing about adding whole numbers or decimals is that we can add by doing the same steps over and over.

Adding Whole Numbers

You can use what you know about place value and addition facts to add whole numbers.

Adding Without Regrouping

EXAMPLE: Add. 264 + 315 = ▓

ONE WAY You can add using place-value models.

MORE HELP
See 36, 104

264 →

315 →

5 hundreds + 7 tens + 9 ones

= 579

A good way to get started in this book is to thumb through the pages. Find these parts.

- **Table of Contents**
  This lists the major sections and sub-sections of the book.

- **Sections and Sub-Sections**
  Each section of the handbook has a short table of contents so you know what is in the section. Sections have several sub-sections and each of these also has its own short table of contents. Notice the color bars along the edges of the pages. Each section has a different color to make it easy to find.

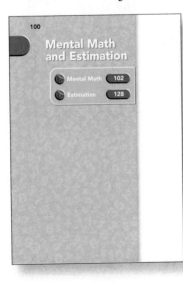

100

Mental Math and Estimation

Mental Math   102
Estimation   128

102

Mental Math

Mental Addition	102
Mental Subtraction	112
Mental Multiplication	118
Mental Division	126

Before you reach for a pencil or look for a calculator, think about whether you really need either.

In this section, you'll learn to do exercises like these in your head.

$$54 + 25 \qquad 64 - 39 \qquad 9 \times 18 \qquad 60 \div 5$$

When you compute in your head, you are doing **mental math.**

Mental Addition

You probably use mental math to add more often than you realize.

Suppose you have 19 rocks in your collection. Then you go on vacation and collect more rocks. You might use mental math to find how many rocks you now have in your collection.

- **Almanac**
  This includes some very helpful tables and lists. It also has hints on how to study, take a test, and use a calculator. Check out all the Almanac entries — you will want to refer to them often.

- **Yellow Pages**
  This part of the handbook has two glossaries. There is a Glossary of Mathematical Terms and a Glossary of Mathematical Symbols. You will find terms and math symbols that your teacher and textbook use.

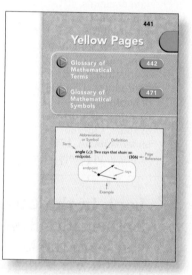

- **Index**
  This is at the very end of the book.

How to Use This Book

There are three ways to find information about the topics in which you are interested.

① Look in the Index.

We listed topics in the Index using any word we thought you might use to describe the topic. For example, you will find "Estimating Sums" under "Estimation" and under "Addition."

② Look in the Glossary.

Mathematics has a language all its own. Once you learn the language, the rest is much easier. Turn to this part of the book whenever you see a word you don't know.

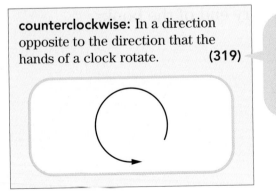

counterclockwise: In a direction opposite to the direction that the hands of a clock rotate.　(319)

Most Glossary entries will give you a page number to go to if you want more information.

③ Look in the Table of Contents.

All the major topics covered in this book are listed in the Table of Contents. If you're looking for a general topic, like Measurement, the Table of Contents is a quick way to find it.

Section (If you want to browse through lots of related topics, start here.)

Sub-section (If you want to browse, but narrow your search, start here.)

Place Value

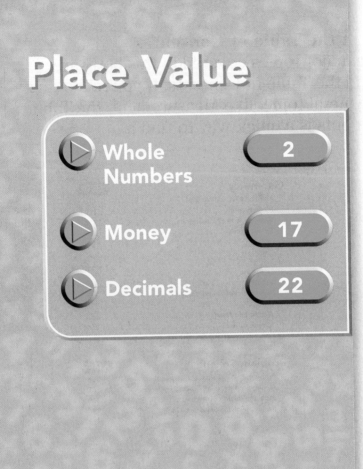

It's /////////
minutes to
///////////.

Without an easy way of writing numbers,
digital watches would be huge!

Imagine you did not have an easy way to write numbers. Suppose you had to write 29 by making 29 marks, like this: ////////////////////////////////.

Calendars and clocks would sure be confusing. Page numbers in books would be confusing, too.

Lucky for us, there is a shorter way to write numbers. You can write numbers large enough to show how many pages are in this book, how many pages are in the whole library, or even how many pages are in the whole world. You can also write numbers tiny enough to show how thin an eyelash is or how much a snowflake weighs.

What's more amazing is that you can do all that with only ten symbols (0, 1, 2, 3, 4, 5, 6, 7, 8, and 9).

Whole Numbers

What are **whole numbers**? They are 0, 1, 2, 3, 4, 5, 6, and so on. Whole numbers can be used to count things, but not parts of things.

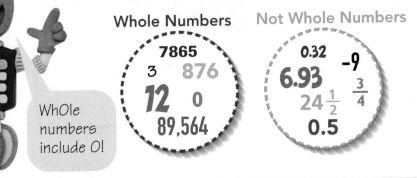

Whole Numbers

7865
3   876
12   0
89,564

Not Whole Numbers

0.32
6.93   -9
24 $\frac{1}{2}$ $\frac{3}{4}$
0.5

WhOle numbers include O!

Place Value: Whole Numbers

Our whole-number system is based on a simple pattern of tens. Each place has ten times the value of the place to its right.

The symbols 0, 1, 2, 3, 4, 5, 6, 7, 8, and 9 are called **digits**. They can be used to write any whole number. **Place value** tells you how much each digit stands for.

Models for Tens and Ones

You can use tens and ones models to show place value for 2-digit numbers.

EXAMPLE: In the number 23, the 2 stands for 2 tens and the 3 stands for 3 ones. Show 23 using models.

Think: 2 tens + 3 ones

ONE WAY You can use bundles of sticks.

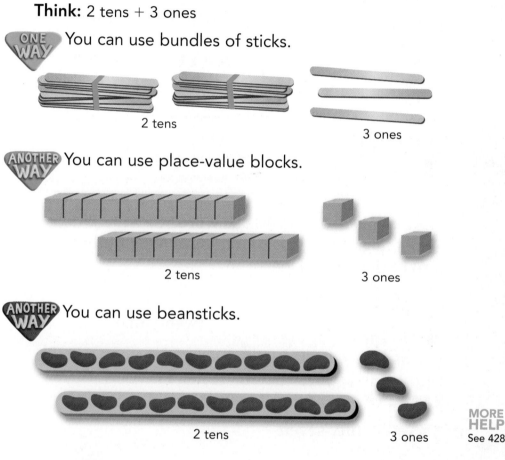

2 tens

3 ones

ANOTHER WAY You can use place-value blocks.

2 tens

3 ones

ANOTHER WAY You can use beansticks.

2 tens

3 ones

MORE HELP See 428

Write: 23

Say: *twenty-three*

Writing Whole Numbers to 99

You can use words instead of digits to write any number. It is longer to use words, but it shows how we say the number. Here are some numbers both ways, with digits and with words.

0 zero	10 ten	20 twenty	30 thirty
1 one	11 eleven	21 twenty-one	40 forty
2 two	12 twelve	22 twenty-two	50 fifty
3 three	13 thirteen	23 twenty-three	60 sixty
4 four	14 fourteen	24 twenty-four	70 seventy
5 five	15 fifteen	25 twenty-five	80 eighty
6 six	16 sixteen	26 twenty-six	90 ninety
7 seven	17 seventeen	27 twenty-seven	
8 eight	18 eighteen	28 twenty-eight	
9 nine	19 nineteen	29 twenty-nine	

Use a hyphen when you use words to write 2-digit numbers greater than 20 that have a digit other than zero in the ones place.

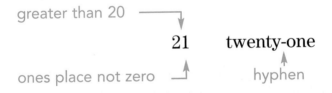

EXAMPLE 1: Write 57 in words.

★ ANSWER: fifty-seven

EXAMPLE 2: Write 80 in words.

★ ANSWER: eighty

Place Value: Hundreds, Tens, and Ones

Count by ones. The next number in this pattern is 100.

97, 98, 99, ■

You can use models for hundreds, tens, and ones to show any 3-digit number. A **place-value chart** tells you how many hundreds, tens, and ones to use.

This is a model for 100.

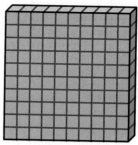

1 hundred

MORE
HELP
See 429

EXAMPLE 1: A supermarket has 258 boxes of cereal on its shelves. Show 258 using a place-value chart and models.

★ **ANSWER:**

Hundreds	Tens	Ones
2	5	8

2 hundreds   5 tens   8 ones

EXAMPLE 2: The supermarket has 285 jars of peanut butter. Show 285 using a place-value chart and models.

★ **ANSWER:**

Hundreds	Tens	Ones
2	8	5

2 hundreds   8 tens   5 ones

Did you notice that both numbers have the same digits but in different orders?

Place Value Through Thousands

You can use place-value models to help you understand greater numbers.

1 thousand is 10 times 1 hundred.	1 hundred is 10 times 1 ten.	1 ten is 10 times 1 one.

Take a ride on the Mean Streak Roller Coaster at Cedar Point Amusement Park in Ohio. You'll go up, down, and around as you travel 5427 feet.

Source: www.rollercoaster.com

The place-value models below show the length of the roller coaster track (in feet).

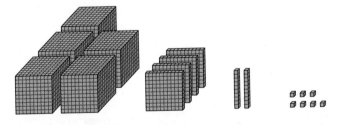

Think: 5 thousands + 4 hundreds + 2 tens + 7 ones

Thousands	Hundreds	Tens	Ones
5	4	2	7

Write: 5427 or 5,427

Say: *five thousand, four hundred twenty-seven*

A four-digit number may be written with or without a comma.

MATH
ALERT

Don't Forget About Zeros

There is a big mistake in my store's ad. I asked that you show the flat screen TV on sale for one thousand thirty dollars.

Zeros may stand for nothing, but that doesn't mean you can leave them out. They keep other digits in the correct places.

Hundreds	Tens	Ones
1	0	3

Think: 1 hundred + 0 tens + 3 ones

Write: 103

Say: *one hundred three*

Thousands	Hundreds	Tens	Ones
1	0	3	0

Think: 1 thousand + 0 hundreds + 3 tens + 0 ones

Write: 1030 or 1,030

Say: *one thousand, thirty*

A Model For One Million

Try to imagine one million marbles. These pictures may help.

The jar holds one thousand marbles.	1000	
The box holds 10 jars. It has 10 times one thousand or ten thousand marbles.	10,000	
The carton holds 10 boxes. It has 10 times ten thousand or one hundred thousand marbles.	100,000	
The crate holds 10 cartons. It has 10 times one hundred thousand or one million marbles.	1,000,000	

MORE HELP See 9

1,000,000		
1,000,000 10 hundred thousands	1,000,000 100 ten thousands	1,000,000 1000 thousands

Place Value Through Millions

Earth is not always the same distance from the Sun. As Earth revolves around the Sun, sometimes it's closer and sometimes it's farther away.

The number in this place-value chart shows the closest distance (in miles) Earth can be to the Sun.

Millions Period			Thousands Period			Ones Period		
Hundreds	Tens	Ones	Hundreds	Tens	Ones	Hundreds	Tens	Ones
	9	1	4	0	2	6	0	0

Source: World Book Encyclopedia

The digits in large numbers are in groups of three places. (You remember the hundreds, tens, and ones places.) The groups are called **periods**. Commas are usually used to separate the periods.

Write: 91,402,600

EXAMPLE: What is the value of the digit **4** in 91,402,600?

★ ANSWER: The digit **4** is in the hundred thousands place. Its value is **4** hundred thousand, or 400,000.

DID YOU KNOW...

that the farthest Earth gets from the Sun is 94,509,200 miles? Source: World Book Encyclopedia

Reading Large Numbers

Reading large numbers is easier than it looks.
You only need to know

- how to read 3-digit numbers, and
- the names of the periods.

In 1967, London Bridge was bought by an American man for $2,469,600. It now stands in Lake Havasu City, Arizona.

EXAMPLE: How do you read 2,469,600?

Millions Period			Thousands Period			Ones Period		
Hundreds	Tens	Ones	Hundreds	Tens	Ones	Hundreds	Tens	Ones
		2	4	6	9	6	0	0

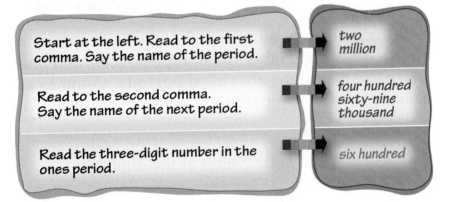

Start at the left. Read to the first comma. Say the name of the period.	two million
Read to the second comma. Say the name of the next period.	four hundred sixty-nine thousand
Read the three-digit number in the ones period.	six hundred

You don't say the name of the ones period.

★ **ANSWER: Say:** *two million, four hundred sixty-nine thousand, six hundred*

"And" Is for Decimals— Not Whole Numbers

When you read a whole number, don't say the word **and**. Use **and** only when you read a decimal point.

Write: 905

Say: *nine hundred five*
(***not*** *nine hundred and five*)

Write: 900.5

Say: *nine hundred*
and *five tenths*

MORE
HELP
See 25

Very Large Numbers

When you study our universe, you will come across very large numbers. For example, the Sun is only one of 200,000,000,000 stars in our galaxy.

Source: kids.infoplease.com

Period Name						
Quintillions	Quadrillions	Trillions	Billions	Millions	Thousands	Ones
			200	000	000	000
		96	000	000	000	000
	20	000	000	000	000	000
14	000	000	000	000	000	000

Write:
200,000,000,000
96,000,000,000,000
20,000,000,000,000,000
14,000,000,000,000,000,000

Say:
two hundred billion
ninety-six trillion
twenty quadrillion
fourteen quintillion

Comparing Whole Numbers

EXAMPLE 1: Jim and Mosi collect animal cards. Jim has collected 28 cards. Mosi has 35 cards in his collection. Who has more animal cards, Jim or Mosi?

ONE WAY You can compare numbers using models.

28   35

It takes more sticks to model 35 than 28. So 35 is greater than 28.

You can write the comparison using the symbols < or >. The mouth of the symbol is open to the greater number.

The hungry hippo always eats the bigger portion.

Write:	Say:
35 > 28	35 **is greater than** 28.
28 < 35	28 **is less than** 35.

ANOTHER WAY You can use a number line.

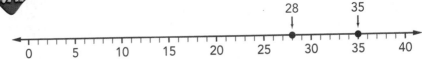

Think: 35 is to the right of 28 on the number line. So, 35 is greater than 28 (35 > 28) and 28 is less than 35 (28 < 35).

★ **ANSWER:** Either way, Mosi has more animal cards.

ANOTHER WAY You can also use what you know about place value to compare two numbers.

EXAMPLE 2: Reggie Jackson hit 563 home runs during his baseball career. Ted Williams hit 521 home runs during his career. Who hit more career home runs? *Source: cnnsi.com*

❶ Line up the place values by lining up the ones.	❷ Begin with the greatest place. Find the first place where the digits are different.	❸ Compare the value of the digits in that place.
563 521	563 521 ↑↑ ⎺⎺ different same	60 is greater than 20. So, 563 > 521.

⭐ **ANSWER:** Reggie Jackson hit more career home runs.

MATH ALERT

Lining Up by Place Value

Be careful when you compare numbers that don't have the same number of digits. Make sure you line up the ones places.

Suppose you want to compare 1246 and 896.

Lined up correctly at the ones place

Lined up incorrectly

When one whole number has more digits than another, it is greater. So, 1246 > 896.

1246
896

🚫 1246
896

Ordering Whole Numbers

It's easier to work with a group of numbers if they are in order. Order can be from greatest to least, or from least to greatest.

ONE WAY You can find each number on a number line to see the order.

EXAMPLE 1: Order the numbers from least to greatest. Then order the numbers from greatest to least.

Average Animal Life Spans	
Animal	Years
Cow	11
Kangaroo	5
Horse	22

Source: Time for Kids
Almanac, 2006

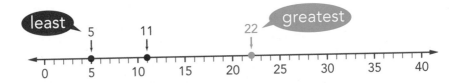

★ **ANSWER:** The order of the numbers from least to greatest is: 5, 11, 22.

To order the numbers from greatest to least, reverse the order of the list.

★ **ANSWER:** The order of the numbers from greatest to least is: 22, 11, 5.

DID YOU KNOW...

that humans and tortoises may be the only well-known animals with life spans of more than 60 years? (Some bacteria and plants far outlive all animals.)

If you know how to compare numbers, you know how to put a group of numbers in order.

EXAMPLE 2: Order the heights from the greatest number of feet to the least.

MORE HELP

See 12–13

Heights of Tall Buildings	
Building	**Height (in feet)**
John Hancock Center Chicago, Illinois	1127
USX Tower Pittsburgh, Pennsylvania	841
Patronas Towers Kuala Lampour, Malaysia	1483

Source: www.infoplease.com

❶ Line up the numbers at the ones place.	❷ Begin to compare at the greatest place.		❸ Compare the remaining numbers. Find the first place where the digits are different.	
1127 841 1483	1127 841 1483	841 is the least because it has the fewest digits.	1127 1483	400 is greater than 100. So, 1483 > 1127.

⭐ **ANSWER:** The order of the heights from greatest to least number of feet is: 1483, 1127, 841.

Ordinal Numbers

You can use **ordinal numbers** to tell you the position of people or things that are in order.

EXAMPLE: Who is the fifth person in line?

Count from the beginning of the line.

Erica is	Ayo is	Kyle is	Isamu is	Maria is
1st.	**2nd.**	**3rd.**	**4th.**	**5th.**

★ **ANSWER:** Maria is the fifth person in line.

You can write an ordinal number for any whole number. Here are some examples.

Ordinal Numbers			
With Digits and Letters	**In Words**	**With Digits and Letters**	**In Words**
1st	first	8th	eighth
2nd	second	9th	ninth
3rd	third	10th	tenth
4th	fourth	20th	twentieth
5th	fifth	25th	twenty-fifth
6th	sixth	31st	thirty-first
7th	seventh	100th	one hundredth

Money

Since ancient times, people have used **money** to make it easier to buy what they needed or wanted. Before money, people traded. For example, a person might trade 10 bags of beans for a pig.

U.S. Coins and Bills

U. S. coins and bills are based on ones, fives, and tens, which make them easy to count. The **dollar** is the basic unit.

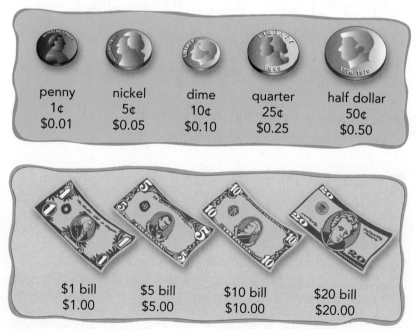

penny	nickel	dime	quarter	half dollar
1¢	5¢	10¢	25¢	50¢
$0.01	$0.05	$0.10	$0.25	$0.50

$1 bill	$5 bill	$10 bill	$20 bill
$1.00	$5.00	$10.00	$20.00

Write: 25¢ or $0.25
Say: *twenty-five cents*

Write: $5.00
Say: *five dollars*

People have different ways to count money. Many people count on from the bill or coin that is worth the most.

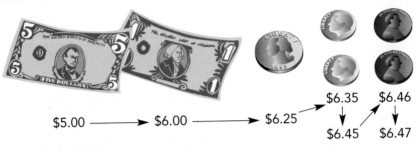

$5.00 ⟶ $6.00 ⟶ $6.25

$6.35 $6.46

$6.45 $6.47

You may have a lot of different bills and coins to count. It helps to sort them.

EXAMPLE: Franklin has these bills and coins. How much money does he have?

 You can sort the bills and coins by value. Then add to find the total amount.

1 Make a pile for each type of bill or coin.

MORE
HELP
See 158

2 Find the value of each pile. Then add all the values.

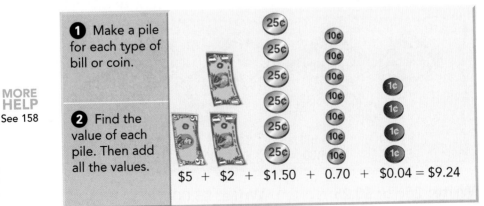

$5 + $2 + $1.50 + 0.70 + $0.04 = $9.24

ANOTHER WAY You can group the coins into one-dollar piles and count them. Then count on.

❶ Sort the bills. Count them from the greatest to the least value.	$5 $6 $7
❷ Group the coins into 1-dollar piles. Count the 1-dollar piles. Then count the coins that are left.	25¢ 25¢ 10¢ 10¢ 25¢ 25¢ 10¢ 10¢ 10¢ 1¢ 1¢ 25¢ 25¢ 10¢ 10¢ 1¢ 1¢ $8.00 $9.00 $9.10 $9.21 $9.20 $9.22 $9.23 $9.24

⭐ **ANSWER:** Either way, Franklin has $9.24.

Write: $9.24

Say: *nine dollars* and *twenty-four cents*

> Remember to say "and" when you read the decimal point.

MATH ALERT

$ and ¢ Do Not Go Together

Don't write $ when you mean ¢, and don't write ¢ when you mean $.

Correct	Not correct
47¢	$0.47¢
or	or
$0.47	0.47¢

Making Change

Cashiers receive money from customers. If the amount they receive is more than the customer owes, they need to give the customer **change.** A cash register makes this job easier because it figures out what the change should be.

ONE WAY Subtract to find the amount of change.

MORE HELP
See 171

EXAMPLE 1: Jenny and her family order food that costs $25.46. She hands the cashier a 20-dollar bill and a 10-dollar bill. The cashier enters "30.00" into the cash register.

The cash register subtracts the amount owed ($25.46) from the amount paid ($30.00).

$$\begin{array}{r} \$30.00 \\ -25.46 \\ \hline \$4.54 \end{array}$$

The cashier counts out the total amount she has given, as she hands out each bill or coin. She begins with the greatest value bill and ends with the least value coin.

Say: $1, $2, $3, $4, $4.25, $4.50, $4.51, $4.52, $4.53, $4.54

Some cashiers do not have a cash register to do the work for them. They need to know how to make change correctly.

ANOTHER WAY The most common way to count change is to count up.

EXAMPLE 2: Vern buys a T-shirt for $7.25. The total cost, including tax, is $7.83. He pays with a 10-dollar bill. How much change should he receive?

1 Begin by saying the amount owed.	$7.83
2 Count up from the amount owed. Use coins to get to the next dollar.	$7.83 → $7.84, $7.85, $7.90, $8.00 〈1¢〉 〈1¢〉 〈5¢〉 〈10¢〉
3 Count up with bills to reach the amount paid.	$8.00 → $9.00, $10.00

★ **ANSWER:** Vern should receive $2.17 in change.

DID YOU KNOW...

that cashiers usually place the bills they are handed on top of the cash register drawer? The cashier counts out the change and the customer checks that it is correct. Then the cashier puts the bills into the drawer.

Decimals

When you write some numbers, you use a dot, called a **decimal point,** to separate the whole number part from the part less than one. Numbers that are written with a decimal point are called **decimals**.

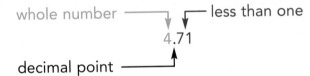

whole number ⎯⎯⎯⎯ less than one

4.71

decimal point ⎯⎯⎯⎯

Dollar signs and decimal points are used to write money amounts. Think of 1 dollar as a whole.

whole number of dollars ⎯⎯⎯ less than one dollar

$4.71

decimal point ⎯⎯⎯⎯

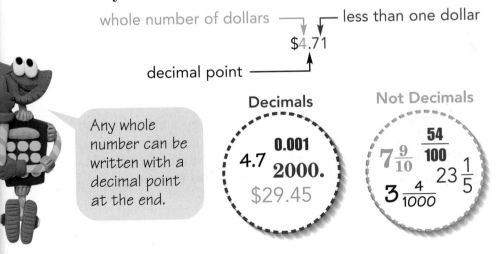

Any whole number can be written with a decimal point at the end.

Decimals

4.7   0.001   2000. $29.45

Not Decimals

$7\frac{9}{10}$ $\frac{54}{100}$ $23\frac{1}{5}$ $3\frac{4}{1000}$

Decimals: Place Value

Decimals follow the same place-value pattern as whole numbers. No matter what place you are looking at, its value is ten times the value of the place to its right.

Models for Ones, Tenths, and Hundredths

ONE WAY One way to help you understand decimals and their place value is to think of money.

    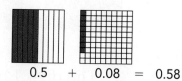

1 dollar   +   0.1 dollar   +   0.01 dollar   = $1.11

ANOTHER WAY You can also use models to show ones, tenths, and hundredths.

1   +   0.1   +   0.01   =   1.11

Write: 1.11

Say: *one and eleven hundredths*

0.6

0.5   +   0.08   =   0.58

Write: 0.6

Say: *six tenths*

Write: 0.58

Say: *fifty-eight hundredths*

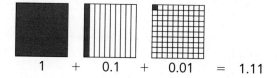

Since each number is less than one, there is a 0 in the ones place.

Decimals: Place-Value Chart

Honolulu, Hawaii has an average rainfall for April of 1.54 inches. *Source: www.nws.noaa.gov*

You can use a place-value chart to help understand the value of each digit.

EXAMPLE: What is the value of each digit in 1.54?

Tens	Ones		Tenths	Hundredths
	1	.	5	4

Think of the models.

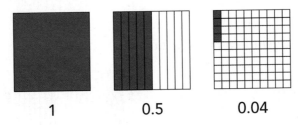

| 1 | 0.5 | 0.04 |

⭐ **ANSWER:** The digit 1 has a value of 1.

The digit 5 has a value of 5 tenths.

The digit 4 has a value of 4 hundredths.

Reading and Writing Decimals

Canadian speed skater,
Catriona Le-May Doan
set the world record for
500 meters in Calgary,
Canada, on December
9, 2001. She skated the
500 meters in 37.22
seconds.

Source: www.infoplease.com

EXAMPLE: Read Catriona's
world record time, in seconds.

Tens	Ones		Tenths	Hundredths
3	7	.	2	2

> The name of every decimal place ends with *ths*.

To read a decimal:

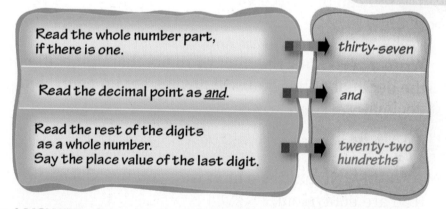

Read the whole number part, if there is one.	thirty-seven
Read the decimal point as *and*.	and
Read the rest of the digits as a whole number. Say the place value of the last digit.	twenty-two hundreths

⭐ **ANSWER: Say:** *thirty-seven and twenty-two hundredths*

When you write a decimal number greater than one,
listen for the word *and*. It tells you where to place
the decimal point.

Say: *five hundred and thirteen hundredths*

Write: 500.13

Equivalent Decimals

Decimals that have the same value are called **equivalent decimals**.

EXAMPLE: Write a decimal equivalent to 0.3.

ONE WAY You can use models.

0.3 (three tenths) of the square is red.

0.30 (thirty hundredths) of the square is red.

ANOTHER WAY You can use number lines.

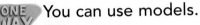

0.0 0.1 0.2 0.3 0.4 0.5 0.6 0.7 0.8 0.9 1.0

0.00 0.10 0.20 0.30 0.40 0.50 0.60 0.70 0.80 0.90 1.00

ANOTHER WAY You can use place value.

Write a zero after the digit or digits that come after the decimal point. You will always get an equivalent decimal.

0.3 = 0.30

Don't add a zero to a whole number part. 3 does not equal 30!

⭐ **ANSWER:** No matter which way you use, 0.3 and 0.30 are equivalent.

Write: 0.3 = 0.30

Say: *Three tenths is equal to thirty hundredths.*

"=" can mean "is equal to" or "is equivalent to."

Comparing Decimals

Comparing decimals is like comparing whole numbers.

EXAMPLE: During a track and field long-jump event, Kim jumped 1.7 meters. Jamila jumped 1.56 meters. Who jumped farther?

MORE HELP
See 12–13

 You can use a number line.

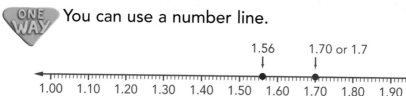

Write $1.7 > 1.56$

Say: *One and seven tenths is greater than one and fifty-six hundredths.*

 You can use models.

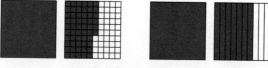

$1.56 < 1.7$

 You can use place value.

❶ Line up the decimal points. Write zero to make an equal number of decimal places.	❷ Begin at the greatest place. Find the first place where the digits are different.	❸ Compare the values of the digits.
1.70 1.56	1.70 1.56	0.7 is greater than 0.5. So, 1.70 > 1.56.

MORE HELP
See 26

⭐ **ANSWER:** No matter which way you use, Kim jumped farther.

Always Look at the Whole Number Parts First!

Be careful when you compare decimals. If the whole number parts are different, you don't need to compare the decimal parts. The decimal with the greater whole number part is always greater.

5.2 is greater than 4.86 because 5 is greater than 4.

Sometimes Greater Isn't Better!

When you run a race, the faster time wins. So, the lower number, not the greater number, is better.

LaToya's time of 48.65 seconds is less than Sarah's time of 49.10 seconds. LaToya wins the race.

Ordering Decimals

If you know how to compare two decimals, you will be able to order a group of decimals.

EXAMPLE: Luis measured the movements of a snail for a science project. Order the distances the snail moved from greatest to least.

MORE HELP
See 14–15

Time	First Hour	Second Hour	Third Hour
Distance	0.25 meter	0.23 meter	0.31 meter

ONE WAY You can use a number line.

least 0.23   0.31 greatest
0.25

0.00   0.05   0.10   0.15   0.20   0.25   0.30   0.35   0.40

ANOTHER WAY You can use place value.

❶ Line up the decimal points.	❷ Begin at the greatest place. Find the first place where the digits are different.		❸ Compare the values of the remaining digits.	
0.25 0.23 0.31	0.25 0.23 0.31	0.3 is greater than 0.2. So, 0.31 is the greatest.	0.25 0.23	0.03 is less than 0.05. So, 0.23 is the least.

★ **ANSWER:** Either way, the order of the distances from greatest to least is 0.31 meter, 0.25 meter, 0.23 meter.

You can write a decimal as a fraction. The denominator will be a multiple of ten, such as 10 or 100.

MORE
HELP
See 90,
210

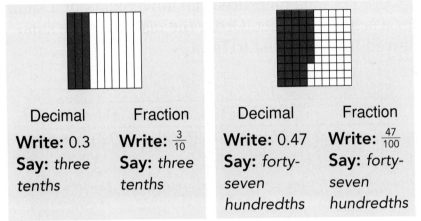

Decimal	Fraction	Decimal	Fraction
Write: 0.3	**Write:** $\frac{3}{10}$	**Write:** 0.47	**Write:** $\frac{47}{100}$
Say: *three tenths*	**Say:** *three tenths*	**Say:** *forty-seven hundredths*	**Say:** *forty-seven hundredths*

After you write a decimal as a fraction, you can sometimes write other fractions that name the same amount.

MORE
HELP
See
220–221

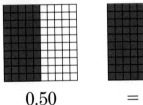 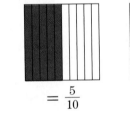 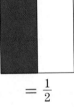

0.50 $= \frac{50}{100}$ $= \frac{5}{10}$ $= \frac{1}{2}$

Sometimes it is easier to think of a number as a fraction. Here are some examples of other decimals written as fractions.

Decimal	Fraction
0.01	$\frac{1}{100}$
0.1	$\frac{1}{10}$
0.25	$\frac{25}{100}$ or $\frac{1}{4}$
0.75	$\frac{75}{100}$ or $\frac{3}{4}$

Decimals and Percents

The word **percent** means *per hundred*. So, 0.30 and $\frac{30}{100}$ and 30% are all ways of naming the same amount.

Decimal	Percent
Write: 0.30	**Write:** 30%
Say: *thirty hundredths*	**Say:** *thirty percent*

Decimal	Percent
Write: 0.47	**Write:** 47%
Say: *forty-seven hundredths*	**Say:** *forty-seven percent*

Here are some other examples of decimals written as percents.

Decimal	Percent
0.01	1%
0.1 or 0.10	10%
0.25	25%
0.5 or 0.50	50%
0.75	75%
1.00	100%

Fifty of the 100 students in the fourth grade are boys. That means that 50% of the students are boys.

Basic Operations

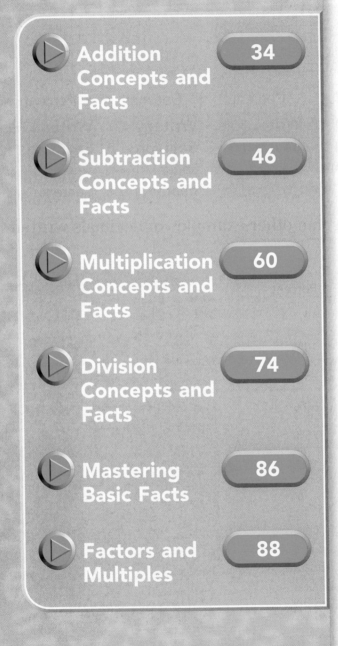

There's something special about the fact that 3 plus 4 is 7. It's true for muffins. It works with dollars and it works with dolls. You can use it with minutes, with hours, with days, and with years. This happens with other facts, too, like $5 - 3 = 2$, $3 \times 4 = 12$, and $8 \div 4 = 2$. Over and over, thousands of times in your life, these basic facts will come in handy.

Do you want to see how to remember and use these facts? Well, you're in the right section. Here, too, you can check out the meaning of the four basic operations: addition, subtraction, multiplication, and division. There's a lot of basic stuff here for you. And that's a fact.

Addition Concepts and Facts

Knowing when and how to **add** whole numbers is a basic skill in mathematics.

Uses for Addition

Let's look at some times when you might want to use addition.

Case 1 You can add to join one amount to another amount.

Case 2 You can add to combine two parts to find the whole amount.

Case 3 When you know one amount and you know how many more are needed to make another amount, you can add to find that other amount.

Addition Words and Symbols

When we talk about addition, it helps if we all use the same words. Numbers to be added are **addends**. When you add two or more addends, the result is called the **sum**. The symbol for addition is the **plus sign**, or the **addition sign (+)**.

You can write numbers in a stack to add them.

$$\begin{array}{r} 9 \\ + 5 \\ \hline 14 \end{array} \quad \text{addends} \quad \begin{array}{r} 5 \\ 4 \\ + 6 \\ \hline 15 \end{array}$$

addends ← → sum

You can also write addition as an **addition sentence**. Write the addends in a row with an addition sign between each. An **equals sign (=)** separates the addends from the sum.

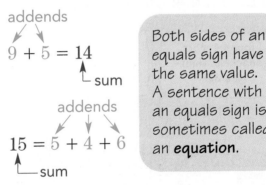

addends

$9 + 5 = 14$

└ sum

addends

$15 = 5 + 4 + 6$

└ sum

Both sides of an equals sign have the same value. A sentence with an equals sign is sometimes called an **equation**.

No matter which way you show addition, you read it the same way.

Write: $5 + 4 + 6 = 15$ or

$$\begin{array}{r} 5 \\ 4 \\ + 6 \\ \hline 15 \end{array}$$

Say: *Five plus four plus six equals fifteen.*

Using an Addition Table

You can use an **addition table** to find the sum of any two 1-digit numbers.

Addition Table										
+	**0**	**1**	**2**	**3**	**4**	**5**	**6**	**7**	**8**	**9**
0	0	1	2	3	4	5	6	7	8	9
1	1	2	3	4	5	6	7	8	9	10
2	2	3	4	5	6	7	8	9	10	11
3	3	4	5	6	7	8	9	10	11	12
4	4	5	6	7	8	9	10	11	12	13
5	5	6	7	8	9	10	11	12	13	14
6	6	7	8	9	10	11	12	13	14	15
7	7	8	9	10	11	12	13	14	15	16
8	8	9	10	11	12	13	14	15	16	17
9	9	10	11	12	13	14	15	16	17	18

EXAMPLE: Use the addition table to find this sum.
$7 + 8 = \blacksquare$

- Find the column labeled *7*. It is shaded blue.
- Find the row labeled *8*. It is shaded yellow.
- The sum is in the green box where the column and row meet.

★ **ANSWER:** $7 + 8 = 15$

Other Ways to Add

There are many ways to find a sum. Use the way that works best for you.

EXAMPLE: Jessie has two fish bowls. He has 8 goldfish in one bowl and 6 goldfish in the other bowl. How many goldfish does Jessie have?

To solve this problem, you can add. $8 + 6 = $ ■

ONE WAY You can draw a picture.

$8 + 6 = 14$

ANOTHER WAY You can use counters. Model each addend. Then count how many in all.

ANOTHER WAY You can use a number line.

1 Find the greater addend, 8.	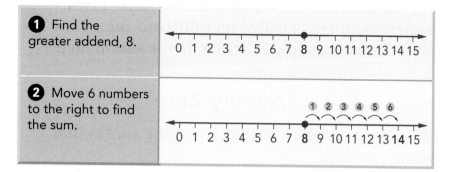
2 Move 6 numbers to the right to find the sum.	

ANOTHER WAY You can count on from the greater addend, 8.

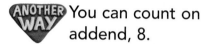 8

9, 10, 11, 12, 13, 14

When you begin with the greater addend, you have fewer numbers to count on.

Count on 6 more numbers.

⭐ **ANSWER:** No matter which way you use to find the sum, Jessie has 14 goldfish.

Addition Fact Strategies

An addition sentence that tells the sum of two 1-digit numbers is called an **addition fact**. Here are some hints to help you remember addition facts.

MORE HELP
See 246

Adding Zero

When you add zero to a number, the sum is that same number.

To master these facts, you need only 1 fact—adding 0 doesn't change anything.

$$0 + 0 = 0$$

$1 + 0 = 1$	$0 + 1 = 1$
$2 + 0 = 2$	$0 + 2 = 2$
$3 + 0 = 3$	$0 + 3 = 3$
$4 + 0 = 4$	$0 + 4 = 4$
$5 + 0 = 5$	$0 + 5 = 5$
$6 + 0 = 6$	$0 + 6 = 6$
$7 + 0 = 7$	$0 + 7 = 7$
$8 + 0 = 8$	$0 + 8 = 8$
$9 + 0 = 9$	$0 + 9 = 9$

4 flowers + 0 flowers = 4 flowers

Turn-Around Facts in Addition

Both of these trains have 9 cubes.

$7 + 2 = 9$ $2 + 7 = 9$

MORE
HELP
See 240

If you change the order of two addends, or *turn them around*, the sum stays the same.

So, when you know an addition fact such as $7 + 2 = 9$, you also know $2 + 7 = 9$.

2 for 1. What a deal!

Adding 1 or 2

When you add 1 to a number, it's like counting. To find $8 + 1$, find the number that is **1 more than** 8.

$$8 + 1 = 9$$

When you add 2 to a number, it is also like counting. To find $8 + 2$, find the number that is **2 more than** 8.

$$8 + 2 = 10$$

Remember the turn-around facts $1 + 8 = 9$ and $2 + 8 = 10$.

I have two more buttons than you have.

I have 8 buttons so you must have 10.

Adding Doubles

Some students think **doubles** are the easiest
addition facts to master.

- A double feature has
  two movies.

- A double-header has
  two games.

- A doubles addition fact has two addends that are
  the same.

$0 + 0 = 0$

$1 + 1 = 2$

$2 + 2 = 4$

$3 + 3 = 6$

$4 + 4 = 8$

$5 + 5 = 10$

$6 + 6 = 12$

$7 + 7 = 14$

$8 + 8 = 16$

$9 + 9 = 18$

Using Doubles to Add

Sometimes you can use doubles facts to learn other facts.

MORE
HELP
See 103

EXAMPLE: $5 + 6 = \blacksquare$

ONE WAY Add 1 to the double 5 + 5.

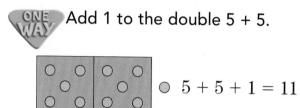 ○ $5 + 5 + 1 = 11$

ANOTHER WAY Subtract 1 from the double 6 + 6.

 $6 + 6 - 1 = 11$

★ ANSWER: Either way, $5 + 6 = 11$.

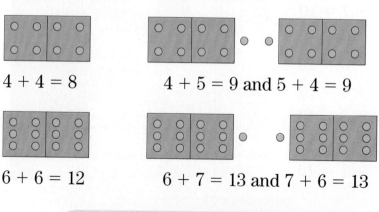

Doubles Facts   **Near Doubles Facts**

$4 + 4 = 8$ $4 + 5 = 9$ and $5 + 4 = 9$

$6 + 6 = 12$ $6 + 7 = 13$ and $7 + 6 = 13$

The sums of all doubles are even numbers.
The sums of near doubles are odd numbers.

MORE
HELP
See 91

Sums of 10

Here are two ways to help you learn addition facts that have a sum of 10.

ONE WAY You can use a ten frame.

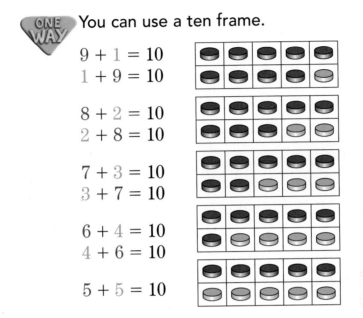

$9 + 1 = 10$
$1 + 9 = 10$

$8 + 2 = 10$
$2 + 8 = 10$

$7 + 3 = 10$
$3 + 7 = 10$

$6 + 4 = 10$
$4 + 6 = 10$

$5 + 5 = 10$

ANOTHER WAY You can color a grid.

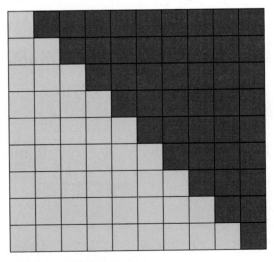

$1 + 9 = 10$
$2 + 8 = 10$
$3 + 7 = 10$
$4 + 6 = 10$
$5 + 5 = 10$
$6 + 4 = 10$
$7 + 3 = 10$
$8 + 2 = 10$
$9 + 1 = 10$

Try this with sums other than 10. You should always get a "step" pattern.

Using Tens to Add

You can use facts with sums of 10 to find sums greater than 10. Think about place value and tens and ones.

MORE HELP
See 3

EXAMPLE 1: $8 + 5 = \blacksquare$

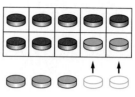

$8 + 5 = 1$ ten 3 ones, or 13

★ **ANSWER:** $8 + 5 = 13$

EXAMPLE 2: $9 + 6 = \blacksquare$

You can use 10 to add 9. Since 9 is 1 less than 10, just add 10 and subtract 1 from the sum.

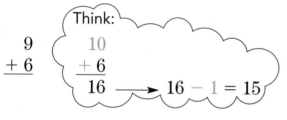

$$\begin{array}{r} 9 \\ + 6 \\ \hline \end{array}$$

Think:
$$\begin{array}{r} 10 \\ + 6 \\ \hline 16 \end{array} \longrightarrow 16 - 1 = 15$$

★ **ANSWER:** $9 + 6 = 15$

When one addend is 9 and the other addend is any 1-digit number other than 0, look what happens.

$9 + 1 = 10$

$9 + 2 = 11$

$9 + 3 = 12$

$9 + 4 = 13$

$9 + 5 = 14$

$9 + 6 = 15$

$9 + 7 = 16$

$9 + 8 = 17$

$9 + 9 = 18$

The last digit in the sum is always one less than the number added to 9.

Subtraction Concepts and Facts

Like addition, **subtraction** is a basic skill in mathematics.

Uses for Subtraction

You can subtract to solve different kinds of problems.

Case 1 You can subtract to take away. The answer tells you how much is left.

Case 2 You can subtract to compare. The answer tells you how many more or how many fewer.

> There are 7 girls in my troop.

> There are 9 girls in my scout troop.

> I can subtract 7 from 9 to find out how many more girls are in her troop than mine.

Case 3 If you know the whole amount and one part, you can subtract to find the other part.

> I ate 9 hot dogs in the contest.

> I ate 4 small hot dogs but the rest were large.

> I can subtract 4 from 9 to find out how many large hot dogs he ate.

MORE
HELP
See 49

> This is like finding the missing addend in an addition sentence.

Subtraction Words and Symbols

There are special words to help you talk about subtraction. When you subtract, the result is called the **difference**. The symbol for subtraction is the **minus sign**, or the **subtraction sign** $(-)$.

You can write numbers in a stack to subtract.

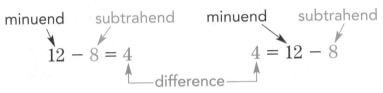

$$
\begin{array}{r}
12 \\
-\ 8 \\
\hline
4
\end{array}
$$

12 ←——— minuend
−8 ←——— subtrahend
4 ←——— difference

The words *minuend* and *subtrahend* are not used very often.

You can also write subtraction as a **subtraction sentence**. Both sides of the equals sign have the same value.

minuend   subtrahend   minuend   subtrahend

$$12 - 8 = 4 \qquad\qquad 4 = 12 - 8$$

difference

No matter which way you show subtraction, you read it the same way.

Write: $12 - 8 = 4$ or
$$
\begin{array}{r}
12 \\
-\ 8 \\
\hline
4
\end{array}
$$

Say: *Twelve minus eight equals four.*

Relating Addition and Subtraction

If you go up 3 steps and then down 3 steps, you're back where you started!

Going down is the opposite of going up. Subtraction is the opposite of addition.

Start with 5.   Add 3.
                 You have 8.

Start with 8.   Subtract 3.
                 You have 5.

This relationship can help you subtract.

Addition Facts	Related Subtraction Facts
$5 + 3 = 8$	$8 - 3 = 5$
$3 + 5 = 8$	$8 - 5 = 3$

Some people find addition easier than subtraction. If you do, when you see subtraction, think about addition.

EXAMPLE: $16 - 9 = $ ■

Think: ■ $+ 9 = 16$

■ $= 7$ because $7 + 9 = 16$.

The number you need to write here is called the **missing addend.**

MORE HELP
See 54

★ **ANSWER:** $16 - 9 = 7$

Ways to Subtract

There are many ways to find the difference between two numbers. Use a method that works best for you.

Using Counters to Subtract

You can act out a subtraction problem by using counters.

Case 1 You can find out how many are left.

EXAMPLE 1: Angela baked 12 muffins. Later, Angela ate 4 of the muffins. How many muffins are left?

Think: $12 - 4 = $ ▪

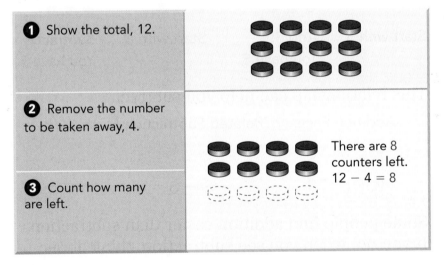

1 Show the total, 12.	
2 Remove the number to be taken away, 4.	There are 8 counters left. $12 - 4 = 8$
3 Count how many are left.	

★ **ANSWER:** There are 8 muffins left.

Case 2 You can compare two numbers.

EXAMPLE 2: Chen lives on a small farm. Every morning he feeds 7 cows and 11 chickens. How many more chickens than cows does he feed?

Think: $11 - 7 = $ ▪

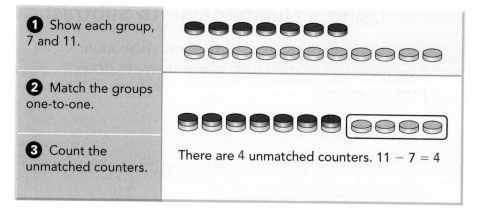

① Show each group, 7 and 11.	
② Match the groups one-to-one.	
③ Count the unmatched counters.	There are 4 unmatched counters. 11 − 7 = 4

⭐ **ANSWER:** Chen feeds 4 more chickens than cows.

Case 3 You can find a missing addend.

EXAMPLE 3: A chess club has 13 members. There are 6 boys, and the rest are girls. How many members are girls?

Think: $6 + \blacksquare = 13$

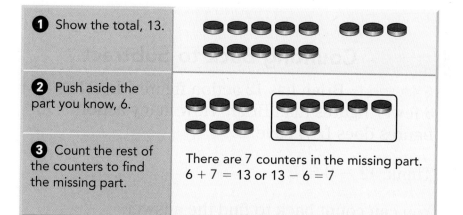

① Show the total, 13.	
② Push aside the part you know, 6.	
③ Count the rest of the counters to find the missing part.	There are 7 counters in the missing part. 6 + 7 = 13 or 13 − 6 = 7

Because addition and subtraction are related, $6 + \blacksquare = 13$ and $13 − 6 = \blacksquare$ are related. That's why finding a missing addend is like subtracting.

⭐ **ANSWER:** There are 7 girls in the chess club.

MORE HELP
See 49, 54

Using a Number Line to Subtract

EXAMPLE: Kim picked 10 flowers. She gave 3 flowers to Lulani. How many flowers does Kim have left?

Think: $10 - 3 = $ ■

You can count back on a number line to find the answer.

1 Find the total, 10.	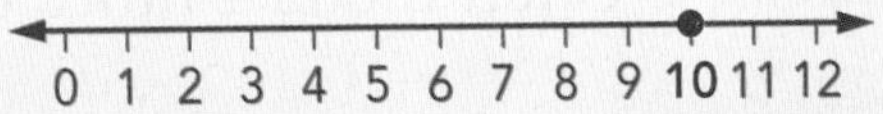 0 1 2 3 4 5 6 7 8 9 10 11 12
2 Move 3 spaces to the left to find the difference.	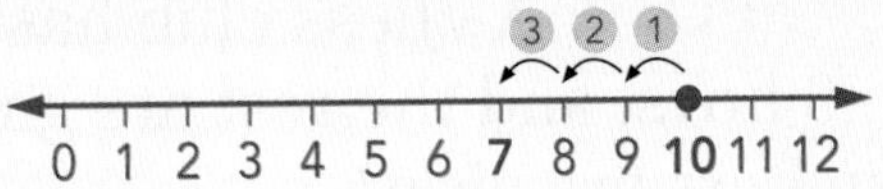 3 2 1 0 1 2 3 4 5 6 7 8 9 10 11 12 $10 - 3 = 7$

⭐ ANSWER: Kim has 7 flowers left.

Counting Back to Subtract

EXAMPLE: Brian has 12 action figures. Levi has 3 fewer figures than Brian. How many action figures does Levi have?

Think: $12 - 3 = $ ■

You can count back to find the answer.

12 11, 10, 9   Count back 3 numbers.

$12 - 3 = 9$

⭐ ANSWER: Levi has 9 action figures.

Using an Addition Table to Subtract

You can use an addition table to find the difference for any subtraction fact.

EXAMPLE: Use the addition table to find this difference. $11 - 8 = $ ■

MORE
HELP
See 37

❶ Find the column that is labeled *8*.

Addition Table

+	0	1	2	3	4	5	6	7	8	9
0	0	1	2	3	4	5	6	7	8	9
1	1	2	3	4	5	6	7	8	9	10
2	2	3	4	5	6	7	8	9	10	11
3	3	4	5	6	7	8	9	10	11	12
4	4	5	6	7	8	9	10	11	12	13
5	5	6	7	8	9	10	11	12	13	14

❷ Find the box in that column with 11.

Addition Table

+	0	1	2	3	4	5	6	7	8	9
0	0	1	2	3	4	5	6	7	8	9
1	1	2	3	4	5	6	7	8	9	10
2	2	3	4	5	6	7	8	9	10	11
3	3	4	5	6	7	8	9	10	11	12
4	4	5	6	7	8	9	10	11	12	13
5	5	6	7	8	9	10	11	12	13	14

❸ The difference is the number at the beginning of that row.

Addition Table

+	0	1	2	3	4	5	6	7	8	9
0	0	1	2	3	4	5	6	7	8	9
1	1	2	3	4	5	6	7	8	9	10
2	2	3	4	5	6	7	8	9	10	11
3	3	4	5	6	7	8	9	10	11	12
4	4	5	6	7	8	9	10	11	12	13
5	5	6	7	8	9	10	11	12	13	14

★ **ANSWER:** $11 - 8 = 3$

A subtraction sentence that has a 1-digit difference and a 1-digit subtrahend is called a **subtraction fact**. Here are some hints to help you remember subtraction facts.

Families of Facts: Addition and Subtraction

Most **fact families** consist of four related facts such as these.

$8 + 3 = 11$ $11 - 3 = 8$

$3 + 8 = 11$ $11 - 8 = 3$

> Each fact uses the same three numbers: 8, 3, and 11.

Doubles have only two facts in their family.

$7 + 7 = 14$ $14 - 7 = 7$

Studying families of facts will help you learn related addition and subtraction facts.

MORE
HELP
See 49,
57

You can use triangular flash cards to help you with families of facts.

Think: 8 + 3 = ■

Say: *11*

Think: 3 + 8 = ■

Say: *11*

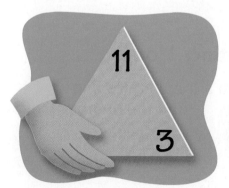

Think: 11 − 3 = ■

Say: *8*

Think: 11 − 8 = ■

Say: *3*

Zeros in Subtraction

Look at the subtraction facts with zero and you will see patterns that make these facts easy to remember.

When you subtract 0 from a number, the difference is the same as the number you subtracted from.

$$0 - 0 = 0$$
$$1 - 0 = 1$$
$$2 - 0 = 2$$
$$3 - 0 = 3$$
$$4 - 0 = 4$$
$$5 - 0 = 5$$
$$6 - 0 = 6$$
$$7 - 0 = 7$$
$$8 - 0 = 8$$
$$9 - 0 = 9$$

When you subtract a number from itself, the difference is 0.

$$0 - 0 = 0$$
$$1 - 1 = 0$$
$$2 - 2 = 0$$
$$3 - 3 = 0$$
$$4 - 4 = 0$$
$$5 - 5 = 0$$
$$6 - 6 = 0$$
$$7 - 7 = 0$$
$$8 - 8 = 0$$
$$9 - 9 = 0$$

Subtracting 1 or 2

When you subtract 1 from a number, it's like counting back. To find $8 - 1$, find the number that is **1 less than** 8.

$$8 - 1 = 7$$

Don't forget the related facts $8 - 7 = 1$ and $8 - 6 = 2$.

When you subtract 2 from a number, it is also like counting back. To find $8 - 2$, find the number that is **2 less than** 8.

$$8 - 2 = 6$$

Using Doubles in Subtraction

If you know addition doubles, then you also know
the related subtraction doubles.

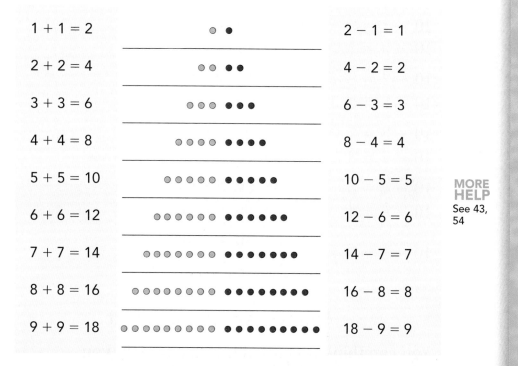

1 + 1 = 2	○ ●	2 − 1 = 1
2 + 2 = 4	○○ ●●	4 − 2 = 2
3 + 3 = 6	○○○ ●●●	6 − 3 = 3
4 + 4 = 8	○○○○ ●●●●	8 − 4 = 4
5 + 5 = 10	○○○○○ ●●●●●	10 − 5 = 5
6 + 6 = 12	○○○○○○ ●●●●●●	12 − 6 = 6
7 + 7 = 14	○○○○○○○ ●●●●●●●	14 − 7 = 7
8 + 8 = 16	○○○○○○○○ ●●●●●●●●	16 − 8 = 8
9 + 9 = 18	○○○○○○○○○ ●●●●●●●●●	18 − 9 = 9

MORE
HELP
See 43,
54

There are only two number sentences for fact
families with doubles.

$$\begin{array}{r} 6 \\ +6 \\ \hline 12 \end{array}$$

$$\begin{array}{r} 12 \\ -6 \\ \hline 6 \end{array}$$

We are
the only
two facts
in our
family.

Subtracting from Ten

You can use a ten frame to help you learn all the subtraction facts for 10.

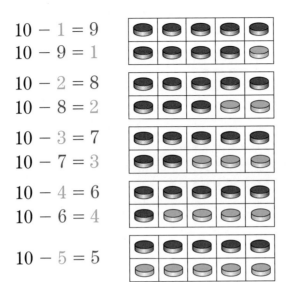

$10 - 1 = 9$
$10 - 9 = 1$

$10 - 2 = 8$
$10 - 8 = 2$

$10 - 3 = 7$
$10 - 7 = 3$

$10 - 4 = 6$
$10 - 6 = 4$

$10 - 5 = 5$

Using Ten to Subtract

You can think about a ten frame to help you subtract from numbers greater than 10.

EXAMPLE: $14 - 8 = \blacksquare$

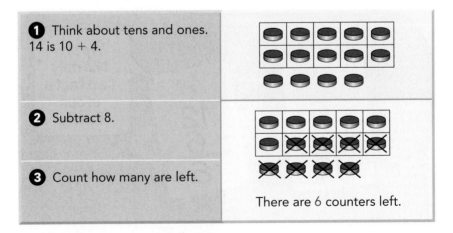

1 Think about tens and ones. 14 is 10 + 4.

2 Subtract 8.

3 Count how many are left.

There are 6 counters left.

★ **ANSWER:** $14 - 8 = 6$

Subtracting 9

When you subtract 9 from a 2-digit number less than 20, look what happens.

$19 - 9 = 10$

$18 - 9 = 9$

$17 - 9 = 8$

6 is one more than 5.

$16 - 9 = 7$

$15 - 9 = 6$

The difference is 1 more than the ones digit of the number you are subtracting from.

$14 - 9 = 5$

$13 - 9 = 4$

$12 - 9 = 3$

$11 - 9 = 2$

3 is one more than 2.

$10 - 9 = 1$

Multiplication Concepts and Facts

Multiplication is a shortcut for addition. When you add, you combine amounts. When you have equal amounts to add, you can **multiply** to find the total.

Uses for Multiplication

Let's look at some times when you might want to use multiplication.

Case 1 You can multiply to join equal groups to find a total.

Case 2 You can multiply equal money amounts to find a total.

Case 3 You can multiply to find the number of objects in an array.

When objects are arranged in equal rows, the arrangement is called an **array**.

Multiplication Words and Symbols

Numbers to be multiplied are **factors**. When you multiply two or more factors, the result is called the **product**. The symbol that stands for multiplication is a **multiplication sign (×)**.

You can write multiplication as a **multiplication sentence**. Write the factors in a row with a multiplication sign between them. An **equals sign (=)** separates the factors from the product.

You can also write numbers vertically to multiply.

MORE
HELP
See 89

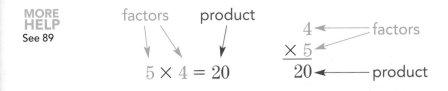

$$5 \times 4 = 20$$

$$\begin{array}{r} 4 \\ \times\ 5 \\ \hline 20 \end{array}$$ ← factors / product

No matter which way you show the multiplication, you read it the same way.

Write: $5 \times 4 = 20$ or $\begin{array}{r} 4 \\ \times\ 5 \\ \hline 20 \end{array}$

Say: *Five times four equals twenty.*

> You can also write a multiplication sentence using a · instead of an ×.
> $5 \cdot 4 = 20$

Some people use these words instead of *factor.*

$\begin{array}{r} 4 \\ \times\ 5 \\ \hline 20 \end{array}$ ← multiplicand (the number being multiplied)
← multiplier (the number multiplied by)

Using a Multiplication Table

You can use a **multiplication table** to find the product of any two 1-digit numbers.

Multiplication Table

×	0	1	2	3	4	5	6	7	8	9
0	0	0	0	0	0	0	0	0	0	0
1	0	1	2	3	4	5	6	7	8	9
2	0	2	4	6	8	10	12	14	16	18
3	0	3	6	9	12	15	18	21	24	27
4	0	4	8	12	16	20	24	28	32	36
5	0	5	10	15	20	25	30	35	40	45
6	0	6	12	18	24	30	36	42	48	54
7	0	7	14	21	28	35	42	49	56	63
8	0	8	16	24	32	40	48	56	64	72
9	0	9	18	27	36	45	54	63	72	81

EXAMPLE: Use the multiplication table to find this product. $6 \times 3 =$ ■

- Find the column labeled *6*. It is shaded blue.
- Find the row labeled *3*. It is shaded yellow.
- The product is in the green box where the column and row meet.

★ ANSWER: $6 \times 3 = 18$

Other Ways to Multiply

There are many ways to find a product. Use the way that works best for you.

EXAMPLE: There are 3 plants on a window sill. There are 4 flowers on each plant. How many flowers are there?

To solve this problem, you can multiply.
$3 \times 4 = \blacksquare$

ONE WAY You can draw a picture.

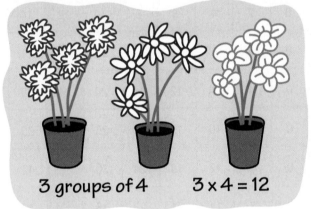

3 groups of 4 $3 \times 4 = 12$

ANOTHER WAY You can skip-count on a number line or a hundred chart.

number line

0 1 2 3 4 5 6 7 8 9 10 11 12 13
1 2 3 4 1 2 3 4 1 2 3 4

hundred chart

1	2	3	4	5	6	7	8	9	10
11	12	13	14	15	16	17	18	19	20
21	22	23	24	25	26	27	28	29	30

You can use addition.

Since 3×4 means 3 groups of 4, 3×4 is the same as $4 + 4 + 4$.

$$4 + 4 + 4 = 12$$

4 is used 3 times.

 **You can make or draw an array.** An array arranges objects in equal rows and columns.

an array using counters

an array drawn on grid paper

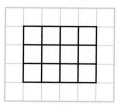

an array made with intersecting lines

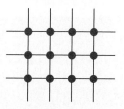

⭐ **ANSWER:** No matter which way you use to find the product, there are 12 flowers.

Multiplication Fact Strategies

A multiplication sentence that tells the product of two 1-digit numbers is called a **multiplication fact**. Here are some hints to help you remember multiplication facts.

Multiplying by 1

When one factor is 1, the product is the same as the other factor.

$$1 \times 1 = 1$$

$1 \times 2 = 2$	$2 \times 1 = 2$
$1 \times 3 = 3$	$3 \times 1 = 3$
$1 \times 4 = 4$	$4 \times 1 = 4$
$1 \times 5 = 5$	$5 \times 1 = 5$
$1 \times 6 = 6$	$6 \times 1 = 6$
$1 \times 7 = 7$	$7 \times 1 = 7$
$1 \times 8 = 8$	$8 \times 1 = 8$
$1 \times 9 = 9$	$9 \times 1 = 9$

$1 \times 3 = 3$ $3 \times 1 = 3$

Multiplying by 0

Multiplying by zero is easy.

$$0 \times 0 = 0$$

$0 \times 1 = 0$	$1 \times 0 = 0$
$0 \times 2 = 0$	$2 \times 0 = 0$
$0 \times 3 = 0$	$3 \times 0 = 0$
$0 \times 4 = 0$	$4 \times 0 = 0$
$0 \times 5 = 0$	$5 \times 0 = 0$
$0 \times 6 = 0$	$6 \times 0 = 0$
$0 \times 7 = 0$	$7 \times 0 = 0$
$0 \times 8 = 0$	$8 \times 0 = 0$
$0 \times 9 = 0$	$9 \times 0 = 0$

Just think of these as *no groups of* something or group *of nothing!*

MORE HELP
See 247

Turn-Around Facts in Multiplication

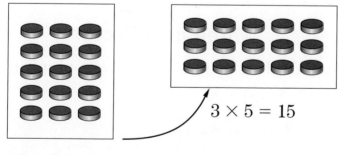

$3 \times 5 = 15$

$5 \times 3 = 15$

The total number of counters is the same in each array. If you reverse the order of two factors, or *turn them around*, the product is the same.

MORE HELP
See 241

Using Doubles in Multiplication

MORE HELP
See 43 You can use what you know about adding doubles to multiply by 2.

EXAMPLE: There are 4 stop signs on Elm Street. There are twice as many stop signs on Grove Street. How many stop signs are on Grove Street?

 You can use the addition doubles fact.

$4 + 4 = 8$

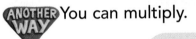 You can multiply.

$2 \times 4 = 8$

Remember, if you know 2×4, you also know 4×2.

⭐ **ANSWER:** Either way, there are 8 stop signs on Grove Street.

Three as a Factor

Knowing doubles can also help you multiply by 3.

EXAMPLE: $3 \times 6 = $ ■

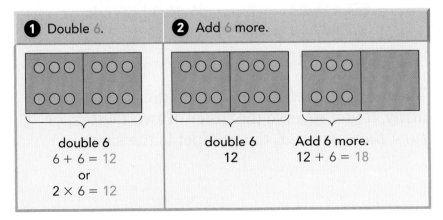

❶ Double 6.

double 6
$6 + 6 = 12$
or
$2 \times 6 = 12$

❷ Add 6 more.

double 6
12

Add 6 more.
$12 + 6 = 18$

⭐ **ANSWER:** $3 \times 6 = 18$

Four as a Factor

What happens when you double a number and then double it again? It's the same as multiplying the number by 4.

MORE
HELP
See 119

EXAMPLE: $4 \times 9 = \blacksquare$

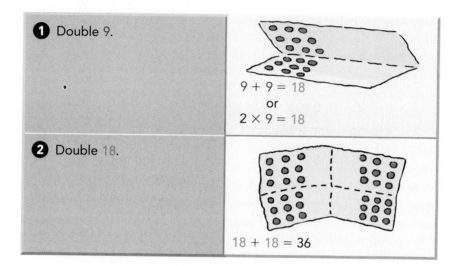

1 Double 9.

$9 + 9 = 18$
or
$2 \times 9 = 18$

2 Double 18.

$18 + 18 = 36$

⭐ **ANSWER:** $4 \times 9 = 36$

Fives Facts

Most students find multiplication facts for 5 easy to remember.

0 × 5 = 0	5 × 0 = 0
1 × 5 = 5	5 × 1 = 5
2 × 5 = 10	5 × 2 = 10
3 × 5 = 15	5 × 3 = 15
4 × 5 = 20	5 × 4 = 20
5 × 5 = 25	5 × 5 = 25
6 × 5 = 30	5 × 6 = 30
7 × 5 = 35	5 × 7 = 35
8 × 5 = 40	5 × 8 = 40
9 × 5 = 45	5 × 9 = 45

Think about nickels. 1 nickel is 5¢, 2 nickels are 10¢, 3 nickels are 15¢, and so on.

Look at the pattern in the list of products. The ones digits have a 0, 5, 0, 5 pattern.

Nifty Nines

You can use patterns to help you learn these multiplication facts for 9.

3 is one less than 4.

$$9 × 4 = 36$$

The sum of 3 and 6 is 9.

1 × 9 = 9	9 × 1 = 9
2 × 9 = 18	9 × 2 = 18
3 × 9 = 27	9 × 3 = 27
4 × 9 = 36	9 × 4 = 36
5 × 9 = 45	9 × 5 = 45
6 × 9 = 54	9 × 6 = 54
7 × 9 = 63	9 × 7 = 63
8 × 9 = 72	9 × 8 = 72
9 × 9 = 81	9 × 9 = 81

The tens digit in the product is always one less than the number you are multiplying by 9. The sum of the two digits in the product is always 9.

Here's an amazing method for using your fingers to help you remember nines facts.

EXAMPLE: $4 \times 9 = \blacksquare$

1. Place both your hands on a table with your palms facing down.

2. Now count 4 fingers from the left and bend this finger.

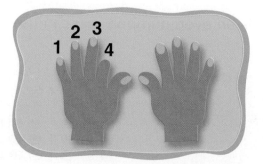

3. Count the number of fingers on each side of the bent finger. Count your thumb as a finger.

The number of fingers on the left is the number of tens in the product.

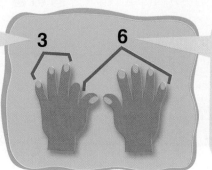

The number of fingers on the right is the number of ones in the product.

★ ANSWER: $4 \times 9 = 36$

Use Facts You Know

MORE
HELP
See 91

When one of the factors is even, use doubling.

EXAMPLE: Toby made 7 packages of apples for the school fair. There are 6 apples in each package. How many apples did Toby have?

To solve the problem, you can multiply.
$7 \times 6 = \blacksquare$

ONE WAY Since 6 is an even number, you can use doubling.

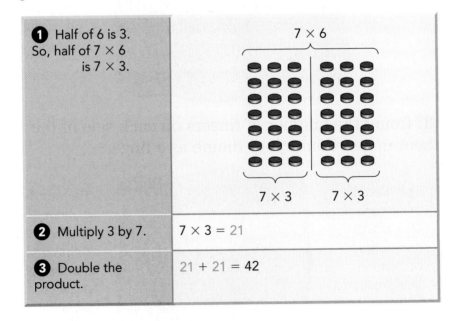

❶ Half of 6 is 3. So, half of 7×6 is 7×3.	
❷ Multiply 3 by 7.	$7 \times 3 = 21$
❸ Double the product.	$21 + 21 = 42$

ANOTHER WAY You can use 6 × 6 and add one more set.

1 Think of 7 sixes as 6 sixes plus 1 more 6.	7×6 ⎨ ... 6×6 ... 6
2 Multiply 6 × 6.	$6 \times 6 = 36$
3 Add 1 more 6.	$36 + 6 = 42$

⭐ **ANSWER:** Either way, Toby had 42 apples.

Division Concepts and Facts

Just like subtraction is the opposite of addition, division is the opposite of multiplication. You can use what you know about multiplication to help you with division.

Uses for Division

You can divide to solve different kinds of problems.

Case 1 You can divide to find the number in each group.

Here are 20 photos I took during the class trip.

You can place them equally on these 5 pages of your album.

I can divide 20 by 5 to find out how many pictures to put on each page.

Case 2 You can divide to find the number of groups.

I baked 42 muffins for the bake sale.

I will pack the muffins 6 to a box.

I can divide 42 by 6 to find out how many boxes you need.

Case 3 If you know one number and how many times greater it is than another number, you can divide to find that other number.

I am 12 years old.

I am 3 times as old as my brother Michael.

I can divide 12 by 3 to find your brother's age.

Case 4 You can divide to compare.

Our apartment building is 48 feet tall.

This tree in front of the building is 8 feet tall.

Then our apartment building must be 6 times as tall as the tree. I know because I divided 48 by 8 and got 6.

Sometimes you can't divide an amount into equal groups. There is a **remainder**.

I thought I could make 4 equal groups using 13 balls.

MORE HELP See 185

Division Words and Symbols

There are two common ways to write division.

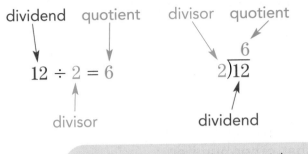

dividend   quotient   divisor   quotient

$$12 \div 2 = 6 \qquad 2\overline{)12}$$

divisor   dividend

MORE HELP
See 212

> You can also show division with a fraction bar. $\frac{12}{2}$ means the same thing as $12 \div 2$.

No matter which way you show division, you read it the same way.

Write: $12 \div 2 = 6$ or $2\overline{)12}^{\,6}$

Read the number "inside the house" first.

Say: *Twelve divided by two equals six.*

> When the division is written using $\overline{)}\,$, you may hear some people read it as: *two goes into twelve six times.*

Six **goes into** forty-two seven times.

What's a gozinta?

Gozinta is not a real math term!

Relating Multiplication and Division

Division is the **opposite** of multiplication, just as subtraction is the opposite of addition.

Multiplication Facts   Related Division Facts

$4 \times 5 = 20$ $20 \div 5 = 4$

$5 \times 4 = 20$ $20 \div 4 = 5$

MORE
HELP
See 49,
62, 82

Some people find multiplication easier than division. If you do, when you see division, think about multiplication.

EXAMPLE: $20 \div 5 = \blacksquare$

Think: $\blacksquare \times 5 = 20$

> The number you need to write here is called the **missing factor**.

$\blacksquare = 4$ because $4 \times 5 = 20$.

So, you know $20 \div 5 = 4$

★ **ANSWER:** $20 \div 5 = 4$

Ways to Divide

There are many ways to find a quotient. Use a method that works best for you.

Using Counters to Divide

You can act out a division problem by using counters.

Case 1 You can use counters to find the number in each group.

EXAMPLE 1: Ravi has 12 rabbits. He puts the same number of rabbits into each of 4 cages. How many rabbits does Ravi put in each cage?

Think: $12 \div 4 = \blacksquare$

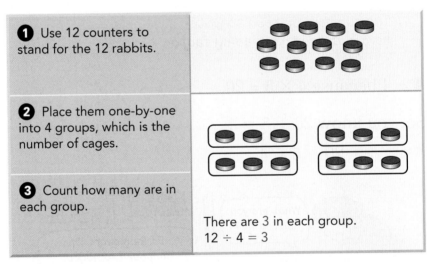

1 Use 12 counters to stand for the 12 rabbits.

2 Place them one-by-one into 4 groups, which is the number of cages.

3 Count how many are in each group.

There are 3 in each group.
$12 \div 4 = 3$

⭐ **ANSWER:** Ravi puts 3 rabbits in each cage.

Case 2 You can use counters to find the number of groups.

EXAMPLE 2: Cindy made 18 jars of jam. She packs them 6 to a carton. How many cartons does Cindy pack with jars of jam?

Think: $18 \div 6 = \blacksquare$

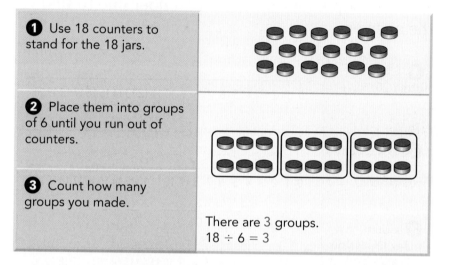

1 Use 18 counters to stand for the 18 jars.	
2 Place them into groups of 6 until you run out of counters.	
3 Count how many groups you made.	There are 3 groups. $18 \div 6 = 3$

⭐ **ANSWER:** Cindy packs 3 cartons with jars of jam.

If you don't have counters, you can draw a picture.

Using a Number Line to Divide

EXAMPLE: Juan blows up 20 balloons. He ties 4 balloons on each picnic table. How many tables have balloons?

Think: $20 \div 4 = \blacksquare$

You can skip-count back on a number line to find the answer.

1 Find the total, 20.	0 1 2 3 4 5 6 7 8 9 10 11 12 13 14 15 16 17 18 19 20
2 Skip-count back by 4 until you reach 0.	0 1 2 3 4 5 6 7 8 9 10 11 12 13 14 15 16 17 18 19 20
3 Count how many times you counted back.	5 4 3 2 1 0 1 2 3 4 5 6 7 8 9 10 11 12 13 14 15 16 17 18 19 20 You counted back 5 times.

⭐ **ANSWER:** There are 5 picnic tables with balloons.

Using a Multiplication Table to Divide

This may be called a **multiplication table,** but you can use it for division facts.

MORE
HELP
See 63

EXAMPLE: Use the multiplication table to divide.

$4\overline{)32}$

1 Find the row that is labeled 4.

Multiplication Table

×	1	2	3	4	5	6	7	8	9
1	1	2	3	4	5	6	7	8	9
2	2	4	6	8	10	12	14	16	18
3	3	6	9	12	15	18	21	24	27
4	4	8	12	16	20	24	28	32	36
5	5	10	15	20	25	30	35	40	45

2 Find the box in that row with 32.

Multiplication Table

×	1	2	3	4	5	6	7	8	9
1	1	2	3	4	5	6	7	8	9
2	2	4	6	8	10	12	14	16	18
3	3	6	9	12	15	18	21	24	27
4	4	8	12	16	20	24	28	32	36
5	5	10	15	20	25	30	35	40	45

3 The quotient is the number at the top of that column.

Multiplication Table

×	1	2	3	4	5	6	7	8	9
1	1	2	3	4	5	6	7	8	9
2	2	4	6	8	10	12	14	16	18
3	3	6	9	12	15	18	21	24	27
4	4	8	12	16	20	24	28	32	36
5	5	10	15	20	25	30	35	40	45

★ **ANSWER:** $4\overline{)32}^{\,8}$

The zeros in the chart have been covered up. That's because you CANNOT divide by zero. Don't try to use a multiplication table to do it. See page 84.

Using Repeated Subtraction to Divide

EXAMPLE: Raymond collects baseball caps. He arranges 24 caps in rows of 8. How many rows of caps does he make?

Think: $24 \div 8 = \blacksquare$

You can use repeated subtraction to find the answer. Start at 24. Keep subtracting 8 until you reach 0. Count how many times you subtracted.

$$
\begin{array}{r}
24 \\
- 8 \quad \text{①} \\
\hline
16 \\
- 8 \quad \text{②} \\
\hline
8 \\
- 8 \quad \text{③} \\
\hline
0
\end{array}
$$

⭐ **ANSWER:** Raymond makes 3 rows of caps.

Division Fact Strategies

A division sentence that has a 1-digit divisor and a 1-digit quotient is called a division fact. Here are some hints to help you remember division facts.

MORE HELP
See 77

Families of Facts: Multiplication and Division

Most **fact families** consist of four related facts such as these.

$6 \times 8 = 48$ $48 \div 8 = 6$

$8 \times 6 = 48$ $48 \div 6 = 8$

> Each fact uses the same three numbers: 6, 8, and 48.

Doubles have only two facts in their family.

$6 \times 6 = 36$ $36 \div 6 = 6$

Studying families of facts will help you learn all the related multiplication and division facts.

You can use triangular flash cards to help you with families of facts.

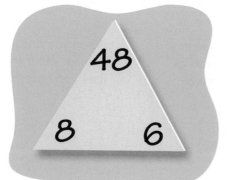

Think: 8 × 6 = ■

Say: 48

Think: 6 × 8 = ■

Say: 48

Think: 48 ÷ 6 = ■

Say: 8

Think: 48 ÷ 8 = ■

Say: 6

One in Division

Look at division facts with 1 and you see patterns that can help you remember these quotients.

When you divide any number by 1, you get that same number.	When you divide a number other than 0 by itself, you get 1.
$0 \div 1 = 0$	
$1 \div 1 = 1$	$1 \div 1 = 1$
$2 \div 1 = 2$	$2 \div 2 = 1$
$3 \div 1 = 3$	$3 \div 3 = 1$
$4 \div 1 = 4$	$4 \div 4 = 1$
$5 \div 1 = 5$	$5 \div 5 = 1$
$6 \div 1 = 6$	$6 \div 6 = 1$
$7 \div 1 = 7$	$7 \div 7 = 1$
$8 \div 1 = 8$	$8 \div 8 = 1$
$9 \div 1 = 9$	$9 \div 9 = 1$

Zero in Division

MORE HELP
See 67, 77, 82

When you divide zero by any number, you get 0.

$0 \div 7 = \blacksquare$

Think of the related multiplication fact:

$\blacksquare \times 7 = 0$

Since $0 \times 7 = 0$, then $0 \div 7 = 0$.

You CANNOT divide a number by zero. Here's why.

$7 \div 0 = \blacksquare$

Think of the related multiplication fact:

$\blacksquare \times 0 = 7$

There is *no* number that you can multiply 0 by and get 7.

Dividing by 2

When you divide a number by 2, you are finding half of it.

> Let's divide the grapes by 2 to share them.

> Let's each take half of them.

There are 18 grapes.

$18 \div 2 = 9$

$\frac{1}{2}$ of 18 is 9.

Each girl gets 9 grapes.

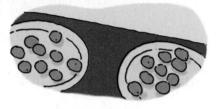

Dividing by 4

When you divide a number by 4, you can divide it by 2 and then divide that quotient by 2.

EXAMPLE: $16 \div 4 = $ ■

❶ Divide 16 by 2. $16 \div 2 = 8$	○ ○ │ ○ ○ ○ ○ │ ○ ○ ○ ○ │ ○ ○ ○ ○ │ ○ ○
❷ Divide 8 by 2. $8 \div 2 = 4$	○ ○ │ ○ ○ ○ ○ │ ○ ○ ● ● │ ○ ○ ● ● │ ○ ○

★ **ANSWER:** $16 \div 4 = 4$

Mastering Basic Facts

It took a lot of time for you to learn all the letters of the alphabet or the numbers to 100. But now, when you look up a word or count things, you don't have to spend time thinking, "What letter comes after *t*?" or "What number comes after *59*?"

It takes time to master addition, subtraction, multiplication, and division facts. But once you do, you will save time during the rest of your life.

Try to master addition and multiplication facts first. Then you can use what you know about related facts to master subtraction and division facts.

Here are two ways to keep track of facts you've mastered.

ONE WAY You can use flash cards.

As you read the front side of a flash card, see if you can name the answer "in a flash." Check by turning the card over.

When you feel you have mastered a fact, remove it from the deck. Keep going until you have no more cards in the deck.

ANOTHER WAY You can use an addition or multiplication table.

Make a copy of each table. Check off all the facts you know. As you learn more facts, check them off. Keep going until you have a table filled with check marks.

Don't forget about turn-around facts. If you know $8 + 2 = 10$, you also know $2 + 8 = 10$.

MORE HELP
See 41, 67

Addition Table

+	0	1	2	3	4	5	6	7	8	9
0	0✓	1✓	2✓	3✓	4✓	5✓	6✓	7✓	8✓	9✓
1	1✓	2✓	3✓	4✓	5✓	6✓	7✓	8✓	9✓	10✓
2	2✓	3✓	4✓	5✓	6✓	7	8	9	10✓	11
3	3✓	4✓	5✓	6✓	7	8	9	10✓	11	12
4	4✓	5✓	6✓	7	8	9	10✓	11	12	13
5	5✓	6✓	7	8	9	10✓	11	12	13	14
6	6✓	7✓	8	9	10✓	11	12✓	13	14	15
7	7✓	8✓	9	10✓	11	12	13	14✓	15	16
8	8✓	9✓	10✓	11	12	13	14	15	16✓	17
9	9✓	10✓	11	12	13	14	15	16	17	18✓

Once you master all the basic facts, you will be able to compute with really large numbers in your head. Believe it or not, you can add numbers such as $3000 + 9000$ faster mentally than on a calculator.

3000 + 9000 = 12,000

The sum is 12,000. What's taking you so long?

I still have more keys to press.

Factors and Multiples

You can look at a carton of eggs and just think *12*. Or you might look more closely at the number *12*.

The eggs form 2 equal rows—12 is an even number.

You could form 3 groups of 4 eggs and learn about factors and multiples.

By studying whole numbers, you can discover useful patterns. These patterns can help you compute. They can help you work with fractions. They can even help mathematicians with secret codes.

Factors

Think of any whole number. No matter which one you pick, there are two whole numbers you can multiply to get your number.

Suppose you picked 7.

$1 \times 7 = 7$ The numbers 1 and 7 are called **factors** of 7.

Since the only other way you can multiply two whole numbers and get 7 is 7×1, 1 and 7 are the only factors of 7.

Some numbers have more than two factors.

EXAMPLE: Find all the factors of 12.

ONE WAY Find all the pairs of whole numbers that can be multiplied to get 12.

MORE HELP
See 92, 93

$1 \times 12 = 12$ One pair of factors of 12 is 1 and 12.

$2 \times 6 = 12$ Another pair of factors of 12 is 2 and 6.

$3 \times 4 = 12$ Another pair is 3 and 4.

ANOTHER WAY Draw arrays to find all the factors of 12.

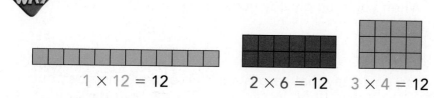

$1 \times 12 = 12$ $2 \times 6 = 12$ $3 \times 4 = 12$

★ **ANSWER:** Either way, the factors of 12 are 1, 2, 3, 4, 6, and 12.

Multiples

When you skip-count, you say multiples of a number. **Multiples** of a number are the products of that number and any whole number.

EXAMPLE: Find the first four multiples of 3 starting with 3.

 ONE WAY Skip count by 3s.

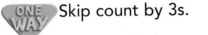

0 1 2 3 4 5 6 7 8 9 10 11 12

ANOTHER WAY Multiply to find multiples of 3.

$1 \times 3 = 3$

$2 \times 3 = 6$

$3 \times 3 = 9$

$4 \times 3 = 12$

⭐ **ANSWER:** Either way, the multiples are 3, 6, 9, 12.

MATH ALERT

Zero as Multiple and Factor

- When you multiply any number by zero, the product is zero.

$0 \times 3 = 0$

You could say that zero is a multiple of any number, but most people don't. So we list the multiples of 3 as 3, 6, 9, and so on.

- Since $0 \times$ any number $= 0$, zero is not a factor of any number *except* itself.

Even and Odd Numbers

- An **even number** has 2 as a factor. An even number of things can be put into pairs.

- An **odd number** does *not* have 2 as a factor. When you try to put an odd number of things into pairs, there is always one left over.

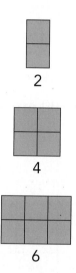

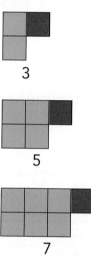

Here are the first 50 counting numbers. The odd numbers are red, and the even numbers are blue.

1	2	3	4	5	6	7	8	9	10
11	12	13	14	15	16	17	18	19	20
21	22	23	24	25	26	27	28	29	30
31	32	33	34	35	36	37	38	39	40
41	42	43	44	45	46	47	48	49	50

Every **even** number has a 0, 2, 4, 6, or 8 in its ones place.

Every **odd** number has a 1, 3, 5, 7, or 9 in its ones place.

Prime Numbers

MORE HELP
See 89

A **prime number** is a whole number greater than zero that has exactly two different factors, one and itself.

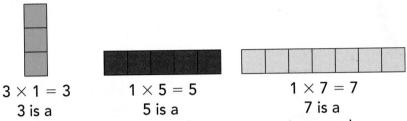

$3 \times 1 = 3$
3 is a
prime number.

$1 \times 5 = 5$
5 is a
prime number.

$1 \times 7 = 7$
7 is a
prime number.

The prime numbers between 1 and 100 are shown in blue.

1	2	3	4	5	6	7	8	9	10
11	12	13	14	15	16	17	18	19	20
21	22	23	24	25	26	27	28	29	30
31	32	33	34	35	36	37	38	39	40
41	42	43	44	45	46	47	48	49	50
51	52	53	54	55	56	57	58	59	60
61	62	63	64	65	66	67	68	69	70
71	72	73	74	75	76	77	78	79	80
81	82	83	84	85	86	87	88	89	90
91	92	93	94	95	96	97	98	99	100

I'm not unlucky,
I'm prime.
Reverse my digits
and I'm still prime!

Composite Numbers

A **composite number** is a whole number greater than zero that has more than two different factors.

MORE HELP
See 89

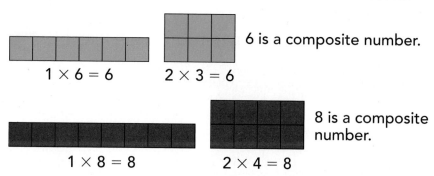

6 is a composite number.

$1 \times 6 = 6$ $2 \times 3 = 6$

8 is a composite number.

$1 \times 8 = 8$ $2 \times 4 = 8$

- All whole numbers greater than one are either prime or composite. Look at the table on page 92. All the numbers that are black are composite numbers, except the number 1.

- All even numbers greater than 2 are composite numbers. Each has at least three factors: 1, 2, and itself.

MORE HELP
See 91

MATH ALERT

One Is Neither Prime Nor Composite

One is not prime because it does not have *exactly* two different factors. It's not composite because it does not have *more than* two factors.

I'm special.

Common Factors

MORE HELP
See 89 When a group of two or more numbers have some factors that are the same, these factors are called **common factors**.

EXAMPLE: Find the common factors of 9 and 12.

❶ Find the factors of 9.	$9 = 1 \times 9$ $9 = 3 \times 3$
❷ Find the factors of 12.	$12 = 1 \times 12$ $12 = 2 \times 6$ $12 = 3 \times 4$
❸ List the factors and find those that are on both lists.	Factors of 9: ①③ 9 Factors of 12: ① 2, ③ 4, 6, 12

⭐ ANSWER: The common factors of 9 and 12 are 1 and 3.

MORE HELP
See 269

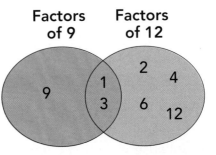

Factors of 9   Factors of 12

The greatest number in a list of common factors is called the **greatest common factor (GCF).** So 3 is the GCF of 9 and 12.

Common Multiples

When a group of two or more numbers have multiples that are the same, these multiples are called **common multiples.**

MORE
HELP
See 90

EXAMPLE: Find four common multiples of 3 and 4.

In this chart, all multiples of 3 are in red squares. All multiples of 4 are in blue circles.

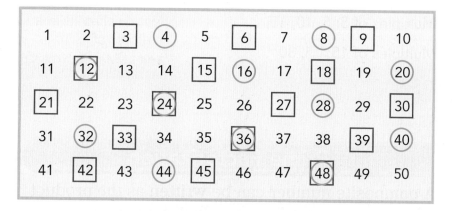

The numbers that have both a red square and a blue circle are the common multiples of 3 and 4.

⭐ **ANSWER:** Four common multiples of 3 and 4 are 12, 24, 36, and 48.

The least number in the list is 12. So 12 is called the **least common multiple (LCM)** of 3 and 4.

MATH ALERT

Sometimes the LCM Is One of the Numbers

Sometimes the least common multiple of a group of numbers is one of the numbers itself. Look at 5 and 15.

Multiples of 5: 5, 10, 15, ...

Multiples of 15: 15, 30, ...

Notice that 15 is a multiple of 5. 15 is the LCM of 5 and 15.

Prime Factorization

A composite number can be written as the product of prime numbers. This is called the **prime factorization** of the number.

EXAMPLE: Find the prime factorization of 18.

 ONE WAY You can find the prime factorization of a number by using a **factor tree**.

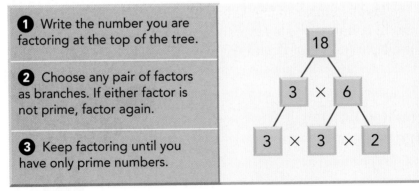

1 Write the number you are factoring at the top of the tree.	18
2 Choose any pair of factors as branches. If either factor is not prime, factor again.	3 × 6
3 Keep factoring until you have only prime numbers.	3 × 3 × 2

No matter which two factors you begin with, you will end up with the same prime factors.

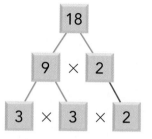

Since 1 is not prime, build factor trees without using 1 as a branch.

ANOTHER WAY You can also find the prime factorization of a number using division.

MORE HELP
See 185

❶ Divide by the least prime number that the number is divisible by.	$2\overline{)18}$ with quotient 9
❷ Keep dividing each quotient by a prime number until you get a quotient of 1.	$2\overline{)18}=9$ $3\overline{)9}=3$ $3\overline{)3}=1$
❸ List all the divisors.	2, 3, 3

If you try a prime number and get a remainder, try a different prime number.

★ **ANSWER:** Either way, the prime factorization of 18 is $2 \times 3 \times 3$.

When you list the prime factors, list them in order from least to greatest.

You can write $2 \times 3 \times 3$ as 2×3^2. Turn the page to find out why.

Exponents

Mathematicians like to find short ways to write things. Suppose you want to add the same number more than once. Instead of writing $5 + 5 + 5$, you can write 3×5. To multiply the same factor more than once, you can use exponents.

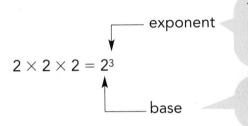

exponent

The **exponent** tells how many times the base is repeated.

$2 \times 2 \times 2 = 2^3$

base

The **base** is the factor that is repeated.

Each edge of the large cube measures 2 units. The large cube is made up of $2 \times 2 \times 2$ (or 2^3, or 8) small cubes. That's why 8 can be called the **cube** of 2.

A **power** of a number tells how many times that number is used as a factor.

MORE HELP See 125

The table shows how to write and read exponents.

Repeated Factors	Write	Say	Standard Form
4×4	4^2	four squared, or four to the second power	16
$2 \times 2 \times 2$	2^3	two cubed, or two to the third power	8
$3 \times 3 \times 3 \times 3$	3^4	three to the fourth power	81

Square Numbers

What shape is each array?

MORE
HELP
See 98

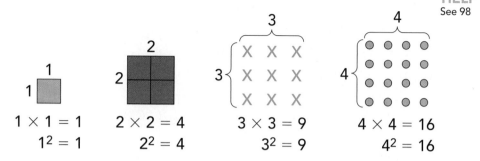

$1 \times 1 = 1$ $2 \times 2 = 4$ $3 \times 3 = 9$ $4 \times 4 = 16$
$1^2 = 1$ $2^2 = 4$ $3^2 = 9$ $4^2 = 16$

Do you see why we say that a product of a number and itself is a **square** number? You can write each square number as a product using an exponent.

Write: $4^2 = 16$

Say: *four squared equals sixteen,* or
four to the second power equals sixteen, or
sixteen is the square of four

The square numbers appear along a diagonal in a multiplication table.

×	0	1	2	3	4	5
0	0	0	0	0	0	0
1	0	1	2	3	4	5
2	0	2	4	6	8	10
3	0	3	6	9	12	15
4	0	4	8	12	16	20
5	0	5	10	15	20	25

Mental Math and Estimation

Some estimates are better than others.

Do you know that you carry a computer with you everywhere you go? That's right—it's your brain. It's an amazing computer. It can add, subtract, multiply, and divide without paper and pencil, without keys or buttons, and without batteries or plugs. Best of all, it can think.

You can figure out a lot of math with your built-in computer. You can calculate exact answers in your head. That's called **mental math**. Another kind of mental math is **estimation**. When you estimate, you figure out *about* how much or *about* how many.

With mental math and estimation, your brain can make computation easier, and it can cut down on mistakes. You'll see how in this section.

Mental Math

Before you reach for a pencil or look for a calculator, think about whether you really need either.

In this section, you'll learn to do exercises like these in your head.

$$54 + 25 \qquad 64 - 39 \qquad 9 \times 18 \qquad 60 \div 5$$

When you compute in your head, you are doing **mental math.**

Mental Addition

You probably use mental math to add more often than you realize.

Suppose you have 19 rocks in your collection. Then you go on vacation and collect more rocks. You might use mental math to find how many rocks you now have in your collection.

Adding Three or More 1-Digit Addends

2004 Summer Olympics

Number of Medals

Country	Gold	Silver	Bronze
Brazil	4	3	3
Cuba	9	7	11
Kazakhstan	1	4	3
Belarus	2	6	7
Sweden	4	1	2

Source: www.athens2004.com

MORE
HELP
See 242

EXAMPLE 1: How many medals did Brazil win?

To solve the problem, add. $4 + 3 + 3 = \blacksquare$

$$\begin{array}{r} 4 \\ 3 \\ + 3 \\ \hline 10 \end{array}$$

$4 + 3 = 7$

$7 + 3 = 10$

> You can only add two addends at a time.

⭐ **ANSWER:** Brazil won a total of 10 medals.

EXAMPLE 2: How many silver medals were won by the five countries on the chart?

Add. $3 + 7 + 4 + 6 + 1 = \blacksquare$

$$\begin{array}{r} 3 \\ 7 \\ 4 \\ 6 \\ + 1 \\ \hline 21 \end{array}$$

$3 + 7 = 10$

$4 + 6 = 10$

> Try to make tens if you can.

$10 + 10 + 1 = 20 + 1$, or 21

⭐ **ANSWER:** The five countries won 21 silver medals.

Adding Tens and Hundreds

You can use basic facts to add tens or hundreds.

EXAMPLE 1: $40 + 80 = $ ■ $400 + 800 = $ ■

If you have 4 of any thing and you add 8 more of the same thing, you get 12 of that thing.

4 apples + 8 apples = 12 apples

4 tens + 8 tens = 12 tens

> 12 tens can be written as **12**0 and is the same as 1 hundred 2 tens.

MORE HELP
See 148–150

4 hundreds + 8 hundreds = 12 hundreds

> 12 hundreds can be written as **12**00 and is the same as 1 thousand 2 hundreds.

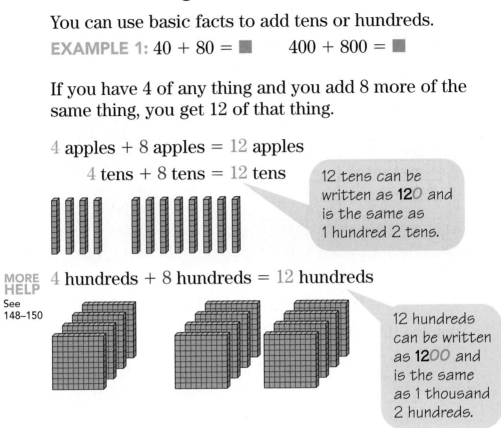

★ **ANSWER:** $40 + 80 = 120$ and $400 + 800 = 1200$

EXAMPLE 2: $500 + 60 + 700 + 30 = $ ■

$$
\begin{array}{r}
500 \\
60 \\
700 \\
+\ 30 \\
\hline
1290
\end{array}
$$

$500 + 700 = 1200$

$60 + 30 = 90$

$1200 + 90 = 1290$

★ **ANSWER:** $500 + 60 + 700 + 30 = 1290$

Adding on Tens and Ones

You may want to add numbers in your head. It can help to think about patterns on a hundred chart.

MORE HELP
See 428

Hundred Chart							
1	2	3	4	5	6	7	8
11	12	13	14	15	16	17	18
21	22	23	24	25	(26)	27	28
31	32	33	34	35	36	37	38
41	42	43	44	45	46	47	48
51	52	53	54	55	56	(57)→58	
61	62	63	64	65	66	67	68
71	72	73	74	75	76	77	78

To add **10**, move **down**.
$26 + 10 = 36$
$26 \downarrow = 36$

To add **1**, move *across*.
$57 + 1 = 58$
$57 \rightarrow = 58$

EXAMPLE: $45 + 32 = \blacksquare$

32 is 3 tens 2 ones. To add tens and ones, think about moving down and then across.

Hundred Chart							
1	2	3	4	5	6	7	8
11	12	13	14	15	16	17	18
21	22	23	24	25	26	27	28
31	32	33	34	35	36	37	38
41	42	43	44	(45)	46	47	48
51	52	53	54	55	56	57	58
61	62	63	64	65	66	67	68
71	72	73	74	(75)→76→77			78

Begin with 45, move **down** 3 tens.
$45 \downarrow\downarrow\downarrow = 75$

From 75, move *across* 2.
$75 \rightarrow \rightarrow = 77$

★ **ANSWER:** $45 + 32 = 77$

Breaking Up Numbers to Add

You can "break up" numbers to make adding easier. Then use mental math to add the parts.

EXAMPLE 1: Add. $42 + 59 = \blacksquare$

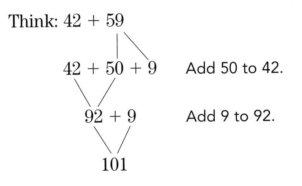

ONE WAY You can break up one addend.

Think: $42 + 59$

$42 + 50 + 9$ Add 50 to 42.

$92 + 9$ Add 9 to 92.

101

ANOTHER WAY You can break up both addends.

Think: $\quad 42 = 40 + 2$
$\quad\;\; +\,59 = 50 + 9$
$\qquad\qquad\; 90 + 11 = 101$

⭐ **ANSWER:** Either way, $42 + 59 = 101$.

EXAMPLE 2: Add. $42 + 70 + 22 + 59 = $ ◼

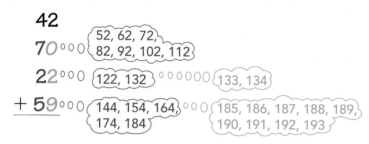

ONE WAY Start with the first addend. Add on the tens and ones from each of the other addends.

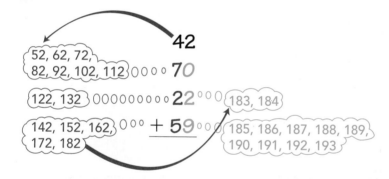

42
70 ° ° ° (52, 62, 72, 82, 92, 102, 112)
22 ° ° ° (122, 132) ° ° ° ° ° ° (133, 134)
+ 59 ° ° ° (144, 154, 164, 174, 184) ° ° ° (185, 186, 187, 188, 189, 190, 191, 192, 193)

ANOTHER WAY Start with the first addend. Add on all the tens. Then add on all the ones.

42
(52, 62, 72, 82, 92, 102, 112) ° ° ° ° 70
(122, 132) ° ° ° ° ° ° ° ° ° 22 ° ° ° (183, 184)
(142, 152, 162, 172, 182) ° ° ° + 59 ° ° ° (185, 186, 187, 188, 189, 190, 191, 192, 193)

⭐ **ANSWER:** Either way, $42 + 70 + 22 + 59 = 193$.

There are lots of ways to add in your head. Use the ways you like, or make up your own ways.

Adding with Compatible Numbers

Compatible numbers can make computation simpler. In addition, compatible numbers are pairs of numbers that give "friendly" sums such as 10, 100, or 1000.

EXAMPLE 1: Add. $40 + 30 + 60 + 50 + 70 = \blacksquare$

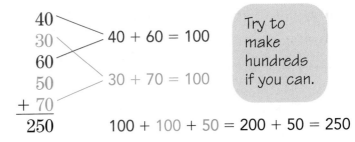

$$\begin{aligned}
40 \\
30 \\
60 \\
50 \\
+\ 70 \\
\hline
250
\end{aligned}$$

$40 + 60 = 100$

$30 + 70 = 100$

Try to make hundreds if you can.

$100 + 100 + 50 = 200 + 50 = 250$

⭐ **ANSWER:** $40 + 30 + 60 + 50 + 70 = 250$

EXAMPLE 2: Add. $350 + 170 + 80 + 650 + 30 = \blacksquare$

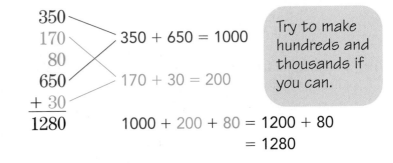

$$\begin{aligned}
350 \\
170 \\
80 \\
650 \\
+\ 30 \\
\hline
1280
\end{aligned}$$

$350 + 650 = 1000$

$170 + 30 = 200$

Try to make hundreds and thousands if you can.

$1000 + 200 + 80 = 1200 + 80$
$= 1280$

⭐ **ANSWER:** $350 + 170 + 80 + 650 + 30 = 1280$

Adding 25s, 50s, and 75s

Do you know how to count by 25?

25, 50, 75, 100, 125, …

You probably do, because you have experience counting quarters. Maybe you save quarters to use for video games or vending machines.

You can add multiples of 25 in your head.

$25 + 75 = 100$ (25¢)   (25¢) (25¢) (25¢)

$50 + 50 = 100$ (25¢) (25¢)   (25¢) (25¢)

Making Compatible Numbers to Add

You can break up numbers to make them compatible.

MORE
HELP
See 106

EXAMPLE: Clark School invites people to visit during Math Week. How many people visited the school on Wednesday and Thursday?

To solve the problem, add. $77 + 28 = \blacksquare$

Math Week at Clark School	
Day	Visitors
Monday	48
Tuesday	63
Wednesday	77
Thursday	28
Friday	64

Think:
$$\begin{array}{r} 77 = 75 + 2 \\ + 28 = 25 + 3 \\ \hline 100 + 5 = 105 \end{array}$$

75 and 25 are compatible numbers.

⭐ **ANSWER:** There were 105 visitors to the school on Wednesday and Thursday.

Adding 9 or 99

You know that 9 is 1 less than 10. You can use this fact to help you add 9 to any number.

EXAMPLE 1: $27 + 9 = \blacksquare$

To add 9, just add 10 and then subtract 1.

$27 + 10 = 37$

$$37 - 1 = 36$$

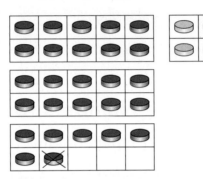

★ **ANSWER:** $27 + 9 = 36$

You can do the same thing with 99 and 100.

EXAMPLE 2: $213 + 99 = \blacksquare$

To add 99, just add 100 and then subtract 1.

$213 + 100 = 313$

$$313 - 1 = 312$$

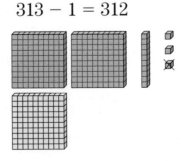

★ **ANSWER:** $213 + 99 = 312$

Give and Take to Add

When you take part of one addend and give it to another addend, you don't change the total.

> We need 2 more books.

> Here, take these.

> We still have the same number of books.

You can use this idea to add numbers mentally.

EXAMPLE: Bart unpacked a carton of 48 math books. Mio unpacked 35 math books. How many math books did they unpack?

To solve the problem, add. $48 + 35 = $ ■

ONE WAY You can make the second addend a multiple of 10.

$$48 + 35$$

It's easier to add 40 than 35. Take 5 from 48 and give it to 35 to make 40.

$-5 \quad +5$

$$43 + 40 = 83$$

ANOTHER WAY You can make the first addend a multiple of 10.

$$48 + 35$$

It's easier to add 50 than 48. Take 2 from 35 and give it to 48 to make 50.

$+2 \quad -2$

$$50 + 33 = 83$$

★ **ANSWER:** They unpacked 83 math books.

Mental Subtraction

Suppose you are playing baseball. You want to know how many runs your team needs to catch up. Knowing how to subtract in your head can come in handy at times like these.

Subtracting Tens and Ones

You may want to subtract numbers in your head. It can help to think about patterns on a hundred chart.

MORE HELP
See 428

Hundred Chart

1	2	3	4	5	6	7	8
11	12	13	14	15	16	17	18
21	22	23	24	25	26	27	28
31	32	33	34	35	(36)	37	38
41	42	43	44	45	46	47	48
51	52	53	54	55	56	57 ← (58)	

To subtract 10, move up.
$36 - 10 = 26$
$36 \uparrow = 26$

To subtract 1, move back.
$58 - 1 = 57$
$58 \leftarrow = 57$

EXAMPLE: $47 - 23 = \blacksquare$

23 is 2 tens 3 ones. To subtract tens and ones, think about moving up and then back.

Hundred Chart

1	2	3	4	5	6	7	8
11	12	13	14	15	16	17	18
21	22	23	24 ← 25 ← 26 ← (27)				28
31	32	From 27, move back 3.			37	38
41	42				(47)	48
51	52	$27 \leftarrow \leftarrow \leftarrow = 24$			57	58

Begin with 47, move up 2 tens
$47 \uparrow\uparrow = 27$

★ **ANSWER:** $47 - 23 = 24$

Subtracting 9 or 99

You know that 9 is 1 less than 10. You can use this fact to help you subtract 9 from any number.

EXAMPLE 1: $26 - 9 = \blacksquare$

To subtract 9, just subtract 10 and add 1.

$26 - 10 = 16$

$16 + 1 = 17$

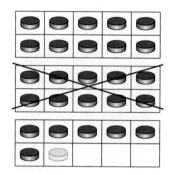

⭐ **ANSWER:** $26 - 9 = 17$

You can do the same thing with 99 and 100.

EXAMPLE 2: $323 - 99 = \blacksquare$

To subtract 99, just subtract 100 and add 1.

$323 - 100 = 223$

$223 + 1 = 224$

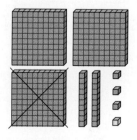

⭐ **ANSWER:** $323 - 99 = 224$

Subtracting in Parts

You can "break up" a number to make subtracting easier. Then use mental math to subtract the parts.

EXAMPLE: How much more does a science fiction book cost than a mystery book?

To solve the problem, subtract. $84 - 56 = $ ■

ONE WAY Break up 56 once.

Think of 56 as 54 + 2. $84 - 54 = 30$

$$\downarrow$$

$$30 - 2 = 28$$

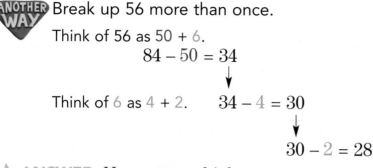

ANOTHER WAY Break up 56 more than once.

Think of 56 as 50 + 6.
$$84 - 50 = 34$$

↓

Think of 6 as 4 + 2. $34 - 4 = 30$

↓

$$30 - 2 = 28$$

⭐ ANSWER: No matter which way you use, a science fiction book costs 28¢ more than a mystery book.

Counting Up to Subtract

Sometimes you can count up to subtract. Count from the number you're subtracting to the number you're subtracting from.

EXAMPLE: Jafar is 12 years old and weighs 115 pounds. When he was 8 years old, he weighed 70 pounds. How much more does Jafar weigh now than he did when he was 8?

To solve, think about how much you need to add to 70 to get to 115.

$70 + 30 = 100$ 30 pounds to reach 100

↓   another 15 pounds

$100 + 15 = 115$ to reach 115

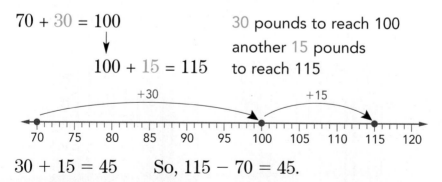

$30 + 15 = 45$ So, $115 - 70 = 45$.

⭐ ANSWER: Jafar weighs 45 pounds more now than when he was 8 years old.

Finding Easier Numbers to Subtract

If you add the same amount to both the number that you're subtracting and to the number you started with, the difference will be the same.

You can use this idea to help you subtract mentally.

EXAMPLE: It was 39 degrees when I got up this morning. By noon, the temperature was 64 degrees. By how many degrees did the temperature rise?

To solve this problem, subtract. $64 - 39 = \blacksquare$

$$64 - 39$$

$+1 \quad +1$

$$65 - 40 = 25$$

Think: Add 1 to 39 to make it 40. Add the same amount to 64 to keep the difference the same.

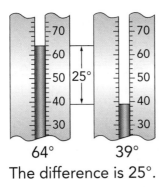

64°   39°
The difference is 25°.

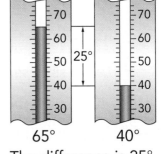

65°   40°
The difference is 25°.

⭐ **ANSWER:** The temperature rose 25 degrees.

Subtracting Multiples of 10 and 100

You can subtract multiples of ten or one hundred
mentally. Just think of their place-value names.

MORE
HELP
See 5

EXAMPLE 1: $90 - 50 = \blacksquare$

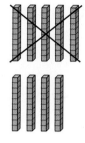

Think of 90 as 9 tens and
　　　　 50 as 5 tens.

9 tens $-$ 5 tens = 4 tens

★ **ANSWER:** $90 - 50 = 40$

EXAMPLE 2: $800 - 300 = \blacksquare$

Think of 800 as 8 hundreds and
　　　　 300 as 3 hundreds.

8 hundreds $-$ 3 hundreds = 5 hundreds

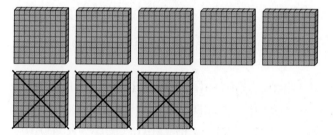

★ **ANSWER:** $800 - 300 = 500$

EXAMPLE 3: $2000 - 400 = \blacksquare$

You can think of 2000 as:
2 thousands　2000
　　　　or
20 hundreds　2000

Think of 2000 as 20 hundreds and
　　　　 400 as 4 hundreds.

20 hundreds $-$ 4 hundreds = 16 hundreds

★ **ANSWER:** $2000 - 400 = 1600$

Mental Multiplication

Do you know the basic multiplication facts? Do you understand place value? If you do, then you can multiply in your head in lots of different situations.

Skip Counting

You can skip count to multiply mentally.

EXAMPLE 1: How many pennies are equal to five quarters?

To solve, multiply. $5 \times 25 =$ ■

Skip count by 25, five times.

25,   50,   75,   100,   125

⭐ **ANSWER:** 125 pennies are equal to five quarters.

EXAMPLE 2: It takes Tom's family 3 days to travel from their home to Lake Geneva. They drive 200 miles a day. How many miles is Lake Geneva from Tom's home?

To solve, multiply. $3 \times 200 =$ ■

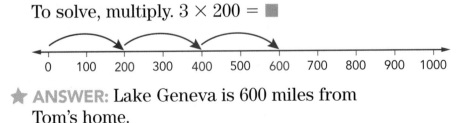

⭐ **ANSWER:** Lake Geneva is 600 miles from Tom's home.

Using Doubles to Multiply by 2, 4, or 8

You can sometimes find a product mentally by doubling one or more times.

The "The Lion King" is performed at The New Amsterdam Theater in New York. Balcony tickets for the evening performance on September 29, 2005 cost $40 each. *Source: www.telecharge.com*

EXAMPLE 1: How much would 2 tickets cost?

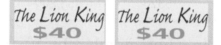

Think: 2×40 is $40 + 40$. $40 + 40 = 80$

⭐ **ANSWER:** Two tickets would cost $80.

EXAMPLE 2: How much would 4 tickets cost?

Think: 4×40 is double 2×40. $80 + 80 = 160$

⭐ **ANSWER:** Four tickets would cost $160.

EXAMPLE 3: How much would 8 tickets cost?

Think: 8×40 is double 4×40. $160 + 160 = 320$

⭐ **ANSWER:** Eight tickets would cost $320.

Multiplying by 10, 100, or 1000

The patterns in the table below show ways to multiply by 10, 100, or 1000 in your head.

Number	Number × 10	Number × 100	Number × 1000
5	50	500	5000
53	530	5300	53,000
532	5320	53,200	532,000

- To multiply a whole number by 10, tack on 1 zero at the right because there is 1 zero in 10.

EXAMPLE 1: $30 \times 10 = \blacksquare$

$30 \times 10 = 300$

> Notice that there are 2 zeros even though you multiplied by 10. That's because 30 has a zero in it!

⭐ **ANSWER:** $30 \times 10 = 300$

- To multiply a whole number by 100, tack on 2 zeros at the right because there are 2 zeros in 100.

EXAMPLE 2: $4 \times 100 = \blacksquare$

$4 \times 100 = 400$

⭐ **ANSWER:** $4 \times 100 = 400$

- To multiply a whole number by 1000, tack on 3 zeros at the right because there are 3 zeros in 1000.

EXAMPLE 3: $72 \times 1000 = \blacksquare$

$72 \times 1000 = 72,000$

⭐ **ANSWER:** $72 \times 1000 = 72,000$

Multiplying with Multiples of 10

When one or both factors are multiples of 10 (like 70, 300, or 8000), you can use basic facts to multiply mentally. Look at these patterns to see how.

MORE HELP

See 66–73

$$5 \times 9 = 45 \qquad\qquad 50 \times 90 = 4500$$
$$5 \times 90 = 450 \qquad\qquad 50 \times 900 = 45{,}000$$
$$5 \times 900 = 4500 \qquad\qquad 500 \times 900 = 450{,}000$$
$$5 \times 9000 = 45{,}000 \qquad 5000 \times 9000 = 45{,}000{,}000$$

To make the multiplication easier, drop the trailing zeros. Multiply. Then put all the trailing zeros back.

Case 1 Sometimes only one factor is a multiple of ten.

EXAMPLE 1: $8 \times 200 = $ ■

❶ Drop the 2 trailing zeros.	8×200
❷ Multiply.	$8 \times 2 = 16$
❸ Put the 2 trailing zeros back.	$8 \times 200 = 1600$

★ **ANSWER:** $8 \times 200 = 1600$

Case 2 Sometimes both factors are multiples of ten.

EXAMPLE 2: $50 \times 400 = $ ■

❶ Drop the 1 trailing zero from 50 and the 2 trailing zeros from 400.	50×400 5×4
❷ Multiply.	$5 \times 4 = 20$
❸ Put the 3 trailing zeros back.	$50 \times 400 = 20{,}000$

★ **ANSWER:** $50 \times 400 = 20{,}000$

The product has 4 zeros. The extra zero came from multiplying 4 and 5 to get 20.

Multiplying by 5

MORE
HELP
See 120,
126

EXAMPLE: Multiply. $5 \times 16 = \blacksquare$

Think about 5×16 as half of 10×16.

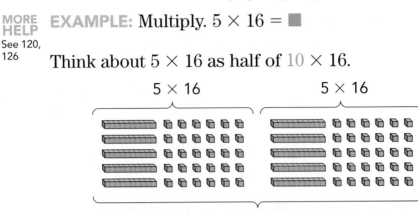

$$5 \times 16 \qquad 5 \times 16$$

$$10 \times 16$$

Multiply 16 by 10. $10 \times 16 = 160$

Divide 160 by 2. $160 \div 2 = 80$

⭐ **ANSWER:** $5 \times 16 = 80$

Multiplying by 9

EXAMPLE: Multiply. $9 \times 15 = \blacksquare$

Think about 9×15 as 15 less than 10×15.

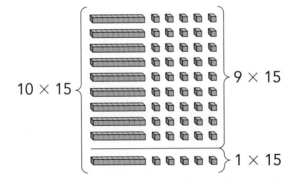

10×15

9×15

1×15

Multiply 15 by 10. $10 \times 15 = 150$

Subtract 15. $150 - 15 = 135$

⭐ **ANSWER:** $9 \times 15 = 135$

Breaking Apart Numbers to Multiply

To multiply a large number mentally, you can break it into smaller parts and multiply each part.

MORE HELP See 121

EXAMPLE 1: The monorail train at Lincoln Park has 5 cars. Each car can hold up to 23 people. What is the greatest number of people the train can hold at one time?

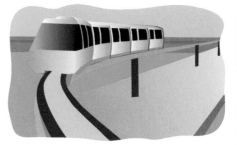

To solve the problem, multiply. $5 \times 23 = \blacksquare$

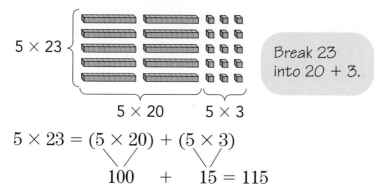

Break 23 into 20 + 3.

$5 \times 20 \qquad 5 \times 3$

$5 \times 23 = (5 \times 20) + (5 \times 3)$

$100 + 15 = 115$

⭐ **ANSWER:** The train can hold up to 115 people at one time.

EXAMPLE 2: Multiply. $4 \times 39 = \blacksquare$

Think of 39 as $40 - 1$.

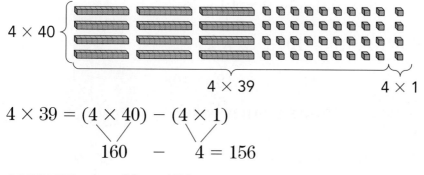

4×40

$4 \times 39 \qquad\qquad 4 \times 1$

$4 \times 39 = (4 \times 40) - (4 \times 1)$

$160 - 4 = 156$

⭐ **ANSWER:** $4 \times 39 = 156$

Multiplying by 11

You can multiply any 1-digit number by 11 in your head. Look at these patterns and see how.

$11 \times 1 = 11$

$11 \times 2 = 22$

$11 \times 3 = 33$

$11 \times 4 = 44$

$11 \times 5 = 55$

$11 \times 6 = 66$

$11 \times 7 = 77$

$11 \times 8 = 88$

$11 \times 9 = 99$

I think I'm seeing double.

No, you're just multiplying by 11.

Multiplying by 12

MORE HELP
See 119–120, 123

To multiply a number by 12, multiply by 10 and by 2 and then add the products.

EXAMPLE: Rosa's mother baked 9 dozen loaves of bread for the PTA bake sale. How many loaves did she bake?

There are 12 loaves of bread in a dozen.

To solve, multiply. $9 \times 12 = \blacksquare$

$9 \times 12 = (9 \times 10) + (9 \times 2)$

$$90 + 18 = 108$$

★ **ANSWER:** Rosa's mother baked 108 loaves of bread.

Three or More Factors

You can multiply a group of numbers mentally, but you can only multiply two numbers at a time. You can change the order of the factors to make the multiplication easier.

MORE HELP
See 241, 243

EXAMPLE 1: Multiply. $5 \times 3 \times 7 \times 2 = \blacksquare$

Think: $5 \times 3 \times 7 \times 2 = (5 \times 2) \times (3 \times 7)$

5 × 3 is 15
15 × 7 is ...

10×21

10 × 21 is easier.

210

⭐ **ANSWER:** $5 \times 3 \times 7 \times 2 = 210$

EXAMPLE 2: The camp swimming pool is 25 meters long, 7 meters wide, and the water is 4 meters deep. What is the volume of the swimming pool?

MORE HELP
See 354–355

To solve the problem, multiply. $25 \times 7 \times 4 = \blacksquare$

Think: $25 \times 4 \times 7$

$100 \times 7 = 700$

Multiplying is easier when one of the factors is 10 or 100.

⭐ **ANSWER:** The volume of the swimming pool is 700 cubic meters.

Mental Division

You may divide in your head more often than you realize it. Suppose you need hamburger rolls for a large party. If the rolls come in packages of 8, you can use mental math to decide how many packages to buy. Of course, it helps to know your eights facts.

Dividing by 2

To divide a number by 2, find half of it.

EXAMPLE: $48 \div 2 = \blacksquare$

Think of 48 as $40 + 8$.

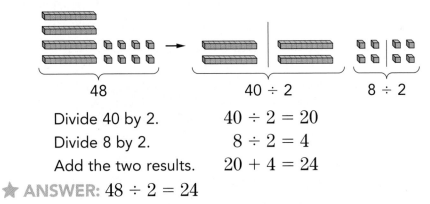

48	$40 \div 2$	$8 \div 2$

Divide 40 by 2.	$40 \div 2 = 20$
Divide 8 by 2.	$8 \div 2 = 4$
Add the two results.	$20 + 4 = 24$

⭐ **ANSWER:** $48 \div 2 = 24$

Dividing by 10

When a number ends in zero, dividing by 10 is easy. Just drop the zero.

$60 \div 10 = 6$

$600 \div 10 = 60$

MORE
HELP
See 120
$340 \div 10 = 34$

Think about the related multiplication sentences.

$6 \times 10 = 60$
$60 \times 10 = 600$
$34 \times 10 = 340$

Dividing Multiples of 10

Sometimes you can use basic division facts to help you divide multiples of 10 (like 50, 600, or 8000) in your head. Look at these patterns to see how.

$$6 \div 3 = 2 \qquad \text{6 ones} \div 3 = \text{2 ones}$$
$$60 \div 3 = 20 \qquad \text{6 tens} \div 3 = \text{2 tens}$$
$$600 \div 3 = 200 \qquad \text{6 hundreds} \div 3 = \text{2 hundreds}$$
$$6000 \div 3 = 2000 \qquad \text{6 thousands} \div 3 = \text{2 thousands}$$

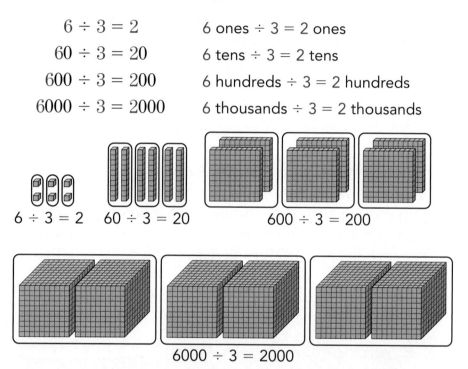

$6 \div 3 = 2 \qquad 60 \div 3 = 20 \qquad\qquad 600 \div 3 = 200$

$6000 \div 3 = 2000$

This shortcut will work when, after all the trailing zeros are dropped, the quotient is a whole number.

EXAMPLE: Divide. $2700 \div 9 = \blacksquare$

❶ Drop the 2 trailing zeros.	$2700 \div 9$
❷ Divide.	$27 \div 9 = 3$
❸ Put the 2 trailing zeros back.	$2700 \div 9 = 300$

★ **ANSWER:** $2700 \div 9 = 300$

MORE HELP
See 82–85

Estimation

When you see words such as *about, close to, just about, a little more than, approximately,* or *almost,* you can be sure that the number given is an **estimate**. An estimate is a number close to the exact amount. Sometimes an estimate is said to be "in the ballpark."

Rounding Numbers

When you **round** a number, you are changing it to a number that is easy to work with, but still close enough to use. A rounded number often has one or more nice, "round" zeros at the end.

Rounding to the Nearest Ten

Rounded numbers give a rough idea of an amount.

ONE WAY You can use a number line.

EXAMPLE 1: Round 57 to the nearest ten.

50 is the closest ten less than 57.　　60 is the closest ten greater than 57.

57

40　　　　　50　　　　　60　　　　　70

⭐ **ANSWER:** 57 is closer to 60 than to 50. So, 57 rounds up to 60.

ANOTHER WAY You can use place value.

EXAMPLE 2: Round 32 to the nearest ten.

❶ Find the tens place.	32
❷ Look at the digit one place to the right.	32
❸ If this digit is 5 or greater, round up. If this digit is less than 5, round down. 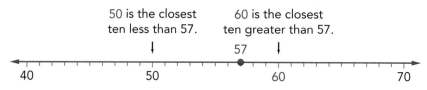	2 is less than 5. Round down.

round up
5 6 7 8 9
0 1 2 3 4
round down

⭐ **ANSWER:** 32 rounds down to 30.

When you round down, the digit in the rounding place stays the same.

Rounding Whole Numbers to the Nearest Hundred or Thousand

EXAMPLE 1: Round 427 to the nearest hundred.

ONE WAY You can use a number line.

400 is the closest hundred less than 427.

500 is the closest hundred greater than 427.

| 427 |

| 200 | 300 | 400 | 500 | 600 | 700 |

427 rounds down to 400.

ANOTHER WAY You can use place value.

❶ Find the hundreds place.	427
❷ Look at the digit one place to the right.	427
❸ If this digit is 5 or greater, round up. If this digit is less than 5, round down.	2 is less than 5. Round down.

★ **ANSWER:** Either way, 427 rounds down to 400.

EXAMPLE 2: Round 2613 to the nearest thousand.

❶ Find the thousands place.	2613
❷ Look at the digit one place to the right.	2613
❸ If this digit is 5 or greater, round up. If this digit is less than 5, round down.	6 is greater than 5. Round up.

★ **ANSWER:** 2613 rounds up to 3000.

You can round a number to any place. You can also round 2613 to 2600 (to the nearest hundred) or to 2610 (to the nearest 10).

Rounding Decimals

You can round decimals the same way you round whole numbers.

EXAMPLE 1: A survey showed that the average person reads 2.8 hours each week. Round this decimal to the nearest whole number.

❶ Find the whole number place.	2.8
❷ Look at the digit one place to the right.	2.8
❸ If this digit is 5 or greater, round up. If this digit is less than 5, round down.	8 is greater than 5. Round up.

⭐ **ANSWER:** 2.8 rounds up to 3.

> You can round decimal money amounts to the nearest dollar: $2.80 rounds to $3.00.

EXAMPLE 2: Round 3.62 to the nearest tenth.

❶ Find the tenths place.	3.62
❷ Look at the digit one place to the right.	3.62
❸ If this digit is 5 or greater, round up. If this digit is less than 5, round down.	2 is less than 5. Round down.

⭐ **ANSWER:** 3.62 rounds down to 3.6.

Sometimes you can estimate to check the reasonableness of an exact answer you've found. Sometimes you estimate *instead* of finding an exact answer.

For example, is $60 enough money to buy a sweater that costs $19 and a pair of pants that cost $28?

You can estimate $19 + $28 to see if the sum is less than $60. You don't have to find the exact sum.

Rounding to Estimate
Sums and Differences

MORE HELP
See 129

EXAMPLE 1: Estimate the sum of $19 and $28 by rounding each to the nearest ten.

$$19 + 28$$
$$\downarrow \quad \downarrow$$
$$20 + 30 = 50$$

> 19 is less than 20 and 28 is less than 30. So, the estimate of 50 is greater than the actual sum. 50 is an **overestimate**.

★ **ANSWER:**
$19 + $28 is about $50.

MORE HELP
See 130

EXAMPLE 2: Estimate the sum of 328 and 462 by rounding to the nearest hundred.

$$328 + 462$$
$$\downarrow \quad \downarrow$$
$$300 + 500 = 800$$

★ **ANSWER:** The sum is about 800.

When you estimate the sum of two or more numbers that have a different number of places, it makes sense to round all of the numbers to the same place.

EXAMPLE 3: Estimate the sum of 546, 78, and 212.

ONE WAY You can estimate by rounding each addend to the nearest hundred.

546 + 78 + 212
 ↓   ↓   ↓
500 + 100 + 200 = 800

⭐ **ANSWER:** The sum of 546, 78, and 212 is about 800.

ANOTHER WAY You can estimate by rounding each addend to the nearest ten.

546 + 78 + 212
 ↓   ↓   ↓
550 + 80 + 210 = 840

⭐ **ANSWER:** The sum of 546, 78, and 212 is about 840.

EXAMPLE 4: About how much more does a fast food meal cost in New York than it does in Dallas?

You can estimate the difference by rounding the cost of each meal to the nearest dollar.

NEW YORK
$5.68

DALLAS
$4.27

$5.68 − $4.27
 ↓   ↓
$6.00 − $4.00 = $2.00

Source: Runzheimer International

⭐ **ANSWER:** The fast food meal costs about $2 more in New York than it does in Dallas.

Front-End Estimation
of Sums and Differences

You can estimate sums and differences using just the front digits. This is called **front-end estimation.**

Case 1 When the numbers have the same number of digits, add the front digits.

EXAMPLE 1: A day camp held registration for 3 days. Each child who registered was to get one of 750 camp hats. Did each child get a hat?

Camp Registration		
Day 1	Day 2	Day 3
347	422	183

To solve, estimate the sum of 347, 422, and 183 using front-end estimation.

$$
\begin{array}{rcr}
347 & \rightarrow & 300 \\
422 & \rightarrow & 400 \\
+\ 183 & \rightarrow & +\ 100 \\
\hline
 & & 800
\end{array}
$$

⭐ **ANSWER:** 800 is greater than 750. All of the children who registered did not get a hat.

When adding, a front-end estimate will always give a sum that is less than the exact sum. This is called an **underestimate.**

EXAMPLE 2: Estimate the difference between 708 and 259 using front-end estimation.

$$
\begin{array}{rcr}
708 & \rightarrow & 700 \\
-\ 259 & \rightarrow & -\ 200 \\
\hline
 & & 500
\end{array}
$$

⭐ **ANSWER:** The difference is about 500.

Case 2 When the numbers have a different number of digits, you can still use front-end estimation.

Find the number with the least number of digits. Use that number to decide where to cut off the front digits in the other numbers.

EXAMPLE 3: Estimate the sum of 137, 29, and 233 using front-end estimation.

$$
\begin{array}{rcl}
137 & \rightarrow & 130 \\
29 & \rightarrow & 20 \\
+\,233 & \rightarrow & +\,230 \\
\hline
 & & 380
\end{array}
$$

Think: 29 has the fewest digits.
Cut off after the tens place.

⭐ ANSWER: The sum is about 380.

EXAMPLE 4: Estimate the difference between 15.4 and 9.3 using front-end estimation.

$$
\begin{array}{rcl}
15.4 & \rightarrow & 15.0 \\
-\,9.3 & \rightarrow & -\,9.0 \\
\hline
 & & 6.0
\end{array}
$$

Think: 9.3 has fewer digits. Cut off after the whole number.

⭐ ANSWER: The difference is about 6.

EXAMPLE 5: About how much would it cost to buy one angel fish which costs $3.49, one guppy which costs $2.25, and one zebra fish which costs $4.25?

To solve, you can estimate the sum using front-end estimation.

$$
\begin{array}{rcl}
\$3.49 & \rightarrow & \$3.00 \\
2.25 & \rightarrow & 2.00 \\
+\,4.25 & \rightarrow & +\,4.00 \\
\hline
 & & \$9.00
\end{array}
$$

⭐ ANSWER: It will cost about $9.00.

Estimating Products

You can check the product displayed on a calculator by estimating. You can also estimate when you don't need an exact answer.

Rounding to Estimate Products

MORE HELP
See 129

Case 1 Estimate by rounding one factor.

EXAMPLE 1: A ticket to the school play costs $5. Lucy sold 74 tickets. Did she collect more than $300?

You can solve by estimating the product of 74 × $5.

74 × $5
↓ ↓
70 × $5 = $350

Only 74 was rounded.

Since 70 is less than 74, 70 × 5 is less than 74 × 5. So, the estimate of $350 is less than the actual product. It is an **underestimate.** That means that Lucy collected more than $350. So, of course, she collected more than $300.

★ **ANSWER:** Lucy collected more than $300.

EXAMPLE 2: The third-grade play was performed on 4 different days. Each day, all 389 tickets were sold. About how many tickets were sold in all?

MORE HELP
See 130

You can solve by estimating the product.

4 × 389
↓ ↓
4 × 400 = 1600

★ **ANSWER:** About 1600 tickets were sold.

*400 is greater than 389. So, the estimate of 1600 is greater than the actual product. 1600 is an **overestimate.** Fewer than 1600 tickets were sold.*

Case 2 Estimate by rounding each factor.

EXAMPLE 3: The school auditorium has 39 rows of 53 seats. About how many seats are in the room?

Round each factor to its greatest place value.

39×53
↓   ↓
$40 \times 50 = 2000$

⭐ **ANSWER:** There are about 2000 seats in the room.

Front-End Estimation of Products

You can multiply the front digits of factors to estimate a product. You will always get an underestimate because it's the same as if you rounded all the factors down.

EXAMPLE: About how much will 8 paintbrushes cost, if each paintbrush costs $1.19?

$8 \times \$1.19$
↓   ↓
$8 \times \$1 = \$8$

⭐ **ANSWER:** 8 paintbrushes will cost about $8.

Suppose you have only $8.25. You're not sure you can buy the paintbrushes with that amount.

You can make your front-end estimate closer to the actual product. Just use more digits.

$8 \times \$1.19$
↓   ↓
$8 \times \$1.10 = \$8.80$

Now you know you don't have enough money!

Estimating Products
Using Compatible Numbers

MORE HELP
See 120–121

When you estimate, look for **compatible numbers**. For multiplication, these are numbers that are easy to multiply.

We get along with everyone.

Any factor is compatible with a multiple of 10, because there are easy shortcuts for multiplying by multiples of 10.

EXAMPLE 1: Chan makes skateboards. He can make 42 skateboards in a week. About how many skateboards can Chan make in 9 weeks?

To solve, you can estimate the product of 9 and 42.

Think: 9 is close to 10.

9×42

$10 \times 42 = 420$

⭐ **ANSWER:** Chan can make about 420 skateboards.

MORE HELP
See 125

EXAMPLE 2: Estimate 4×26.

Think: 26 is close to 25.

4×26

$4 \times 25 = 100$

When you multiply by 25, think about quarters. Four quarters are the same as $1.00. So, $4 \times 25 = 100$.

⭐ **ANSWER:** 4×26 is a little more than 100.

Estimating Quotients

Estimation can be useful if you want to check the reasonableness of your quotient. It can also be helpful if you just want to know how many digits there are in your quotient.

Estimating Quotients Using Compatible Numbers

Look for **compatible numbers** when you estimate quotients. Compatible numbers are numbers that are easy to divide.

EXAMPLE: There are 437 people signed up for a city tour in double-decker buses. The tour company will use 6 buses. On average, about how many people will ride on each bus?

MORE HELP
See 82–85, 285

To solve, estimate $437 \div 6$.

Look for a basic fact.

$437 \div 6$

$\downarrow \quad \downarrow$

$420 \div 6 = 70$

Think: 43 is close to 42.

$42 \div 6 = 7$

Since $437 > 420$, $420 \div 6$ is less than $437 \div 6$. So, the estimate of 70 is less than the actual quotient. It is an **underestimate**. That means that, on average, more than 70 people will ride on each bus.

★ **ANSWER:** On average, more than 70 people will ride on each bus.

Using Multiples of 10 to Estimate Quotients

MORE HELP
See 120–121, 129

You can use what you know about multiplying and dividing with multiples of 10 to help you estimate quotients.

Since multiplication is the opposite of division, you can use multiplication to find the number of digits in a quotient. You can also multiply to estimate a quotient.

EXAMPLE: There are 637 pencils in stock in the school supply store. Each box holds 8 pencils. About how many boxes of pencils are in stock?

To solve, you can estimate the quotient of 637 ÷ 8.

1 Multiply the divisor by 10, 100, and 1000, to find the number of digits in the quotient.	$8 \times 10 = 80$ —— 637 $8 \times 100 = 800$ $8 \times 1000 = 8000$	637 is between 80 and 800, so the quotient is between 10 and 100. It has two digits.
2 Multiply the rounded 2-digit numbers by 8.	$8 \times 10 = 80$ $8 \times 20 = 160$ $8 \times 30 = 240$ $8 \times 40 = 320$ $8 \times 50 = 400$ $8 \times 60 = 480$ $8 \times 70 = 560$ —— 637 $8 \times 80 = 640$ $8 \times 90 = 720$	637 is between 560 and 640 but is closer to 640. The quotient is close to 80.

★ **ANSWER:** There are about 80 boxes of pencils in the school supply store.

Estimating with Fractions

When you estimate, use **benchmarks**—numbers that are easy to work with. Common benchmarks for estimating with fractions are 0, $\frac{1}{2}$, and 1.

MORE
HELP
See 224

Benchmark Fractions

A number line or a picture can help you decide whether a fraction is closest to 0, $\frac{1}{2}$, or 1.

- $\frac{1}{8}$ is closest to 0.

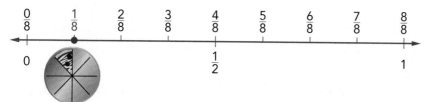

- $\frac{6}{10}$ is closest to $\frac{1}{2}$.

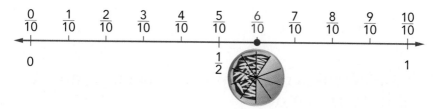

- $\frac{11}{12}$ is closest to 1.

Estimating Sums and Differences of Fractions Less than One

MORE HELP
See 141, 227, 232 **EXAMPLE 1:** Yuki's mother needs 2 yards of green fabric for her quilt pattern. She has a piece $\frac{7}{8}$ yard long and a piece $\frac{3}{8}$ yard long. Does she have enough green fabric?

To solve, estimate the sum of $\frac{7}{8}$ and $\frac{3}{8}$.

Think: $\frac{7}{8}$ is close to 1. $\frac{3}{8}$ is close to $\frac{1}{2}$.

$$\frac{7}{8} + \frac{3}{8}$$
$$\downarrow \quad \downarrow$$
$$1 + \frac{1}{2} = 1\frac{1}{2}$$

Since $\frac{7}{8}$ is less than 1 and $\frac{3}{8}$ is less than $\frac{1}{2}$, $1\frac{1}{2}$ is an **overestimate**. She has less than $1\frac{1}{2}$ yards.

★ **ANSWER:** $1\frac{1}{2}$ yards is less than 2 yards. Yuki's mother does not have enough green fabric.

EXAMPLE 2: Yuki's mother cuts $\frac{1}{3}$ yard of yellow fabric from a piece that measures $\frac{7}{8}$ yard. About how much yellow fabric does she have left over?

To solve, estimate the difference between $\frac{7}{8}$ and $\frac{1}{3}$.

Think: $\frac{7}{8}$ is close to 1. $\frac{1}{3}$ is close to $\frac{1}{2}$.

$$\frac{7}{8} - \frac{1}{3}$$
$$\downarrow \quad \downarrow$$
$$1 - \frac{1}{2} = \frac{1}{2}$$

★ **ANSWER:** Yuki's mother will have about $\frac{1}{2}$ yard of yellow fabric left over.

Estimating Sums and Differences of Mixed Numbers

Let's see.
For one batch I need:
$3\frac{9}{16}$ pounds of peanuts
$1\frac{7}{8}$ pounds of hazelnuts
$2\frac{1}{8}$ pounds of cashews

EXAMPLE 1: About how much does the batch weigh?

MORE HELP See 141, 230–231, 234–235

To solve, estimate the sum of $3\frac{9}{16}$, $1\frac{7}{8}$, and $2\frac{1}{8}$.
Use benchmark fractions.

$$3\frac{9}{16} \rightarrow 3\frac{1}{2} \qquad \frac{9}{16} \text{ is about } \frac{1}{2}. \quad 3 + \frac{1}{2} = 3\frac{1}{2}$$

$$1\frac{7}{8} \rightarrow 2 \qquad \frac{7}{8} \text{ is about } 1. \quad 1 + 1 = 2$$

$$+ 2\frac{1}{8} \rightarrow + 2 \qquad \frac{1}{8} \text{ is about } 0. \quad 2 + 0 = 2$$

$$7\frac{1}{2}$$

⭐ **ANSWER:** One batch weighs about $7\frac{1}{2}$ pounds.

EXAMPLE 2: About how many more pounds of peanuts than cashews are in a batch?

To solve, estimate $3\frac{9}{16} - 2\frac{1}{8}$.
Use benchmark fractions.

$$3\frac{9}{16} \rightarrow 3\frac{1}{2} \qquad \frac{9}{16} \text{ is about } \frac{1}{2}. \quad 3 + \frac{1}{2} = 3\frac{1}{2}$$

$$- 2\frac{1}{8} \rightarrow - 2 \qquad \frac{1}{8} \text{ is about } 0. \quad 2 + 0 = 2$$

$$1\frac{1}{2}$$

⭐ **ANSWER:** There are about $1\frac{1}{2}$ more pounds of peanuts than cashews.

Computing with Whole Numbers and Decimals

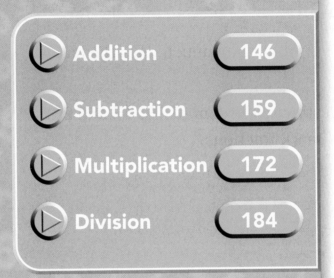

Which is easier, counting or computing? Before you answer, imagine this: You have filled a 40-page book with 12 stickers on each page. You want to know how many stickers are in your book. It sure would be faster to multiply 12 by 40 than to count every single one of the 480 stickers. You would also be less likely to make a mistake.

Adding, subtracting, multiplying, and dividing may seem like a lot of work. However, they actually make things easier.

Addition

In many number systems, adding can be very complicated. In our system, the nice thing about adding whole numbers or decimals is that we can add by doing the same steps over and over.

Adding Whole Numbers

You can use what you know about place value and addition facts to add whole numbers.

Adding Without Regrouping

EXAMPLE: Add. $264 + 315 = $ ■

ONE WAY You can add using place-value models.

MORE HELP
See 36, 104

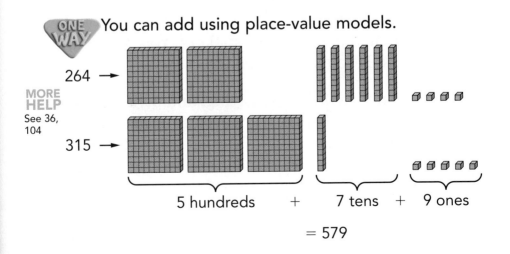

264 →

315 →

5 hundreds   +   7 tens   +   9 ones

= 579

ANOTHER WAY You can line up the addends. Then add each column starting at the right.

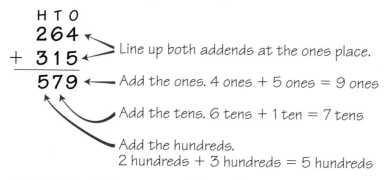

H T O
```
  264
+ 315
  579
```

Line up both addends at the ones place.

Add the ones. 4 ones + 5 ones = 9 ones

Add the tens. 6 tens + 1 ten = 7 tens

Add the hundreds.
2 hundreds + 3 hundreds = 5 hundreds

The **H, T,** and **O** above the columns stand for hundreds, tens, and ones.

★ **ANSWER:** Either way, $264 + 315 = 579$.

MATH ALERT

Line Up the Digits to Add

Be sure to line up the ones, line up the tens, and so on. You can turn a piece of lined paper sideways to help you keep the columns straight.

correct way
```
  208
+  51
  259
```

```
  208
+  51
  718
```
incorrect way

MORE HELP
See 5, 13

You can also use graph paper to help you line up the digits. When you line up the places correctly, you are sure to add ones to ones, tens to tens, and hundreds to hundreds.

Regrouping Ones

Suppose you have 12 one-dollar bills. You could trade 10 of them for 1 ten-dollar bill. You would still have the same amount of money. **Regrouping** is like trading bills. You get different numbers of tens and ones, but the total amount is the same.

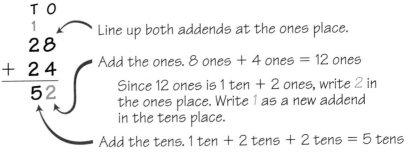

12 ones → 1 ten + 2 ones

Regrouping is sometimes called **renaming**.

MORE HELP
See 104

Adding—Regrouping Ones

When you add, sometimes the sum of the ones may be 10 or greater. But only one digit can go in the ones place in the sum. So you regroup the ones.

EXAMPLE: The United States has 28 endangered species of reptiles and 24 endangered species of amphibians. How many species is this?

Source: International Union for the Conservation of Nature

When there are very few of a kind of animal left in the world, they are called an *endangered species*.

To solve the problem, add. $28 + 24 = $ ■

```
  T O
  1        Line up both addends at the ones place.
  2 8
+ 2 4      Add the ones. 8 ones + 4 ones = 12 ones
-----
  5 2      Since 12 ones is 1 ten + 2 ones, write 2 in
           the ones place. Write 1 as a new addend
           in the tens place.

           Add the tens. 1 ten + 2 tens + 2 tens = 5 tens
```

⭐ ANSWER: There are 52 endangered species of reptiles and amphibians in the United States.

Regrouping Tens

Suppose you have 12 ten-dollar bills. You could trade 10 of them for 1 one-hundred-dollar bill. You would have fewer bills, but you would still have $120. This is like **regrouping** 12 tens as 1 hundred plus 2 tens.

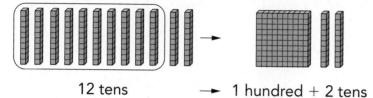

12 tens   →   1 hundred + 2 tens

Adding—Regrouping Tens

When you add, the sum of the tens may be 10 or greater. But only one digit can go in the tens place of the sum. That's when you regroup the tens so that there is only one digit in each place.

EXAMPLE: Al and Kate each collect comic books. Al has 273 comic books. Kate has 153 more than Al. How many comic books does Kate have?

MORE HELP
See 104

To solve the problem, add. $273 + 153 = $

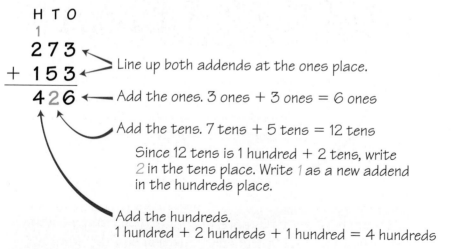

```
  H T O
  1
  2 7 3
+ 1 5 3
  4 2 6
```

Line up both addends at the ones place.

Add the ones. 3 ones + 3 ones = 6 ones

Add the tens. 7 tens + 5 tens = 12 tens

Since 12 tens is 1 hundred + 2 tens, write 2 in the tens place. Write 1 as a new addend in the hundreds place.

Add the hundreds.
1 hundred + 2 hundreds + 1 hundred = 4 hundreds

★ ANSWER: Kate has 426 comic books.

Adding with More Than One Regrouping

When you add, you may need to regroup more than once.

Socks: 267 pairs
Bicycle Shorts: 343
Boys' Bicycles: 56
Girls' Bicycles: 97

Closing Sale!
Everything
must go!

Sweaters: 476
Bike Helmets: 340
Girls' Shirts: 605
Boys' Shirts: 909

EXAMPLE 1: How many bicycles are on sale?

MORE HELP See 104

To solve, add. 56 + 97 = ■

> To estimate the sum, round each addend to the nearest ten. 60 + 100 = 160

```
  H T O
  1 1
    5 6
+   9 7
  1 5 3
```

Line up both addends at the ones place.

Add the ones. 6 ones + 7 ones = 13 ones

Since 13 ones is 1 ten + 3 ones, write 3 in the ones place. Write 1 as a new addend in the tens place.

Add the tens. 1 ten + 5 tens + 9 tens = 15 tens

Since 15 tens is 1 hundred + 5 tens, write 5 in the tens place. Write 1 as a new addend in the hundreds place.

Add the hundreds.
1 hundred + 0 hundreds = 1 hundred

> Since there are no hundreds to add, you can just write the new hundred in the hundreds place in the sum.

★ **ANSWER:** There are 153 bicycles on sale.

> 153 is close to the estimate, 160.

EXAMPLE 2: How many pairs of socks and bicycle shorts are on sale?

To solve this problem, add. 267 + 343 = ■

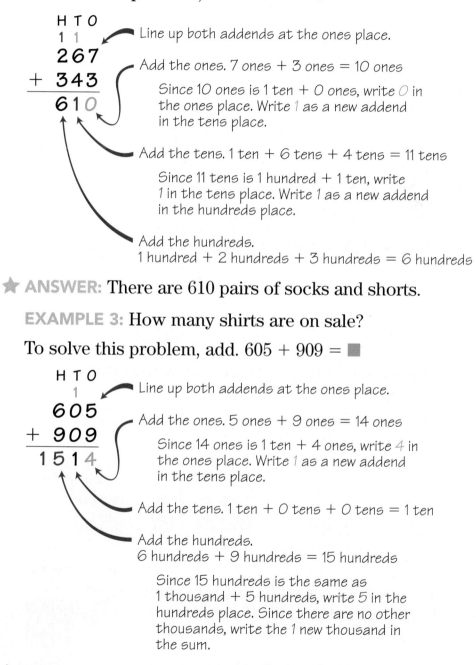

```
  H T O
  1 1
   2 6 7
+  3 4 3
   6 1 0
```

Line up both addends at the ones place.

Add the ones. 7 ones + 3 ones = 10 ones

Since 10 ones is 1 ten + 0 ones, write 0 in the ones place. Write 1 as a new addend in the tens place.

Add the tens. 1 ten + 6 tens + 4 tens = 11 tens

Since 11 tens is 1 hundred + 1 ten, write 1 in the tens place. Write 1 as a new addend in the hundreds place.

Add the hundreds.
1 hundred + 2 hundreds + 3 hundreds = 6 hundreds

★ ANSWER: There are 610 pairs of socks and shorts.

EXAMPLE 3: How many shirts are on sale?

To solve this problem, add. 605 + 909 = ■

```
  H T O
    1
   6 0 5
+  9 0 9
 1 5 1 4
```

Line up both addends at the ones place.

Add the ones. 5 ones + 9 ones = 14 ones

Since 14 ones is 1 ten + 4 ones, write 4 in the ones place. Write 1 as a new addend in the tens place.

Add the tens. 1 ten + 0 tens + 0 tens = 1 ten

Add the hundreds.
6 hundreds + 9 hundreds = 15 hundreds

Since 15 hundreds is the same as 1 thousand + 5 hundreds, write 5 in the hundreds place. Since there are no other thousands, write the 1 new thousand in the sum.

★ ANSWER: There are 1514 shirts on sale.

Sometimes You Don't Need to Regroup

You should regroup only when the sum of the digits in any place is 10 or greater.

The answer should be 96. What did I do wrong?

Checking Addition

To check addition, you can change the order of the addends.

EXAMPLE: Does 234 + 479 = 703? Add in a different order to check.

MORE HELP See 240

```
  11          11
 234         479
+479        +234
 703         713
```

I do it a little differently. First I add by starting at the top. Then I add again by starting at the bottom of each column.

713 does not equal 703. So, you need to add again to decide if either sum is correct.

★ **ANSWER:** No, the correct sum is 713.

Column Addition

Here's how to add more than two numbers.

EXAMPLE: Add. 66 + 37 + 48 + 53 = ■

MORE
HELP
See 103,
240, 242

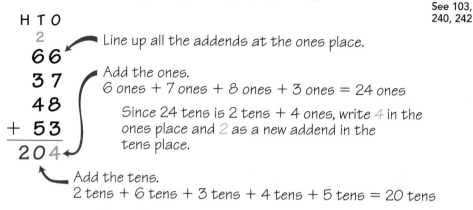

H T O
```
    2
  6 6
  3 7
  4 8
+ 5 3
─────
2 0 4
```

Line up all the addends at the ones place.

Add the ones.
6 ones + 7 ones + 8 ones + 3 ones = 24 ones

Since 24 tens is 2 tens + 4 ones, write 4 in the ones place and 2 as a new addend in the tens place.

Add the tens.
2 tens + 6 tens + 3 tens + 4 tens + 5 tens = 20 tens

Since 20 tens is 2 hundreds + 0 tens, write 0 in the tens place and 2 in the hundreds place.

★ **ANSWER:** 66 + 37 + 48 + 53 = 204

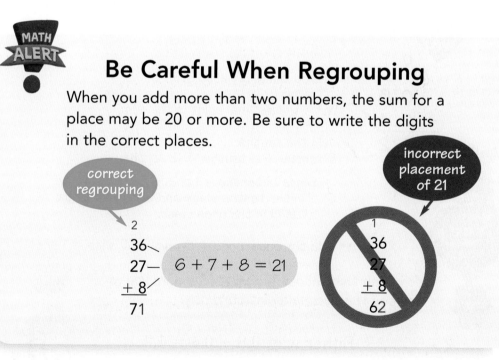

MATH ALERT

Be Careful When Regrouping

When you add more than two numbers, the sum for a place may be 20 or more. Be sure to write the digits in the correct places.

correct regrouping

```
  2
 36
 27      6 + 7 + 8 = 21
+ 8
────
 71
```

incorrect placement of 21

```
  1
 36
 27
+ 8
────
 62
```

Adding Decimal Numbers

If you know how to add whole numbers, then you can add decimals. Line up the decimal points. That will make the numbers in all places line up correctly.

- Start from the right and add each column.
- Regroup when the digits in a column total 10 or more.

Adding Tenths

MORE
HELP
See 22,
23

EXAMPLE 1: Add. $0.8 + 0.4 = $ ■

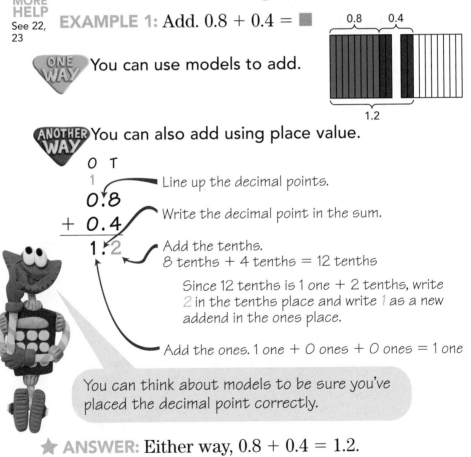

ONE WAY You can use models to add.

ANOTHER WAY You can also add using place value.

O T
1
0.8
+ 0.4
1.2

Line up the decimal points.

Write the decimal point in the sum.

Add the tenths.
8 tenths + 4 tenths = 12 tenths

Since 12 tenths is 1 one + 2 tenths, write 2 in the tenths place and write 1 as a new addend in the ones place.

Add the ones. 1 one + 0 ones + 0 ones = 1 one

You can think about models to be sure you've placed the decimal point correctly.

⭐ **ANSWER:** Either way, $0.8 + 0.4 = 1.2$.

EXAMPLE 2: At a local competition, a gymnast scored 4.6 for the floor exercises. She received a score that was 0.5 higher for the balance beam. What score did she receive on the balance beam?

To solve the problem, add 4.6 and 0.5.

ONE WAY You can use models to add.

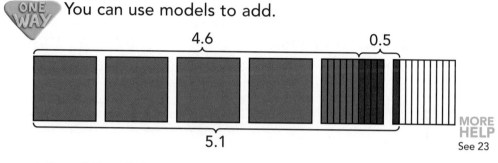

4.6   0.5

5.1

MORE HELP
See 23

$$4.6 + 0.5 = 5.1$$

ANOTHER WAY You can also add using place value.

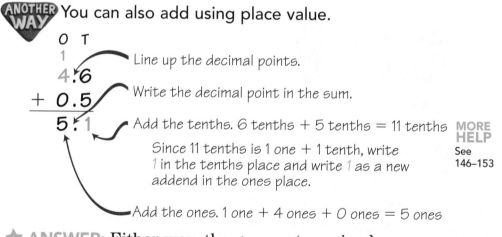

O T

1

4.6

+ 0.5

5.1

Line up the decimal points.

Write the decimal point in the sum.

Add the tenths. 6 tenths + 5 tenths = 11 tenths

Since 11 tenths is 1 one + 1 tenth, write 1 in the tenths place and write 1 as a new addend in the ones place.

Add the ones. 1 one + 4 ones + 0 ones = 5 ones

MORE HELP
See
146–153

⭐ **ANSWER:** Either way, the gymnast received a score of 5.1 on the balance beam.

Adding Hundredths

EXAMPLE 1: Liza's pet hedgehog weighs 0.34 pounds more than the average guinea pig. How much does her pet weigh?

To solve the problem, add. $1.54 + 0.34 =$ ■

Average Weight of Small Animals (in Pounds)	
Animal	Weight
Chinchilla	1.50
Guinea Pig	1.54
Ferret	2.04
Domestic Rabbit	8.00

Source: Comparisons: The Diagram Group

 You can use models to add.

MORE HELP
See 23

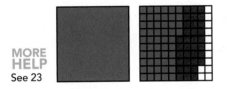

$$1.54 + 0.34 = 1.88$$

ANOTHER WAY You can also add using place value.

MORE HELP
See 146–153, 165

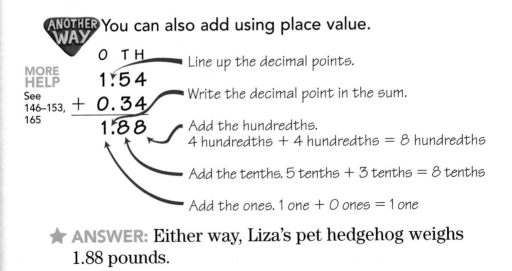

O T H ── Line up the decimal points.
1.5 4
+ 0.3 4 ── Write the decimal point in the sum.
1.8 8 ── Add the hundredths.
4 hundredths + 4 hundredths = 8 hundredths

Add the tenths. 5 tenths + 3 tenths = 8 tenths

Add the ones. 1 one + 0 ones = 1 one

⭐ **ANSWER:** Either way, Liza's pet hedgehog weighs 1.88 pounds.

EXAMPLE 2: Flora's mouse weighs 0.79 ounces. Her gerbil weighs 3.41 ounces more than her mouse. How much does her gerbil weigh?

To solve the problem, add. $3.41 + 0.79 = \blacksquare$

ONE WAY You can use models to add.

MORE HELP
See 23

$3.41 + 0.79 = 4.20$

ANOTHER WAY You can also add using place value.

MORE HELP
See 146–153

```
  O T H
  1  1
  3.41       Line up the decimal points.
+ 0.79       Write the decimal point in the sum.
  4.20       Add the hundredths.
```

Add the hundredths.
1 hundredth + 9 hundredths = 10 hundredths

Since 10 hundredths is 1 tenth + 0 hundredths, write 0 in the hundredths place and write 1 in the tenths place.

Add the tenths.
1 tenth + 4 tenths + 7 tenths = 12 tenths

Since 12 tenths is 1 one + 2 tenths, write 2 in the tenths place and write 1 in the ones place.

Add the ones. 1 one + 3 ones + 0 ones = 4 ones

★ **ANSWER: Either way, Flora's gerbil weighs 4.20 ounces.**

Estimate the sum to make sure your answer is reasonable.

$$
\begin{array}{r}
3.41 \rightarrow \quad 3 \\
+\ 0.79 \rightarrow +\ 1 \\
\hline
4.20 \quad\quad 4
\end{array}
$$

The exact answer, 4.20, is close to 4. The answer is reasonable.

MORE HELP
See 132–133

What to Do with a Ragged Right Side

MORE HELP
See 26

When you line up decimal points, the right side of the addends may look uneven, or **ragged**. To make all the decimal numbers have the same number of places, you can tack on zeros.

```
  1
  0.4
+ 0.57
```

Write equivalent decimals for 1, 0.4, and 0.57 so that all three numbers have the same number of decimal places.

```
  1.00
  0.40
+ 0.57
  1.97
```

Remember, a whole number can be written with a decimal point at the end. 1 = 1.00

Adding Money

MORE HELP
See 17

When you add dollars and cents, you are really adding decimals. Just remember to write a dollar sign as well as a decimal point in the sum.

EXAMPLE: Suppose you buy a notebook for $2.59 and a package of markers for $2. What is the total cost, not including sales tax?

To solve the problem, add. $2.59 + $2 = ■

```
  $2.59
+  2.00
  $4.59
```

You can tack on 0 dimes and 0 pennies without changing the amount.

 ANSWER: The total cost is $4.59.

Subtraction

You can invent your own method for subtraction or use a standard method. Sometimes you might combine methods. The important thing to remember is that subtraction is the opposite of addition. What you put together in addition, you separate in subtraction.

MORE
HELP
See
112–117

Subtracting Whole Numbers

You can use what you know about place value and subtraction facts to subtract any two whole numbers.

If you know how to subtract tens and ones, you also know how to subtract hundreds, thousands, millions, and even billions!

Subtracting Without Regrouping

EXAMPLE: How many more libraries are there in Illinois than in Michigan?

To solve, subtract.
366 − 263 = ■

Libraries	
State	Number
New York	436
Illinois	366
Pennsylvania	317
Iowa	293
Michigan	263

Source: American Library Directory, 1999

 You can subtract using place-value models.

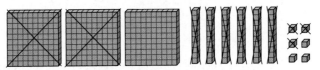

1 hundred + 0 tens + 3 ones

> Be sure to start by showing the greater amount. Then take away the models for the number you are subtracting.

ANOTHER WAY You can also line up the numbers and subtract each column starting at the right.

MORE
HELP
See 112, 117

```
  H T O        Line up both numbers at the ones place.
  3 6 6
              Subtract the ones. 6 ones − 3 ones = 3 ones
− 2 6 3
  1 0 3        Subtract the tens. 6 tens − 6 tens = 0 tens

              Subtract the hundreds.
              3 hundreds − 2 hundreds = 1 hundred
```

⭐ **ANSWER:** Either way, there are 103 more libraries in Illinois than in Michigan.

Regrouping Tens as Ones

Suppose you have a ten-dollar bill and you owe your brother $2. You could trade the ten-dollar bill for 10 one-dollar bills and pay the $2. Regrouping is like trading bills. When you subtract, if you don't have enough ones, you can get more ones by regrouping a ten.

> When you regroup 1 ten as 10 ones, you don't change the value.

EXAMPLE: Regroup 45 so that you can subtract 7.

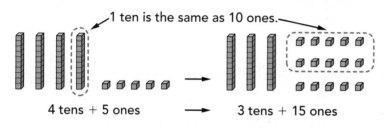

4 tens + 5 ones → 3 tens + 15 ones

Subtracting—Regrouping Tens as Ones

EXAMPLE: Eldridge made 45 meatballs. Before he could show anyone, the dog ate some of the meatballs. Only 7 meatballs were left. How many meatballs did the dog eat?

To solve the problem, subtract. 45 − 7 = ■

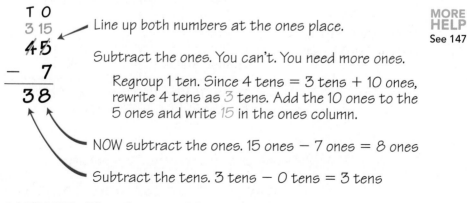

MORE HELP
See 147

★ **ANSWER:** The dog ate 38 meatballs.

Regrouping Hundreds as Tens

Sometimes you need to **regroup** hundreds as tens to subtract. That's like trading 1 one-hundred dollar bill for 10 ten-dollar bills.

EXAMPLE: Regroup 243 to subtract 180.

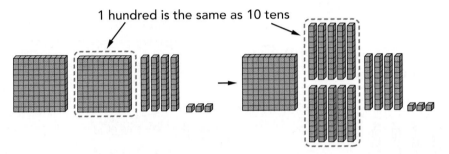

1 hundred is the same as 10 tens

2 hundreds + 4 tens + 3 ones → 1 hundred + 14 tens + 3 ones

Subtracting—Regrouping Hundreds as Tens

EXAMPLE: How many more school days do Japanese students have each year than U.S. students?

To solve the problem, subtract. 243 − 180 = ■

Annual School Days	
Country	Number of Days
China	251
Japan	243
Korea	220
Russia	210
United States	180

Source: The Top 10 of Everything 1999 by Russell Ash, DK Publishing, Inc.

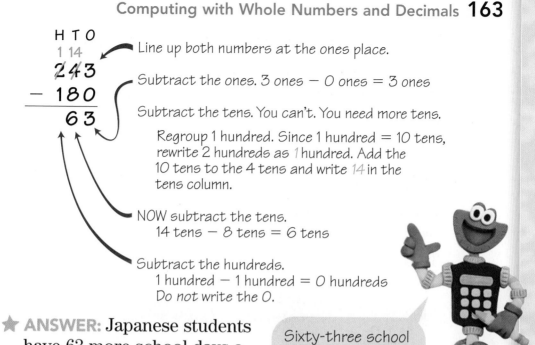

H T O
1 14
2̶4̶3

− 180

63

Line up both numbers at the ones place.

Subtract the ones. 3 ones − 0 ones = 3 ones

Subtract the tens. You can't. You need more tens.

Regroup 1 hundred. Since 1 hundred = 10 tens, rewrite 2 hundreds as *1* hundred. Add the 10 tens to the 4 tens and write *14* in the tens column.

NOW subtract the tens.
14 tens − 8 tens = 6 tens

Subtract the hundreds.
1 hundred − 1 hundred = 0 hundreds
Do not write the 0.

★ **ANSWER:** Japanese students have 63 more school days a year than U.S. students.

Sixty-three school days—that's more than 12 weeks!

Checking Subtraction

To check that your answer is correct, add it to the number you subtracted. The sum should be the same as the number you subtracted from. If it isn't, try subtracting again.

MORE HELP
See 49, 54

EXAMPLE: Does 613 − 195 = 418? Check using addition.

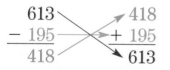

613
− 195
418

418
+ 195
613

★ **ANSWER:** 613 = 613, so 613 − 195 = 418.

Subtracting with Two Regroupings

When you subtract, you may need to regroup more than once.

EXAMPLE: In 1960, the baseball player Ted Williams hit a 475-foot home run. Seven years earlier, Mickey Mantle had hit a home run in the same ballpark that traveled 510 feet. How much farther did the ball travel for Mickey Mantle?

Source: www.baseball-almanac.com

To solve the problem, subtract. $510 - 475 = $ ■

> Remember. Line up the digits in the ones place to avoid errors.

```
 H T O
   10
 4 0 10
 5 1 0
− 4 7 5
   3 5
```

Line up both numbers at the ones place.

Subtract the ones. You can't. You have 0 ones.

Regroup 1 ten. Rewrite 1 ten 0 ones as 1 ten 10 ones.

NOW subtract the ones.
10 ones − 5 ones = 5 ones

Subtract the tens. You can't. You need more tens.

Regroup 1 hundred. Since 5 hundreds = 4 hundreds + 10 tens, rewrite 5 hundreds as 4 hundreds. Write 10 tens in the tens column.

NOW subtract the tens.
10 tens − 7 tens = 3 tens

Subtract the hundreds.
4 hundreds − 4 hundreds = 0 hundreds. Do *not* write the 0.

★ ANSWER: The ball traveled 35 feet farther for Mickey Mantle.

Regroup When Necessary

When you subtract, always regroup when you need
to. A common mistake people make is to just subtract
the smaller digit from the larger digit!

**MORE
HELP**
See 241

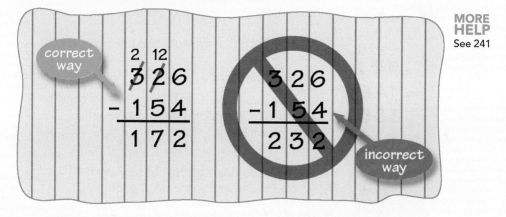

You cannot subtract 2
from 5 in this exercise.

Subtraction would be
a lot easier if I didn't
need the right answer.

Subtracting Across Zeros

Sometimes you have to regroup more than once before you can even begin subtracting.

MORE HELP
See
132–133,
161–163

EXAMPLE 1: Subtract. 501 − 146 = ■

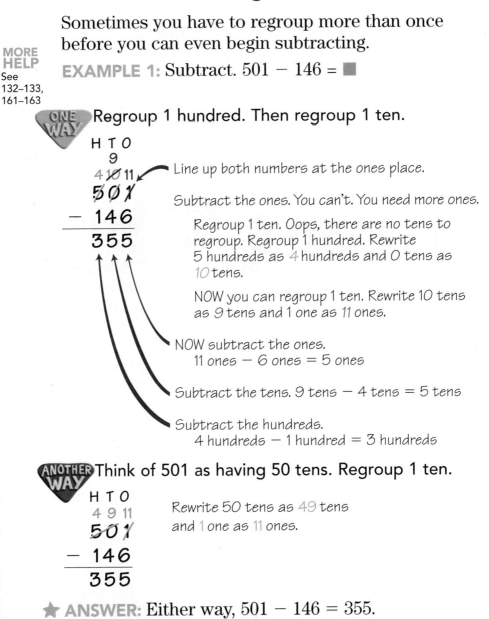

ONE WAY Regroup 1 hundred. Then regroup 1 ten.

H T O

Line up both numbers at the ones place.

Subtract the ones. You can't. You need more ones.

Regroup 1 ten. Oops, there are no tens to regroup. Regroup 1 hundred. Rewrite 5 hundreds as 4 hundreds and 0 tens as 10 tens.

NOW you can regroup 1 ten. Rewrite 10 tens as 9 tens and 1 one as 11 ones.

NOW subtract the ones.
11 ones − 6 ones = 5 ones

Subtract the tens. 9 tens − 4 tens = 5 tens

Subtract the hundreds.
4 hundreds − 1 hundred = 3 hundreds

ANOTHER WAY Think of 501 as having 50 tens. Regroup 1 ten.

H T O

Rewrite 50 tens as 49 tens and 1 one as 11 ones.

★ **ANSWER:** Either way, 501 − 146 = 355.

EXAMPLE 2: Hank Aaron made 3771 hits in his career in baseball. How many more hits would he have needed to make to reach 4000 hits?

Source: www.baseball-reference.com

To solve the problem, subtract. $4000 - 3771 = \blacksquare$

Regroup three times.

ONE WAY

$$
\begin{array}{r}
{\scriptstyle 9\ 9} \\
{\scriptstyle 3\ \cancel{10}\ \cancel{10}\ 10} \\
4\,\cancel{0}\,\cancel{0}\,\cancel{0} \\
-\ 3\,7\,7\,1 \\
\hline
2\,2\,9
\end{array}
$$

Line up both numbers at the ones place.

Subtract the ones. You can't. You need more ones.

There are no tens or hundreds to regroup.

Regroup 1 thousand. Rewrite 4 thousands as 3 thousands and 0 hundreds as 10 hundreds.

Regroup 1 hundred. Rewrite 10 hundreds as 9 hundreds and 0 tens as 10 tens.

NOW you can regroup 1 ten. Rewrite 10 tens as 9 tens and 0 ones as 10 ones.

NOW subtract the ones.
10 ones − 1 one = 9 ones

Subtract the tens. 9 tens − 7 tens = 2 tens

MORE HELP
See 114

Subtract the hundreds.
9 hundreds − 7 hundreds = 2 hundreds

Subtract the thousands.
3 thousands − 3 thousands = 0 thousands

ANOTHER WAY **Think of 4000 as 400 tens. Regroup 1 ten.**

$$
\begin{array}{r}
{\scriptstyle 3\ 9\ 9\ 10} \\
4\,0\,0\,\cancel{0} \\
-\ 3\,7\,7\,1 \\
\hline
2\,2\,9
\end{array}
$$

Rewrite 400 tens as 399 tens and 0 ones as 10 ones.

I prefer using mental math.
$4000 - 3000 = 1000$
$1000 - 700 = 300$
$300 - 70 = 230$
$230 - 1 = 229$

★ **ANSWER:** Either way, Hank Aaron needed 229 more hits.

Subtracting Decimal Numbers

MORE HELP
See 22 If you know how to subtract whole numbers, then you can subtract decimals. Line up the decimal points. That will make the numbers in all places line up correctly.

Subtracting Tenths

EXAMPLE 1: Jack's stride is 0.5 meter long. His father's stride is 0.8 meter long. How much shorter is Jack's stride?

To solve the problem, subtract. $0.8 - 0.5 =$ ■

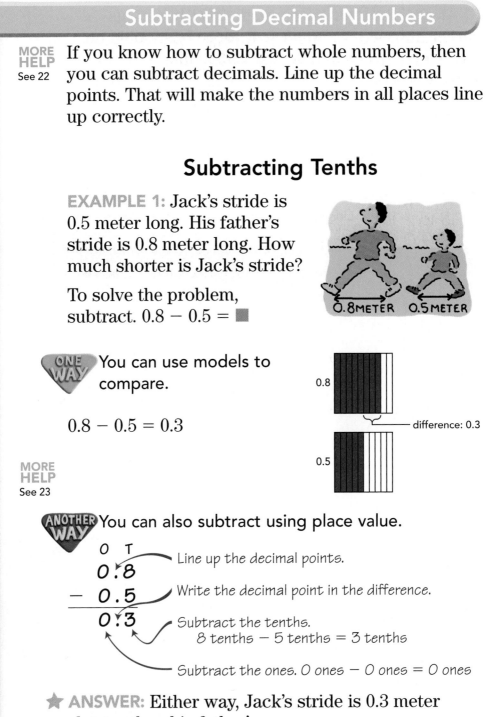

0.8METER 0.5METER

ONE WAY You can use models to compare.

$0.8 - 0.5 = 0.3$

0.8

difference: 0.3

0.5

MORE HELP
See 23

ANOTHER WAY You can also subtract using place value.

```
  O  T
 0.8      Line up the decimal points.
- 0.5      Write the decimal point in the difference.
 0.3      Subtract the tenths.
              8 tenths − 5 tenths = 3 tenths
          Subtract the ones. O ones − O ones = O ones
```

★ **ANSWER:** Either way, Jack's stride is 0.3 meter shorter than his father's.

EXAMPLE 2: In 1978, Americans drank an average of 7.1 ounces of milk per person per day. In 2003, Americans drank an average of 5.2 ounces of milk per person per day. What is the difference in the amount of milk Americans drank per day in 1978 and in 2003? *Source: www.ers.usda.gov*

To solve the problem, subtract. $7.1 - 5.2 = $ ■

ONE WAY You can use models to subtract.

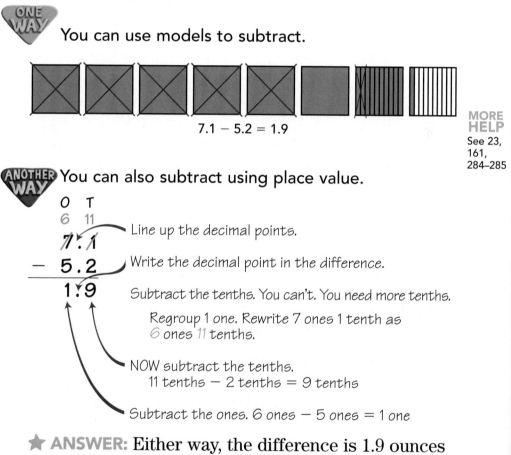

$7.1 - 5.2 = 1.9$

MORE HELP
See 23, 161, 284–285

ANOTHER WAY You can also subtract using place value.

$$\begin{array}{r} \overset{0}{6}\ \overset{T}{11} \\ \cancel{7}.\cancel{1} \\ -\ 5.2 \\ \hline 1.9 \end{array}$$

Line up the decimal points.

Write the decimal point in the difference.

Subtract the tenths. You can't. You need more tenths.

Regroup 1 one. Rewrite 7 ones 1 tenth as 6 ones 11 tenths.

NOW subtract the tenths.
11 tenths − 2 tenths = 9 tenths

Subtract the ones. 6 ones − 5 ones = 1 one

★ **ANSWER:** Either way, the difference is 1.9 ounces of milk.

Subtracting Hundredths

Olympic 100-Meter Dash Winners		
Name	**Time** (in seconds)	**Year**
Justin Gatlin	9.85	2004
Maurice Green	9.87	2000
Donovan Bailey	9.84	1996
Linford Christie	9.96	1992
Carl Lewis	9.92	1988

Source: www.infoplease.com

EXAMPLE: Justin Gatlin won the men's 100-meter dash in the 2004 Olympics. What was the difference between Gatlin's time and the time of Carl Lewis in 1988?

To solve the problem, subtract. $9.92 - 9.85 = \blacksquare$

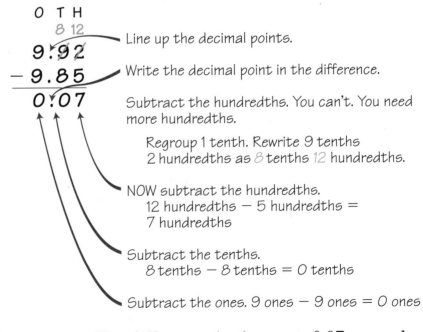

O T H

    8 12
  9.9̷2̷
− 9.85
  0.07

Line up the decimal points.

Write the decimal point in the difference.

Subtract the hundredths. You can't. You need more hundredths.

Regroup 1 tenth. Rewrite 9 tenths 2 hundredths as 8 tenths 12 hundredths.

NOW subtract the hundredths. 12 hundredths − 5 hundredths = 7 hundredths

Subtract the tenths. 8 tenths − 8 tenths = 0 tenths

Subtract the ones. 9 ones − 9 ones = 0 ones

★ **ANSWER:** The difference in time was 0.07 second.

Sometimes You Need to Tack on Zeros in Order to Subtract

When you line up decimal points, the right side may be uneven. To make all the decimal numbers have the same number of places, you can tack on zeros.

MORE
HELP
See 26,
158

$$\begin{array}{r} 2.3 \\ -\ 1.09 \end{array}$$

Write equivalent decimals for 2.3 and 1.09 so that both numbers have the same number of decimal places.

$$\begin{array}{r} {}^{2\ 10} \\ 2.3\cancel{0} \\ -\ 1.09 \\ \hline 1.21 \end{array}$$

Subtracting Money

MORE
HELP
See 17

When you subtract dollars and cents, you are really subtracting decimals. Just remember to write the dollar sign as well as the decimal point in the difference.

EXAMPLE: How much more does a jumbo bucket of popcorn cost than a large bucket?

Jumbo
$3.49
Large
$2

To solve the problem, subtract.
$3.49 − $2 = ■

$$\begin{array}{r} \$3.49 \\ -\ 2.00 \\ \hline \$1.49 \end{array}$$

You can tack on 0 dimes and 0 pennies without changing the value.

★ **ANSWER:** A jumbo bucket costs $1.49 more.

Multiplication

MORE HELP
See 2-7, 60–73

You can't memorize the answer to every possible multiplication problem. That's the bad news. The good news is that you don't have to! You can use what you know about place value and multiplication facts to multiply greater numbers.

Multiplying with No Regrouping

EXAMPLE: On Monday, the circus gave backstage tours to 2 groups of 123 children. How many children took the backstage tour on Monday?

To solve, multiply. $2 \times 123 = $ ■

ONE WAY You can use models to find the product.

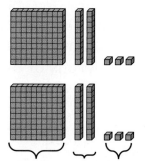

2 hundreds + 4 tens + 6 ones = 246

ANOTHER WAY You can multiply ones, multiply tens, multiply hundreds, and then add.

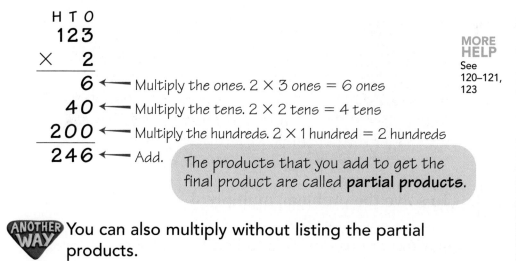

```
  H T O
  1 2 3
×     2
─────────
      6  ◄── Multiply the ones. 2 × 3 ones = 6 ones
    4 0  ◄── Multiply the tens. 2 × 2 tens = 4 tens
  2 0 0  ◄── Multiply the hundreds. 2 × 1 hundred = 2 hundreds
─────────
  2 4 6  ◄── Add.
```

MORE HELP
See
120–121,
123

The products that you add to get the final product are called **partial products**.

ANOTHER WAY You can also multiply without listing the partial products.

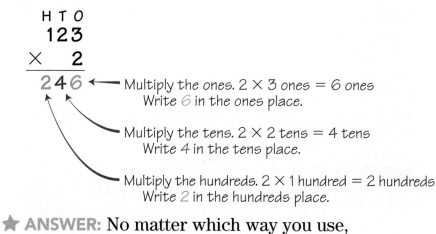

```
  H T O
  1 2 3
×     2
─────────
  2 4 6  ◄── Multiply the ones. 2 × 3 ones = 6 ones
              Write 6 in the ones place.
```

Multiply the tens. 2 × 2 tens = 4 tens
Write 4 in the tens place.

Multiply the hundreds. 2 × 1 hundred = 2 hundreds
Write 2 in the hundreds place.

★ **ANSWER:** No matter which way you use, 246 children took the backstage tour on Monday.

MORE
HELP
See 120,
123,
172–173
EXAMPLE: Film comes in rolls of 24 exposures. Elliot used 4 rolls of film during a trip to the mountains. How many pictures did he take?

To solve the problem, multiply. $4 \times 24 = \blacksquare$

ONE WAY You can use models to find the product.

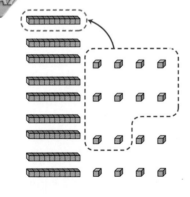

$4 \times 24 = 96$

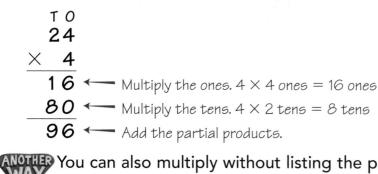

ANOTHER WAY You can also multiply by finding and listing all the partial products, and then adding.

```
 T O
 2 4
×  4
─────
 1 6  ◄─── Multiply the ones. 4 × 4 ones = 16 ones
 8 0  ◄─── Multiply the tens. 4 × 2 tens = 8 tens
─────
 9 6  ◄─── Add the partial products.
```

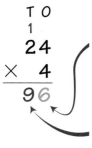

ANOTHER WAY You can also multiply without listing the partial products.

```
 T O
 1
 2 4
×  4
─────
 9 6
```

Multiply the ones. 4 × 4 ones = 16 ones

Since 16 is 1 ten + 6 ones, write 6 in the ones place of the product and write 1 above the tens place, so that you won't forget it.

Multiply the tens. 4 × 2 tens = 8 tens

Add the 8 tens to the 1 ten you already have. Write the 9 in the tens place of the product.

★ **ANSWER:** No matter which way you use, Elliot took 96 pictures.

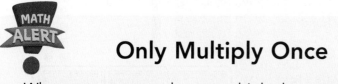

MATH ALERT

Only Multiply Once

When you regroup, do not multiply the regrouped tens again.

```
 1  ◄─── This 1 ten comes from multiplying the ones by 4.
 2 4    (4 × 4 ones = 16 ones)
×  4    Do not multiply it again. Multiply tens and then
 9 6    add on the 1 ten.
```

Multiplying a 3-Digit Number

EXAMPLE: Dana needs 139 beads to make a necklace. How many beads does she need for 3 necklaces?

To solve the problem, multiply. $3 \times 139 = \blacksquare$

ONE WAY You can use models to show the multiplication.

MORE HELP
See 120, 172–173

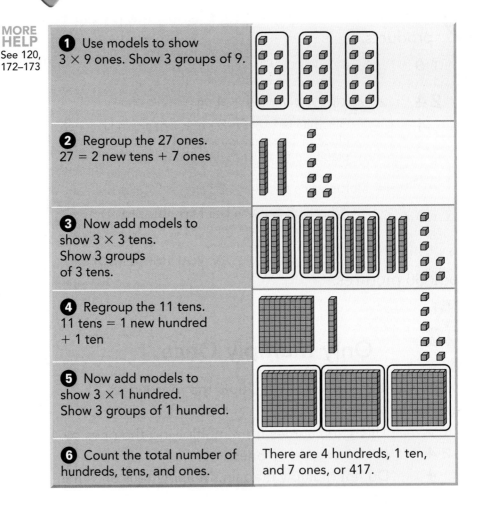

1 Use models to show 3×9 ones. Show 3 groups of 9.

2 Regroup the 27 ones.
27 = 2 new tens + 7 ones

3 Now add models to show 3×3 tens. Show 3 groups of 3 tens.

4 Regroup the 11 tens.
11 tens = 1 new hundred + 1 ten

5 Now add models to show 3×1 hundred. Show 3 groups of 1 hundred.

6 Count the total number of hundreds, tens, and ones. | There are 4 hundreds, 1 ten, and 7 ones, or 417.

ANOTHER WAY You can also multiply by finding all the partial products, and then adding.

```
H T O
1 3 9
×    3
─────────
   2 7  ←── Multiply the ones. 3 × 9 ones = 27 ones
   9 0  ←── Multiply the tens. 3 × 3 tens = 9 tens
 3 0 0  ←── Multiply the hundreds. 3 × 1 hundred = 3 hundreds
─────────
 4 1 7  ←── Add the partial products.
```

ANOTHER WAY You can also multiply without listing the partial products.

MORE HELP
See 175

```
  H T O
  1 2
  1 3 9
×      3
─────────
  4 1 7
```

Multiply the ones. 3 × 9 ones = 27 ones

Since 27 is 2 tens + 7 ones, write *7* in the ones place of the product and write *2* above the tens place, so that you will remember it.

Multiply the tens. 3 × 3 tens = 9 tens

Add the 9 tens to the 2 tens you already have. Since 11 tens is 1 hundred + 1 ten, write *1* in the tens place of the product and write *1* above the hundreds place, so that you will remember it.

Multiply the hundreds. 3 × 1 hundred = 3 hundreds

Add the 3 hundreds to the 1 hundred you already have. Write *4* in the hundreds place of the product.

★ **ANSWER:** No matter which way you use, Dana needs 417 beads for 3 necklaces.

Zeros in Factors and Products

Zero may mean nothing, but it sure helps to keep digits in line.

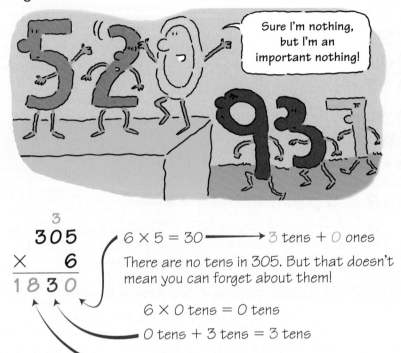

Sure I'm nothing, but I'm an important nothing!

$$
\begin{array}{r}
\overset{3}{305} \\
\times \quad 6 \\
\hline
1830
\end{array}
$$

$6 \times 5 = 30 \longrightarrow 3$ tens + 0 ones

There are no tens in 305. But that doesn't mean you can forget about them!

6×0 tens = 0 tens

0 tens + 3 tens = 3 tens

$6 \times 300 = 1800 \longrightarrow 1$ thousand + 8 hundreds

MORE
HELP
See 136

To check your answer, compare it with an estimate. 6×305 should be a little more than 6×300, or 1800. The product 1830 seems reasonable.

Multiplying Money

Multiply dollars and cents the same way you multiply whole numbers. Just remember to write a dollar sign and a decimal point in the product.

MORE
HELP
See 17,
26, 136

EXAMPLE: How much do 4 hair clips cost?

To find the answer, multiply. 4 × $2.35 = ■

MORE
HELP
See 416

```
  1 2
$2.35
×   4
$9.40
```

An estimate shows that the exact product should be more than 4 × $2, or $8. So, $9.40 is reasonable.

★ **ANSWER:** The 4 hair clips cost $9.40.

You can use a calculator to multiply 2.35 by 4.

The calculator shows the answer as 9.4. When you write the answer, remember to write the dollar sign and decimal point. Tack on a zero in the cents place.

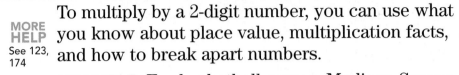

Multiplying by a 2-Digit Number

MORE
HELP
See 123,
174

To multiply by a 2-digit number, you can use what you know about place value, multiplication facts, and how to break apart numbers.

EXAMPLE: For basketball games, Madison Square Garden sets up seats on the floor. Sections 11 and 12 together have 15 rows with 28 seats in each row. How many seats are in these two sections?

Source: www.thegarden.com

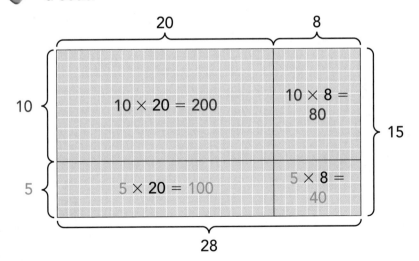

To solve the problem, multiply. $15 \times 28 = \blacksquare$

ONE WAY You can draw a model. Each small square is a seat.

The total number of seats is:

$40 + 100 + 80 + 200 = 420$

ANOTHER WAY You can also multiply by the ones and the tens. List all the partial products and add to find the product.

```
    T O
    2 8
  × 1 5
    4 0
  1 0 0
    8 0
  2 0 0
  4 2 0
```

Multiply by the ones.
5 × 8 = 40
5 × 20 = 100

Multiply by the tens.
10 × 8 = 80
10 × 20 = 200

Add the partial products.

MORE HELP
See 120, 172–175

ANOTHER WAY You can also multiply without listing every partial product.

```
   T O
   4
   2 8
 × 1 5
 1 4 0
```

Multiply by the ones. 5 × 28 = ■
5 × 8 = 40 ⟶ 0 ones with 4 tens to regroup
5 × 20 = 100 ⟶ 10 tens + 4 tens = 14 tens
14 tens = 1 hundred 4 tens

So, 5 × 28 = 140.

```
   T O
   4
   2 8
 × 1 5
 1 4 0
 2 8 0
 4 2 0
```

Multiply by the tens. 10 × 28 = ■
10 × 8 = 80 ⟶ 8 tens + 0 ones
10 × 20 = 200 ⟶ 2 hundreds

So, 10 × 28 = 280.

Add the partial products.

★ **ANSWER: No matter which way you use, there are 420 seats in sections 11 and 12.**

What to Do with Regrouped Tens

Be careful with regrouped tens.

When you multiply 4 × 9, ⟶ you regroup 3 tens.

When you multiply 3 × 9, you regroup again. Now you have 2 tens.

```
    2
    ⨉
   2 9
 ⨉ 3 4
 1 1 6
 8 7 0
 9 8 6
```

It helps to cross out the regrouped 3 tens once you add them to the multiplied tens from 4 × 2 tens. That way, you won't add them again by mistake.

Lattice Multiplication

Here's another method you can use to multiply.

EXAMPLE: Multiply. 32 × 41 = ■

Draw a grid. Write one factor on top. Write the other factor on the right. Show the diagonals in each square.

In each square, write a product. Multiply the digit at the top of the column by the digit to the right of the row. Write 1-digit products with a 0 in front.

The diagonal line separates the digits in each product. 3 × 4 = 12

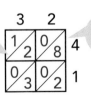

Write 8 as 08.

Add along the diagonals. Begin at the lower right. For 2-digit sums, add the tens digit to the digits in the next diagonal.

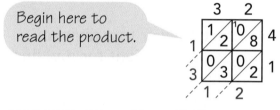

$1 + 0 + 2 + 0 = 3$

Begin here to add the diagonals.

$8 + 0 + 3 = 11$

To read the product, begin at the left and end at the bottom right.

Begin here to read the product.

⭐ ANSWER: $32 \times 41 = 1312$

Checking Multiplication

It is always a good idea to check your answer.

EXAMPLE: Does $52 \times 13 = 676$?

You can check by reversing the factors.

$$
\begin{array}{r} 1 \\ 13 \\ \times 52 \\ \hline 26 \\ 650 \\ \hline 676 \end{array}
\qquad
\begin{array}{r} 52 \\ \times 13 \\ \hline 156 \\ 520 \\ \hline 676 \end{array}
$$

Both products are the same, so you can be more sure that the answer 676 is correct.

MORE
HELP
See 240

⭐ ANSWER: Yes. $52 \times 13 = 676$

Division

MORE HELP
See 74–85

Suppose you need an exact answer to a division problem, but the numbers are not right for dividing in your head and you don't have a calculator. Relax! You can always use some step-by-step methods. You only need paper and pencil and a little patience.

Dividing by a 1-Digit Number

You can use what you know about place value and division facts to help you divide by a 1-digit divisor. The same steps work with any size dividend.

Remainders in Division

Sometimes when you divide, you can't make equal groups. You have things left over. The part left over is called the **remainder**.

MORE
HELP
See 75,
78–79

EXAMPLE 1: Akio and his friend want to share 9 pens equally. How many pens will each boy get?

To solve the problem, divide 9 by 2.

$$\begin{array}{r} 4 \ \text{R1} \\ 2\overline{)9} \\ -8 \\ \hline 1 \end{array}$$

$2 \times 5 = 10$
There aren't enough pens for each boy to get 5.

$2 \times 4 = 8$
Each boy gets 4 pens and there is 1 left over. Write *4* as the quotient and *R1* to stand for the remainder of 1.

⭐ **ANSWER:** Akio and his friend each get 4 pens. There is 1 pen left over.

EXAMPLE 2: A chef uses 5 small tomatoes for each salad that she makes. How many salads can she make with 17 small tomatoes?

To solve, divide 17 by 5.

$$\begin{array}{r} 3 \ \text{R2} \\ 5\overline{)17} \\ -15 \\ \hline 2 \end{array}$$

$5 \times 4 = 20$
There aren't enough tomatoes for 4 salads.

$5 \times 3 = 15$
There are enough tomatoes for 3 salads with 2 tomatoes left over. Write *3* as the quotient and *R2* to stand for the remainder of 2.

⭐ **ANSWER:** The chef can make 3 salads. She will have 2 tomatoes left over.

Dividing Hundreds, Tens, and Ones (No Regrouping)

EXAMPLE: It is 248 miles from Kansas City to Tulsa, Oklahoma. If you travel the same number of miles each day, how many miles would you travel in each of 2 days? *Source: World Almanac, 1998*

To solve this problem, divide 248 by 2.

ONE WAY You can use models to find the answer.

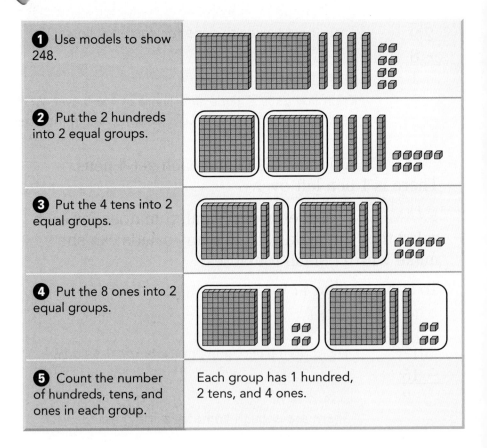

❶ Use models to show 248.	
❷ Put the 2 hundreds into 2 equal groups.	
❸ Put the 4 tens into 2 equal groups.	
❹ Put the 8 ones into 2 equal groups.	
❺ Count the number of hundreds, tens, and ones in each group.	Each group has 1 hundred, 2 tens, and 4 ones.

ANOTHER WAY You can divide 248 by 2 without using models.

MORE
HELP
See 77

❶ Divide the hundreds.
$200 \div 2 = \blacksquare$ hundreds
2×1 hundred $= 200$
Write *1* in the hundreds place.
Write *200* under 248.
Subtract and compare.
$248 - 200 = 48$
There are 48 ones left.
48 is greater than 2.
Keep dividing.

$$2\overline{)248} \quad^{1}$$
$$-200 \longleftarrow 2 \times 1 \text{ hundred}$$
$$48 \longleftarrow 248 - 200$$

❷ Divide the tens.
$40 \div 2 = \blacksquare$ tens
2×2 tens $= 40$
Write *2* in the tens place.
Write *40* under 48.
Subtract and compare.
$48 - 40 = 8$
There are 8 ones left.
8 is greater than 2.
Keep dividing.

$$2\overline{)248} \quad^{12}$$
$$-200$$
$$48$$
$$-40 \longleftarrow 2 \times 2 \text{ tens}$$
$$8 \longleftarrow 48 - 40$$

❸ Divide the ones.
$8 \div 2 = \blacksquare$ ones
2×4 ones $= 8$
Write *4* in the ones place.
Write *8* under 8.
Subtract and compare.
$8 - 8 = 0$
There are 0 ones left.
You are finished dividing.

$$2\overline{)248} \quad^{124}$$
$$-200$$
$$48$$
$$-40$$
$$8$$
$$-8 \longleftarrow 2 \times 4 \text{ ones}$$
$$0 \longleftarrow 8 - 8$$

★ **ANSWER:** Either way, you would travel 124 miles each day.

Dividing with Regrouping and a Remainder

EXAMPLE: The PTA bought 55 math handbooks. They want to divide the books equally among the 3 fourth-grade classes. Any leftovers will go to the library. How many books will each class get? How many leftovers will go to the library?

To solve this problem, divide 55 by 3.

ONE WAY You can use models to find the answer.

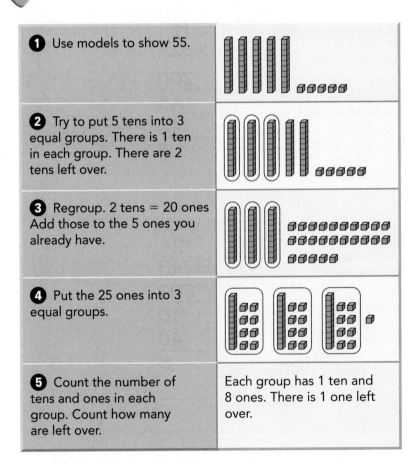

1 Use models to show 55.	
2 Try to put 5 tens into 3 equal groups. There is 1 ten in each group. There are 2 tens left over.	
3 Regroup. 2 tens = 20 ones Add those to the 5 ones you already have.	
4 Put the 25 ones into 3 equal groups.	
5 Count the number of tens and ones in each group. Count how many are left over.	Each group has 1 ten and 8 ones. There is 1 one left over.

ANOTHER WAY You can divide 55 by 3 without using models.

1 Divide the tens.
50 ÷ 3 = ■ tens

Multiply to estimate.
3 × ■ tens = 50
3 × 1 ten = 30
3 × 2 tens = 60
Use 3 × 1 ten.   2 tens is too much.

Write *1* in the tens place.
Write *30* under 55.

Subtract and compare.
55 − 30 = 25
There are 25 ones remaining.
25 is greater than 3.
Keep dividing.

$$\begin{array}{r} 1 \\ 3\overline{)55} \\ -30 \quad \leftarrow 3 \times 1 \text{ ten} \\ \hline 25 \quad \leftarrow 55 - 30 \end{array}$$

2 Divide the ones.
25 ÷ 3 = ■ ones

Multiply to estimate.
3 × ■ ones = 25
3 × 8 ones = 24
3 × 9 ones = 27
Use 3 × 8 ones.   9 ones is too much.

Write *8* in the ones place.
Write *24* under 25.

Subtract and compare.
25 − 24 = 1
1 is less than 3.
There are not enough ones
to divide again.
You are finished dividing.
The remainder is 1.

$$\begin{array}{r} 18 \text{ R1} \\ 3\overline{)55} \\ -30 \\ \hline 25 \\ -24 \quad \leftarrow 3 \times 8 \text{ ones} \\ \hline 1 \quad \leftarrow 25 - 24 \end{array}$$

You keep dividing
until the remainder is
less than the divisor.

★ **ANSWER:** Either way, each class will get 18 books,
and there will be 1 book left over for the library.

Zeros in the Quotient

MORE HELP
See 139

Sometimes you need to write a zero in the quotient to show that there is nothing in that place. If you estimate the quotient and pay attention to place value, you can handle zeros like they're nothing.

EXAMPLE: A millipede has 4 legs on each body segment. How many segments would a millipede with 436 legs have?

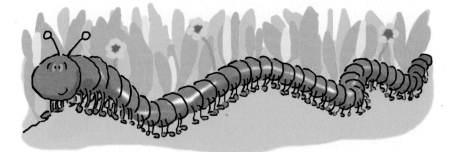

Millipede means "1000 feet." But, no one has ever found a millipede with that many feet.

To find the answer, divide 436 by 4.
Estimate first.

436 is about 400.

$$436 \div 4 \rightarrow 400 \div 4 = 100$$

The exact quotient should be a little more than 100.

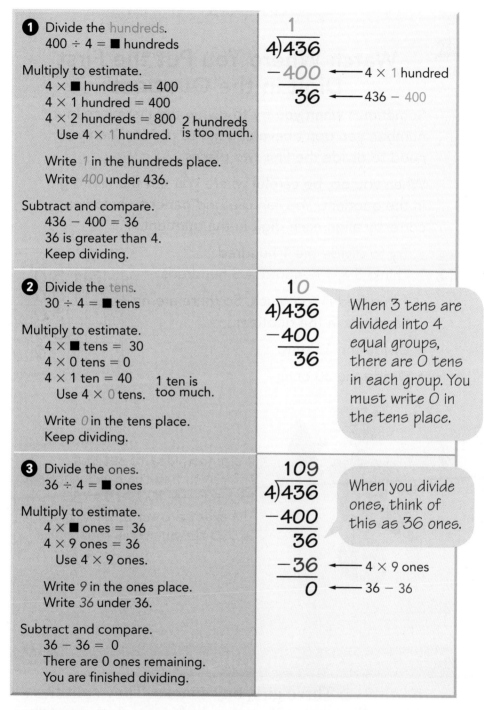

❶ Divide the hundreds.
   400 ÷ 4 = ■ hundreds

Multiply to estimate.
   4 × ■ hundreds = 400
   4 × 1 hundred = 400
   4 × 2 hundreds = 800   2 hundreds
      Use 4 × 1 hundred.   is too much.

Write 1 in the hundreds place.
Write 400 under 436.

Subtract and compare.
   436 − 400 = 36
   36 is greater than 4.
   Keep dividing.

```
    1
4)436
−400   ←— 4 × 1 hundred
  36   ←— 436 − 400
```

❷ Divide the tens.
   30 ÷ 4 = ■ tens

Multiply to estimate.
   4 × ■ tens = 30
   4 × 0 tens = 0
   4 × 1 ten = 40   1 ten is
      Use 4 × 0 tens.   too much.

Write 0 in the tens place.
Keep dividing.

```
   10
4)436
−400
  36
```

When 3 tens are divided into 4 equal groups, there are 0 tens in each group. You must write 0 in the tens place.

❸ Divide the ones.
   36 ÷ 4 = ■ ones

Multiply to estimate.
   4 × ■ ones = 36
   4 × 9 ones = 36
      Use 4 × 9 ones.

Write 9 in the ones place.
Write 36 under 36.

Subtract and compare.
   36 − 36 = 0
   There are 0 ones remaining.
   You are finished dividing.

```
  109
4)436
−400
  36
−36   ←— 4 × 9 ones
   0   ←— 36 − 36
```

When you divide ones, think of this as 36 ones.

★ **ANSWER:** The millipede would have 109 body segments.

MORE
HELP
See 139

Watch Where You Put the First Digit in the Quotient

Sometimes when you try to divide the first place in a number, you don't have enough to divide. Then you need to divide the first two places.

When you do, be careful where you put the first digit in the quotient. You can use grid paper to help you correctly align each digit in the quotient.

- Try to divide the 1 hundred.

  Think: 5 × 1 hundred = 5 hundreds

  1 hundred is too much. So there are no hundreds in the quotient.

- Divide the 13 tens.

- Divide the 30 ones.

```
        2 6
5)1 3 0
  1 0 0
    3 0
  - 3 0
        0
```

It's a good idea to estimate before you find the exact quotient.
130 ÷ 5 → 100 ÷ 5 = 20
The exact answer of 26 is close to 20, so the answer is reasonable.

Dividing Money

MORE
HELP
See 17

EXAMPLE: Three girls buy snacks. They split the $6.15 bill equally. How much does each girl pay?

To solve the problem, divide $6.15 by 3.

ONE WAY You can use bills and coins as models.

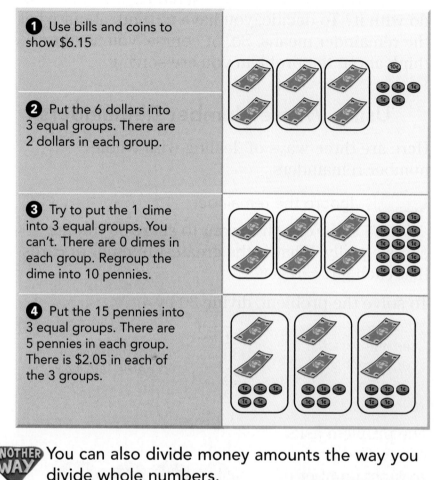

1 Use bills and coins to show $6.15	
2 Put the 6 dollars into 3 equal groups. There are 2 dollars in each group.	
3 Try to put the 1 dime into 3 equal groups. You can't. There are 0 dimes in each group. Regroup the dime into 10 pennies.	
4 Put the 15 pennies into 3 equal groups. There are 5 pennies in each group. There is $2.05 in each of the 3 groups.	

ANOTHER WAY You can also divide money amounts the way you divide whole numbers.

MORE HELP
See 190

Make sure you place the decimal point correctly in the quotient.

$$
\begin{array}{r}
\$2.05 \\
3\overline{)\$6.15} \\
-6\ 00 \\
\hline
15 \\
-15 \\
\hline
0
\end{array}
$$

When 1 dime is divided into 3 equal groups, there are 0 dimes in each group. Write a *0* in the quotient.

★ **ANSWER:** Either way, each girl paid $2.05.

When you divide and get a remainder, what do you do with it? To decide, you have to think about what the remainder means. So, of course, you need to think about the problem you are solving.

Using Whole Number Remainders

Here are three ways of dealing with whole number remainders.

MORE
HELP
See 185

Case 1 Ignore the remainder.

EXAMPLE 1: Four girls want to share 30 trading cards equally. What is the greatest number of cards that each girl can get?

To solve the problem, divide 30 by 4.

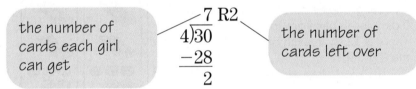

the number of cards each girl can get

$$\begin{array}{r} 7 \text{ R}2 \\ 4\overline{)30} \\ -28 \\ \hline 2 \end{array}$$

the number of cards left over

The problem asks you to find the greatest number of cards each girl can get. There aren't enough for each of them to get 8. It wouldn't make sense to cut up the extra cards and share the pieces. So, the remainder is not part of the answer. Just use the quotient to answer the question.

★ **ANSWER:** Each girl can get 7 cards.

Case 2 The answer is the next greater whole number.

EXAMPLE 2: Juice boxes come in packages of 9. There are 32 students in your class. You want to have a juice box for each student. How many packages should you buy?

To solve the problem, divide 32 by 9.

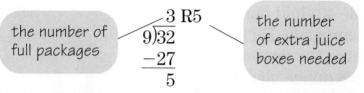

the number of full packages

$$\begin{array}{r} 3 \text{ R5} \\ 9\overline{)32} \\ -27 \\ \hline 5 \end{array}$$

the number of extra juice boxes needed

If you buy 3 packages, 5 students will not get juice. You need to buy another package.

★ **ANSWER:** You need to buy 4 packages of juice boxes.

Case 3 Use the remainder as the answer.

EXAMPLE 3: A family has 248 photos to put in their album. They will put 6 photos on each page. How many photos will be on the last page?

MORE
HELP
See 192

To solve the problem, divide 248 by 6.

the number of full pages

$$\begin{array}{r} 41 \text{ R2} \\ 6\overline{)248} \\ -240 \\ \hline 8 \\ -6 \\ \hline 2 \end{array}$$

the number of photos on the last page

★ **ANSWER:** There will be 2 photos on the last page.

Writing Remainders as Part of the Quotient

Sometimes when you divide to find the answer to a problem, you need to write the remainder as part of the quotient.

MORE HELP
See 185, 210, 218

Case 1 You can write the remainder as a fraction.

EXAMPLE 1: Pablo made 43 fluid ounces of lemonade. He then poured the lemonade into 8-ounce glasses until the pitcher was empty. How many glasses did he fill?

To solve the problem, divide 43 by 8.

$$\begin{array}{r} 5 \text{ R3} \\ 8\overline{)43} \\ -40 \\ \hline 3 \end{array}$$

The result shows that Pablo can fill 5 glasses. Three ounces will be left over. These last 3 ounces will fill $\frac{3}{8}$ of another glass.

To write a remainder as a fraction, use the remainder as the numerator, and the divisor as the denominator.

$$\frac{\text{remainder}}{\text{divisor}} = \frac{3}{8}$$

Write the quotient as a mixed number by including the fraction as part of the quotient. The quotient is $5\frac{3}{8}$.

★ **ANSWER:** Pablo filled $5\frac{3}{8}$ glasses with lemonade.

Case 2 You can write the remainder as a decimal.

EXAMPLE 2: Ana pays $7 for 4 pounds of potato salad. How much does 1 pound cost?

MORE
HELP
See 30,
139, 185

To solve the problem, divide 7 by 4.

$$\begin{array}{r} 1 \text{ R3} \\ 4\overline{)7} \\ -4 \\ \hline 3 \end{array}$$

The result shows you that 1 pound of potato salad costs $1 plus part of a dollar because there is $3 left over when you divide.

You can write the remainder as a decimal part of a dollar. First write it as a fraction.

Think: $\frac{\text{remainder}}{\text{divisor}} = \frac{3}{4}$

Then write the fraction as a decimal.

$\frac{3}{4} = 0.75$

Write the quotient as a decimal number by including the decimal as part of the quotient.

⭐ **ANSWER:** A pound of potato salad costs $1.75.

I know that if 4 pounds cost $8, 1 pound would cost $8 ÷ 4, or $2. Since the 4 pounds cost only $7, I know that 1 pound costs a little less than $2. So, the answer $1.75 makes sense.

Dividing by Tens

MORE HELP
See 139, 192, 194

Sometimes you need to divide by a multiple of ten like 10, 20, 30, 40, 50, and so on.

EXAMPLE: All of the students in Skyline School are going by bus to a park for a field trip. A total of 675 students and teachers need to get to the park. A school bus holds 40 people. How many buses does the school need to use?

To solve, divide 675 by 40.

1 Try to divide the hundreds.
600 ÷ 40 = ■ hundreds

Multiply to estimate.
40 × ■ hundreds = 600
40 × 1 hundred = 4000
1 hundred is too much.
Can't divide the hundreds.

$$40\overline{)675}$$

Since you can't divide the hundreds, the quotient will not have a digit in the hundreds place.

2 Divide the tens.
670 ÷ 40 = ■ tens

Multiply to estimate.
40 × ■ tens = 670
40 × 1 ten = 400
40 × 2 tens = 800
Use 40 × 1 ten.   2 is too much.

Write 1 in the tens place.
Write 400 under 675.

Subtract and compare.
675 − 400 = 275
275 is greater than 40.
Keep dividing.

$$
\begin{array}{r}
1 \\
40\overline{)675} \\
-400 \quad \longleftarrow 40 \times 1\ \text{ten} \\
\hline
275 \quad \longleftarrow 675 - 400
\end{array}
$$

3 Divide the ones.
$275 \div 40 = \blacksquare$ ones

Multiply to estimate.
$40 \times \blacksquare$ ones $= 275$
40×6 ones $= 240$
40×7 ones $= 280$ 7 is too much.

Use 40×6 ones.
Write 6 in the ones place.
Write 240 under 275.

Subtract and compare.
$275 - 240 = 35$
35 is less than 40.
You are finished dividing.
The remainder is 35.

$$
\begin{array}{r}
16 \ \text{R}35 \\
40)\overline{675} \\
-400 \\
\hline
275 \\
-240 \longleftarrow 40 \times 6 \text{ ones} \\
\hline
35 \longleftarrow 275 - 240
\end{array}
$$

If the school uses 16 buses, 35 students will be left behind. You need one more bus.

MORE HELP
See 195

⭐ ANSWER: The school needs to use 17 buses.

You can check if the exact answer is reasonable. Estimate by using compatible numbers.

$675 \div 40 \longrightarrow 800 \div 40 = 20$

The exact answer should be less than 20 because 675 is less than 800.

Seventeen is reasonable. It is less than the estimate of 20.

Other Ways to Divide

There is more than one way to divide using multiplication and subtraction. Whichever method you use, you should get the same answer.

Using Repeated Subtraction

MORE
HELP
See 82, 139

EXAMPLE: Divide 185 by 4.

ONE WAY You can list all the estimates above the dividend.

❶ Estimate the quotient.	$\dfrac{30}{4\overline{)185}}$
❷ Multiply your estimate by the divisor. If the product is less than the dividend, subtract. If the product is greater than the dividend, lower your estimate.	$\begin{array}{r} 30 \\ 4\overline{)185} \\ -120 \quad\leftarrow 4\times30 \\ \hline 65 \end{array}$
❸ Keep estimating, multiplying, and subtracting until the difference is less than the divisor.	$\begin{array}{r} 6 \\ 10 \\ 30 \\ 4\overline{)185} \\ -120 \\ \hline 65 \\ -40 \quad\leftarrow 4\times10 \\ \hline 25 \\ -24 \quad\leftarrow 4\times6 \\ \hline 1 \end{array}$
❹ Add all the estimates to get the whole number part of the quotient. The remainder is the final difference.	$30 + 10 + 6 = 46$ The quotient is 46. The remainder is 1.

This is sometimes called the **pyramid method** of dividing.

1 is less than 4. You can stop dividing.

ANOTHER WAY You can list all the estimates on the side.

❶ Estimate the quotient.	$4\overline{)185}$ 30
❷ Multiply your estimate by the divisor. If the product is less than the dividend, subtract. If the product is greater than the dividend, lower your estimate.	$4\overline{)185}$ 30 -120 ←—— 4 × 30 $\overline{65}$
❸ Keep estimating, multiplying, and subtracting until the difference is less than the divisor.	$4\overline{)185}$ 30 -120 $\overline{65}$ 10 -40 ←—— 4 × 10 $\overline{25}$ 6 -24 ←—— 4 × 6 $\overline{1}$
❹ Add all the estimates to get the quotient. The remainder is the final difference.	30 + 10 + 6 = 46 The quotient is 46. The remainder is 1.

I used different estimates:

$4\overline{)185}$ 20
-80
$\overline{105}$ 20
-80
$\overline{25}$ 6
-24
$\overline{1}$

But I still got the same answer, 46 R1. Choose estimates that are easy for you to multiply.

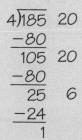

⭐ **ANSWER:** Either way, the answer is 46 R1.

Bring-Down Method

EXAMPLE: Chicago's Navy Pier is home to one of the tallest Ferris wheels in the world. It is 150 feet tall. Each of its 40 gondolas can hold up to 6 passengers. What is the least number of gondolas needed for 84 passengers? *Source: Theme Parks Interest Group*

To solve the problem, divide 84 by 6.

1 Divide the tens. Multiply to estimate. $6 \times \blacksquare = 8$ $6 \times 1 = 6$ $6 \times 2 = 12$ 2 is too much. Use 6×1. Write *1* in the tens place. Write *6* under the 8. Subtract and compare. $8 - 6 = 2$ This remainder is less than the divisor. Keep dividing. Bring down the 4 ones.	$\begin{array}{r} 1 \\ 6\overline{)84} \\ -6\downarrow \\ \hline 24 \end{array}$
2 Divide the ones. Multiply to estimate. $6 \times \blacksquare = 24$ $6 \times 4 = 24$ Write *4* in the ones place. Write *24* under 24. Subtract and compare. $24 - 24 = 0$ You are finished dividing. There is no remainder.	$\begin{array}{r} 14 \\ 6\overline{)84} \\ -6 \\ \hline 24 \\ -24 \\ \hline 0 \end{array}$

★ **ANSWER:** At least 14 gondolas are needed.

EXAMPLE 2: Divide 773 by 3.

1 Divide the hundreds.	$\begin{array}{r} 2 \\ 3\overline{)773} \\ -6 \\ \hline 17 \end{array}$
Multiply to estimate. $3 \times \blacksquare = 7$ $3 \times 1 = 3$ $3 \times 2 = 6$ Use 3×2.	
Write 2 in the hundreds place. Write 6 under the 7.	

Subtract and compare.
  $7 - 6 = 1$
  This remainder is less
  than the divisor. Keep dividing.
  Bring down the 7 tens.	

2 Divide the tens.	$\begin{array}{r} 25 \\ 3\overline{)773} \\ -6 \\ \hline 17 \\ -15 \\ \hline 23 \end{array}$
Multiply to estimate. $3 \times \blacksquare = 17$ $3 \times 5 = 15$	
Write 5 in the tens place. Write 15 under 17.	

Subtract and compare.
  $17 - 15 = 2$
  This remainder is less than
  the divisor. Keep dividing.
  Bring down the 3 ones.	

3 Divide the ones.	$\begin{array}{r} 257 \text{ R2} \\ 3\overline{)773} \\ -6 \\ \hline 17 \\ -15 \\ \hline 23 \\ -21 \\ \hline 2 \end{array}$
Multiply to estimate. $3 \times \blacksquare = 23$ $3 \times 7 = 21$	
Write 7 in the ones place. Write 21 under 23.	

Subtract and compare.
  $23 - 21 = 2$
  This remainder is less than
  the divisor. Write 2 as the remainder.	

⭐ **ANSWER:** When you divide 773 by 3, you get 257 R2.

Using Short Division

MORE HELP
See 185

Some people use **short division** when dividing by a 1-digit number. In this method they do the multiplication and subtraction mentally. They write down only the quotients and the remainders.

EXAMPLE: An animal-park train is carrying 780 children and adults through the park. The train has 4 big passenger cars. If each car is carrying the same number of people, how many people are in each?

To solve, divide 780 by 4. $4\overline{)780}$

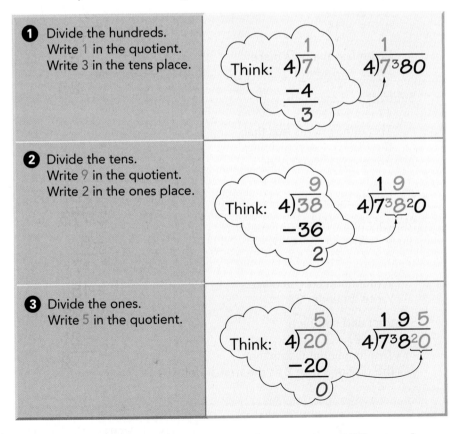

1 Divide the hundreds. Write 1 in the quotient. Write 3 in the tens place.	Think: $4\overline{)7}$ -4 3 $\quad$ $4\overline{)7^{3}80}$ with 1 above
2 Divide the tens. Write 9 in the quotient. Write 2 in the ones place.	Think: $4\overline{)38}$ -36 2 $\quad$ $4\overline{)7^{3}8^{2}0}$ with 1 9 above
3 Divide the ones. Write 5 in the quotient.	Think: $4\overline{)20}$ -20 0 $\quad$ $4\overline{)7^{3}8^{2}0}$ with 1 9 5 above

★ **ANSWER:** Each passenger car is carrying 195 people.

Checking Division

Whether you find a quotient using a calculator, paper and pencil, or by dividing mentally, it makes sense to check that your answer is correct.

One way to check division is to use multiplication. This works because multiplication is the opposite, or **inverse**, of division.

MORE
HELP
See 77

EXAMPLE 1: Is this quotient correct?

$135 \div 3 = 45$

Multiply the quotient by the divisor. If the product equals the dividend, the quotient is correct.

divisor   quotient
$$3 \times 45 = 135$$
dividend

★ **ANSWER:** $135 = 135$, so the division is correct.

EXAMPLE 2: Is this a correct answer?

$$\begin{array}{r} 16 \text{ R2} \\ 3\overline{)47} \end{array}$$

Multiply the quotient by the divisor. Then add the remainder. If the result equals the dividend, the quotient and remainder are correct.

divisor   quotient   remainder
$$3 \times 16 = 48 \qquad 48 + 2 = 50 \textbf{ not} \text{ the dividend}$$

★ **ANSWER:** 50 does not equal 47, so 16 R2 is not correct. You should divide again.

$$\begin{array}{r} 15 \text{ R2} \\ 3\overline{)47} \end{array}$$

Divisibility

A number is **divisible** by another number if the remainder is zero when you divide. There are patterns that make it easier to tell whether one number is divisible by another. These are known as **divisibility rules**. You can use these rules to test any number.

EXAMPLE: The Mighty Mathletes Math Club is planning a party. They want to put 126 people at tables so that all the tables are full. They also want to put the same number at each table. Should they put 2, 3, 4, 5, 6, 9, or 10 people at each table?

To solve this problem, you need to know whether 126 is divisible by 2, 3, 4, 5, 6, 9, or 10.

Divisor	Rule	Test with 126
2	The number is even. (The ones digit is 0, 2, 4, 6, or 8.)	126: the ones digit is 6. 6 is an even number. So, 126 is divisible by 2.
3	The sum of the digits is divisible by 3.	126: $1 + 2 + 6 = 9$ 9 is divisible by 3. So, 126 is divisible by 3.
4	The number formed by the last two digits is divisible by 4.	126: the last two digits are 26. 26 is not divisible by 4. So, 126 is not divisible by 4.
5	The ones digit is 0 or 5.	126: the ones digit is not 0 or 5. So, 126 is not divisible by 5.
6	The number is divisible by 2 and by 3.	126: is divisible by 2 and 3. So, 126 is divisible by 6.
9	The sum of the digits is divisible by 9.	126: $1 + 2 + 6 = 9$ 9 is divisible by 9. So, 126 is divisible by 9.
10	The ones digit is 0.	126: the ones digit is not 0. So, 126 is not divisible by 10.

★ **ANSWER:** The Math Club can put 126 people at tables that seat 2, 3, 6, or 9 people and every table will be full and all tables will have the same number of people.

Fractions

You have probably used fractions many times. "We're about halfway there." "I'll give you half of my sandwich."

In this section, you'll see that some things about fractions are like whole numbers and some things are very different. You'll see why $\frac{1}{2}$ is greater than $\frac{1}{3}$ even though 2 is less than 3 and why you can't add and subtract fractions the way you add and subtract whole numbers.

Once you see how fractions are different from whole numbers, you're well on your way to mastering fractions. You may even be more than halfway there.

Fraction Concepts

A **fraction** is a number that stands for part of something. It is made up of two parts.

The **denominator** tells how many *equal* parts are in the whole.

$$\frac{3}{4}$$

The **numerator** tells how many of those equal parts the fraction stands for.

4 equal parts

3 of the 4 equal parts

$\frac{3}{4}$

When you use fractions to describe part of a whole, the whole can be a single thing or a group of things.

Case 1 You can use a fraction to name a part of a single thing.

EXAMPLE 1: What fraction of the pizza has a mushroom topping?

The whole pizza has 8 equal slices.

3 slices have a mushroom topping.

$\dfrac{3}{8}$ ←—— slices that have a mushroom topping
←—— equal slices in the whole pizza

⭐ **ANSWER:** $\frac{3}{8}$ of the pizza has a mushroom topping.

Case 2 You can use a fraction to name part of a group of things.

EXAMPLE 2: What fraction of the animals are birds?

There are 8 animals in the group.

3 of the animals are birds.

$\dfrac{3}{8}$ ←—— birds in the group
←—— animals in the whole group

⭐ **ANSWER:** $\frac{3}{8}$ of the animals in the group are birds.

Reading and Writing Fractions

EXAMPLE: Read $\frac{2}{3}$.

> First read the numerator. Just say the number.

→ *two*

> Then read the denominator. Use words like *thirds, fourths, twelfths,* and so on.

→ *thirds*

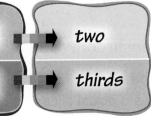

★ **ANSWER: two thirds**

Birds are the third most popular pet in America. $\frac{2}{5}$ of all pet birds are parakeets. $\frac{1}{20}$ of all pet birds are canaries. *Source: American Pet Products Manufacturers Association, Inc.*

MORE HELP
See 16

Write: $\frac{2}{5}$
Say: *two fifths*

Write: $\frac{1}{20}$
Say: *one twentieth*

> Words like *third, fourth,* and *fifth* are used in two different ways. They can show position, such as "fourth in line." They can also show equal parts, such as "The pizza is divided into fourths."

Models for Fractions

EXAMPLE: Model $\frac{3}{4}$.

ONE WAY You can use a circle as a fraction model.

❶ Draw a circle.	❷ Divide it into 4 equal parts.	❸ Color 3 of the parts.

ANOTHER WAY You can use a rectangle to model a fraction.

❶ Draw a rectangle.	❷ Divide it into 4 equal parts.	❸ Color 3 of the parts.

There are many other ways to divide a rectangle into 4 equal parts. Here are two other ways.

★ **ANSWER:** No matter which way you model $\frac{3}{4}$, there should be 4 equal parts and 3 of the parts should be marked.

MATH ALERT

Always Check for Equal Parts

We're each getting $\frac{1}{6}$ of the pizza.

Each slice is **NOT** $\frac{1}{6}$ of the pizza since the slices are not *equal*. Here's how the pizza could have been divided into sixths.

Fractions on a Number Line

Any fraction can be shown on a number line.

EXAMPLE: Show $\frac{1}{4}$ on a number line.

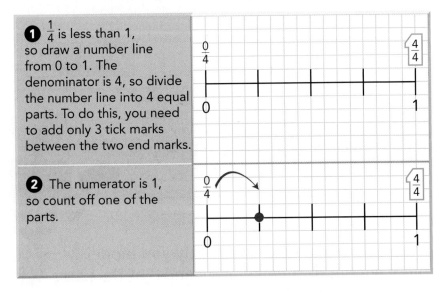

❶ $\frac{1}{4}$ is less than 1, so draw a number line from 0 to 1. The denominator is 4, so divide the number line into 4 equal parts. To do this, you need to add only 3 tick marks between the two end marks.

❷ The numerator is 1, so count off one of the parts.

⭐ **ANSWER:**

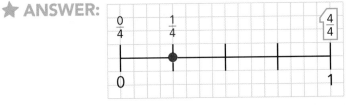

Fraction of a Group

A fraction can describe a part of a group. Sometimes you need to find out how many objects the fraction stands for.

Zoe is copying the work of artist Lori Van Houten. She paints on squares of paper and later puts the squares together to make a picture.

Case 1 Sometimes the fraction has a numerator of 1.

EXAMPLE 1: Zoe makes 16 squares. She uses mostly green on $\frac{1}{8}$ of the squares. How many squares are mostly green?

To solve, find $\frac{1}{8}$ of 16.

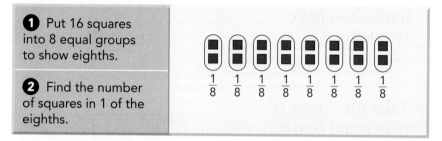

1 Put 16 squares into 8 equal groups to show eighths.

2 Find the number of squares in 1 of the eighths.

$\frac{1}{8}$ $\frac{1}{8}$ $\frac{1}{8}$ $\frac{1}{8}$ $\frac{1}{8}$ $\frac{1}{8}$ $\frac{1}{8}$ $\frac{1}{8}$

⭐ **ANSWER:** Zoe makes 2 squares that are mostly green.

Case 2 Sometimes the numerator is greater than 1.

EXAMPLE 2: Zoe uses mostly brown on $\frac{3}{8}$ of her 16 squares. How many squares are mostly brown?

To solve, find $\frac{3}{8}$ of 16.

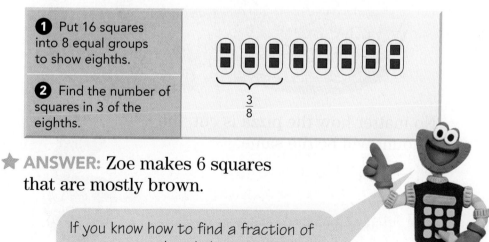

1 Put 16 squares into 8 equal groups to show eighths.

2 Find the number of squares in 3 of the eighths.

$\frac{3}{8}$

⭐ **ANSWER:** Zoe makes 6 squares that are mostly brown.

If you know how to find a fraction of a group, you already know something about multiplying fractions. $\frac{3}{8}$ of 16 is the same as $\frac{3}{8} \times 16$.

Fractions Equal to 1

When the numerator and denominator of a fraction are the same, the fraction is equal to 1.

- Take one sheet of paper and fold it into two equal parts. You have two halves.

$$\frac{2}{2} = 1$$

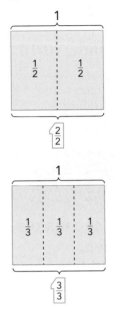

- Take one sheet of paper and fold it into three equal parts. You have three thirds.

$$\frac{3}{3} = 1$$

Can you cut it into 6 slices? I'm not hungry enough to eat 8.

No matter how the pizza is cut, the amount will be the same.

$$\frac{8}{8} = 1 \text{ and } \frac{6}{6} = 1$$

There's no end to the fractions you can make that equal 1.

$$\frac{1}{1}, \frac{2}{2}, \frac{3}{3}, \cdots \frac{100}{100} \cdots$$

Fractions Greater than 1

Sometimes you will need to describe a whole and a part. You can use a **mixed number**. A mixed number has a whole number (not 0) mixed with a fraction.

whole number part

$1\frac{1}{2}$

fraction part

Write: $1\frac{1}{2}$

Say: *one and one half*

MORE
HELP
See 25

Mixed numbers are greater than 1. Here are some ways you can picture the mixed number $1\frac{1}{2}$.

Reading a mixed number is like reading a decimal. You say *and* after the whole number. $1\frac{1}{2}$ is 1 *and* 1 half. 1.5 is 1 *and* 5 tenths.

• Olu used $1\frac{1}{2}$ sheets of poster board for his social studies project.

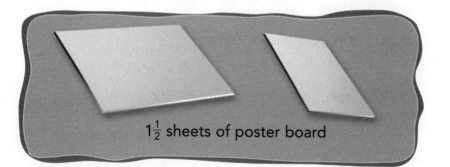

$1\frac{1}{2}$ sheets of poster board

• Jacob used $1\frac{1}{2}$ cups of milk to make pudding.

• Sarah used $1\frac{1}{2}$-inch nails on her bird house.

$1\frac{1}{2}$ cups of milk

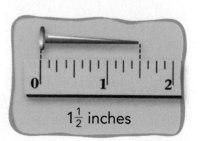

$1\frac{1}{2}$ inches

Think of $1\frac{1}{2}$ as 1 whole and $\frac{1}{2}$, or $1 + \frac{1}{2}$.

Writing a Fraction as a Whole or Mixed Number

If a fraction has a numerator greater than the denominator, the fraction is greater than 1.

A fraction greater than 1 can be written as a whole number or a mixed number.

EXAMPLE: Write $\frac{7}{3}$ as a mixed number.

ONE WAY You can use a drawing to picture the fraction.

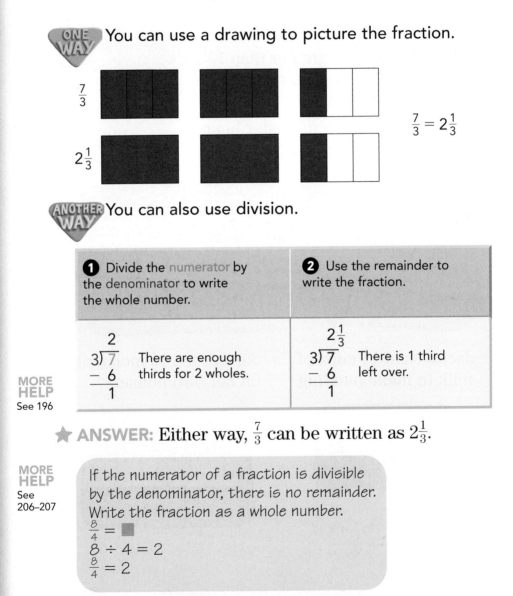

$\frac{7}{3}$

$2\frac{1}{3}$

$$\frac{7}{3} = 2\frac{1}{3}$$

ANOTHER WAY You can also use division.

❶ Divide the numerator by the denominator to write the whole number.	❷ Use the remainder to write the fraction.
$\begin{array}{r} 2 \\ 3\overline{)7} \\ -6 \\ \hline 1 \end{array}$ There are enough thirds for 2 wholes.	$\begin{array}{r} 2\frac{1}{3} \\ 3\overline{)7} \\ -6 \\ \hline 1 \end{array}$ There is 1 third left over.

MORE HELP
See 196

⭐ **ANSWER:** Either way, $\frac{7}{3}$ can be written as $2\frac{1}{3}$.

MORE HELP

See 206–207

If the numerator of a fraction is divisible by the denominator, there is no remainder. Write the fraction as a whole number.

$\frac{8}{4} = \blacksquare$

$8 \div 4 = 2$

$\frac{8}{4} = 2$

Writing a Whole or
Mixed Number as a Fraction

EXAMPLE: Write $2\frac{3}{4}$ as a fraction.

ONE WAY You can use a picture.

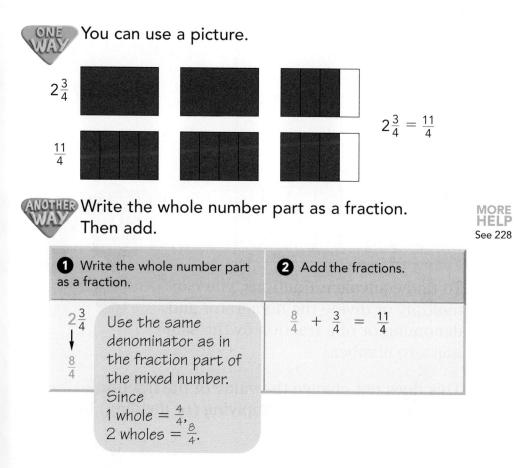

$2\frac{3}{4}$

$\frac{11}{4}$

$2\frac{3}{4} = \frac{11}{4}$

ANOTHER WAY Write the whole number part as a fraction. Then add.

MORE
HELP
See 228

❶ Write the whole number part as a fraction.	❷ Add the fractions.
$2\frac{3}{4}$ ↓ $\frac{8}{4}$ Use the same denominator as in the fraction part of the mixed number. Since 1 whole = $\frac{4}{4}$, 2 wholes = $\frac{8}{4}$.	$\frac{8}{4} + \frac{3}{4} = \frac{11}{4}$

⭐ **ANSWER:** Either way, $2\frac{3}{4}$ can be written as $\frac{11}{4}$.

Equivalent Fractions

Equivalent fractions name the same amount.
$\frac{1}{2}$, $\frac{2}{4}$, and $\frac{4}{8}$ are equivalent fractions.

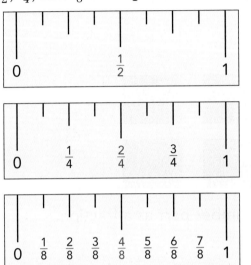

Knowing about equivalent fractions can help you read the markings on a ruler.

MORE HELP
See 66, 84

To find equivalent fractions, you can multiply or divide the numerator and denominator of a fraction by the same nonzero number.

This does not change the value of the fraction, because you are just multiplying (or dividing) by 1.

$$\frac{1}{2} = \frac{1 \times \boxed{3}}{2 \times \boxed{3}} = \frac{3}{6} \qquad\qquad \frac{2}{4} = \frac{2 \div \boxed{2}}{4 \div \boxed{2}} = \frac{1}{2}$$

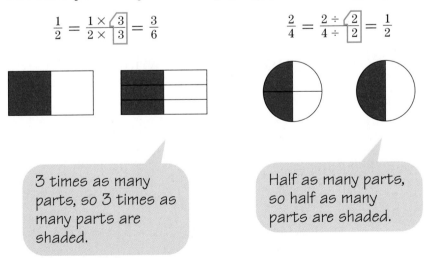

3 times as many parts, so 3 times as many parts are shaded.

Half as many parts, so half as many parts are shaded.

Writing a Fraction in Simplest Form

A fraction is in **simplest form** when its numerator and denominator have no common factors other than 1.

EXAMPLE: A student survey shows that 6 out of 18 children in the class said they would go to a theme park for their vacation this year.

Write $\frac{6}{18}$ in simplest form.

ONE WAY You can draw a picture.

Draw the simplest picture that shows the same amount.

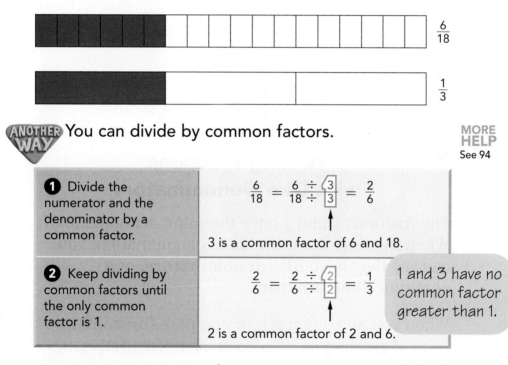

$\frac{6}{18}$

$\frac{1}{3}$

ANOTHER WAY You can divide by common factors.

MORE HELP
See 94

❶ Divide the numerator and the denominator by a common factor.

$$\frac{6}{18} = \frac{6 \div 3}{18 \div 3} = \frac{2}{6}$$

3 is a common factor of 6 and 18.

❷ Keep dividing by common factors until the only common factor is 1.

$$\frac{2}{6} = \frac{2 \div 2}{6 \div 2} = \frac{1}{3}$$

2 is a common factor of 2 and 6.

1 and 3 have no common factor greater than 1.

⭐ **ANSWER:** Either way, $\frac{6}{18}$ in simplest form is $\frac{1}{3}$.

A fraction in simplest form may have a numerator greater than 1. For example, $\frac{2}{5}$, $\frac{6}{7}$, and $\frac{5}{12}$ are all in simplest form.

Finding the Numerator
for an Equivalent Fraction

MORE
HELP
See 220

EXAMPLE: Find the missing numerator. $\frac{2}{3} = \frac{\blacksquare}{15}$

Think: $\frac{2 \times \boxed{?}}{3 \times \boxed{?}} = \frac{\blacksquare}{15}$

❶ Find the missing factor in the denominator.	$3 \times ? = 15$	The missing factor is 5 since $3 \times 5 = 15$.
❷ Use the missing factor to find the missing numerator.	$\frac{2 \times 5}{3 \times 5} = \frac{10}{15}$	

Multiplying the numerator and denominator by the same number is the same as multiplying the fraction by 1.

⭐ **ANSWER:** The missing numerator is 10.

Writing Fractions
with Like Denominators

The fractions $\frac{2}{3}$ and $\frac{1}{3}$ have the same denominator, 3. When fractions have the same denominators, you can say they have **like denominators**, or a **common denominator**.

When you add, subtract, or compare fractions, it helps if you rewrite the fractions as fractions with like denominators. You can use what you know about equivalent fractions to do this.

Case 1 One denominator is a multiple of the other.

MORE HELP
See 90, 220, 222

EXAMPLE 1: Rewrite $\frac{1}{2}$ and $\frac{3}{8}$ with like denominators.

❶ Use 8 as a common denominator because 8 is a multiple of itself and 2.	$\frac{3}{8} = \frac{3}{8}$ You don't have to change $\frac{3}{8}$.
❷ Rewrite $\frac{1}{2}$ with a denominator of 8.	$\frac{1}{2} = \frac{\blacksquare}{8}$ $\frac{1 \times \boxed{4}}{2 \times \boxed{4}} = \frac{4}{8}$

★ **ANSWER:** Fractions with like denominators for $\frac{1}{2}$ and $\frac{3}{8}$ are $\frac{4}{8}$ and $\frac{3}{8}$.

Case 2 Neither denominator is a multiple of the other.

EXAMPLE 2: Rewrite $\frac{2}{3}$ and $\frac{1}{4}$ with like denominators.

ONE WAY You can use models.

Both models must have the same number of equal parts.

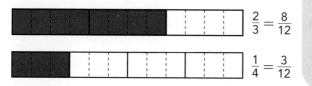

$\frac{2}{3} = \frac{8}{12}$

$\frac{1}{4} = \frac{3}{12}$

> If you can't think of a denominator to use, multiply the two denominators you have! $3 \times 4 = 12$

ANOTHER WAY You can use any common multiple of the denominators as the common denominator.

$\frac{2}{3} = \frac{2 \times \boxed{4}}{3 \times \boxed{4}} = \frac{8}{12}$ $\frac{1}{4} = \frac{1 \times \boxed{3}}{4 \times \boxed{3}} = \frac{3}{12}$

> 12 is a common multiple of 3 and 4.

★ **ANSWER:** Fractions with like denominators for $\frac{2}{3}$ and $\frac{1}{4}$ are $\frac{8}{12}$ and $\frac{3}{12}$.

MORE HELP
See 95, 222

Comparing and Ordering Fractions

Sometimes you need to compare fractions. If you know how to compare two fractions, you can also order a group of fractions.

Comparing Fractions

MORE
HELP
See 12

Case 1 You can compare fractions with like denominators.

EXAMPLE 1: In a swim camp, $\frac{7}{10}$ of the children were girls and $\frac{3}{10}$ were boys. Were there more boys or more girls in the camp?

To solve the problem, compare $\frac{7}{10}$ and $\frac{3}{10}$.

ONE WAY You can use models to compare.

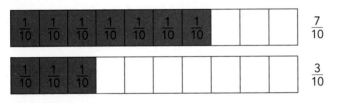

Write: $\frac{7}{10} > \frac{3}{10}$
Say: *Seven tenths is greater than three tenths.*

ANOTHER WAY You can compare the numerators of fractions with like denominators.

$7 > 3$, so $\frac{7}{10} > \frac{3}{10}$

That makes sense, because 7 of anything is greater than 3 of the same thing.

★ **ANSWER:** Either way, there were more girls than boys.

Case 2 You can compare fractions with unlike denominators.

EXAMPLE 2: Which is greater, $\frac{1}{3}$ or $\frac{1}{2}$?

ONE WAY You can use models.

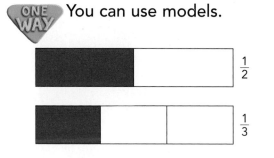

$\frac{1}{2}$

$\frac{1}{3}$

Write: $\frac{1}{2} > \frac{1}{3}$

Say: *One half is greater than one third.*

ANOTHER WAY You can compare equivalent fractions.

❶ Find equivalent fractions with the same denominator.	❷ Compare the numerators.
$\frac{1 \times 2}{3 \times 2} = \frac{2}{6}$ — same denominator $\frac{1 \times 3}{2 \times 3} = \frac{3}{6}$	3 is greater than 2. $\frac{3}{6} > \frac{2}{6}$ So $\frac{1}{2} > \frac{1}{3}$

⭐ **ANSWER:** Either way, $\frac{1}{2}$ is greater than $\frac{1}{3}$.

MATH ALERT

Be Sure You Use the Same-Size Whole

When you compare two fractions, make sure the wholes are the same size.

 Even though $\frac{1}{2}$ is greater than $\frac{1}{4}$, $\frac{1}{2}$ of a small sandwich can be smaller than $\frac{1}{4}$ of a large sandwich.

Ordering Fractions

If you know how to compare two fractions, you also know how to order a group of fractions.

MORE HELP
See 14, 220, 222–223

EXAMPLE: A survey taken of people who have dinner at restaurants shows these results. Which of these three drinks is served the least?

$\frac{1}{10}$ drink milk $\frac{1}{4}$ drink water $\frac{2}{5}$ drink soda

❶ Find fractions with like denominators.	❷ Compare the numerators.
Multiples of 4: 4, 8, 12, 16, 20, ... Multiples of 5: 5, 10, 15, 20, ... Multiples of 10: 10, 20, ... 20 is the least common denominator. $\frac{1}{10} = \frac{2}{20}$ $\frac{1}{4} = \frac{5}{20}$ $\frac{2}{5} = \frac{8}{20}$	$8 > 5 > 2$ $\frac{8}{20} > \frac{5}{20} > \frac{2}{20}$, so $\frac{2}{5} > \frac{1}{4} > \frac{1}{10}$. $\frac{1}{10}$ is less than $\frac{1}{4}$ or $\frac{2}{5}$.

★ **ANSWER:** Milk is served least of the three drinks.

Ordering Unit Fractions

A **unit fraction** has 1 as its numerator. $\frac{1}{2}, \frac{1}{3}, \frac{1}{4}$, and $\frac{1}{5}$ are all unit fractions.

When you divide something into more and more equal parts, the size of each part gets smaller, but the denominator of the fraction gets larger.

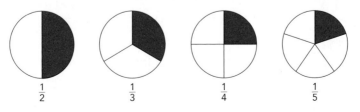

$\frac{1}{2}$ $\frac{1}{3}$ $\frac{1}{4}$ $\frac{1}{5}$

Computing with Fractions

You can use what you know about adding and subtracting whole numbers to help you add and subtract fractions. You'll also use what you know about mixed numbers and equivalent fractions.

Adding Fractions

When you add 1 *frog* to 2 *frogs*, you have 3 *frogs*. The number of *frogs* changes, but they are still *frogs*.

When you add 1 *fourth* to 2 *fourths*, you have 3 *fourths*. The number of *fourths* changes, but they are still *fourths*.

When you add 1 *dog* to 2 *cats* you need to think about adding *pets*. When you add 1 *third* to 2 *fourths*, you need to think about finding fractions with like denominators.

Adding Fractions
with Like Denominators

If the fractions have like denominators, add the numerators and keep the denominator the same.

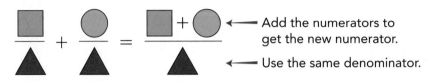

$\dfrac{\blacksquare}{\blacktriangle} + \dfrac{\bigcirc}{\blacktriangle} = \dfrac{\blacksquare + \bigcirc}{\blacktriangle}$ ⟵ Add the numerators to get the new numerator.

⟵ Use the same denominator.

EXAMPLE: Lee is baking two different kinds of muffins. He uses $\frac{3}{8}$ of a stick of butter for one kind and $\frac{3}{8}$ of a stick of butter for the other kind. How much butter does Lee use in all?

To solve the problem, add. $\frac{3}{8} + \frac{3}{8} = \blacksquare$

ONE WAY You can use models to find the sum.

$\dfrac{3}{8} + \dfrac{3}{8} = \dfrac{6}{8}$

| $\frac{1}{8}$ | $\frac{1}{8}$ | $\frac{1}{8}$ | $\frac{1}{8}$ | $\frac{1}{8}$ | $\frac{1}{8}$ | |

| $\frac{1}{4}$ | $\frac{1}{4}$ | $\frac{1}{4}$ | |

$\dfrac{3}{4}$

MORE HELP
See 221

Why can't I find my answer in any of these choices?

$\frac{6}{8}$ is equivalent to $\frac{3}{4}$.

ANOTHER WAY You can also add without models.

❶ Write the denominator of the like fractions.	❷ Add the numerators.	❸ Write the sum in simplest form.
$\dfrac{3}{8} + \dfrac{3}{8} = \dfrac{}{8}$	$\dfrac{3}{8} + \dfrac{3}{8} = \dfrac{6}{8}$	$\dfrac{6}{8} \rightarrow \dfrac{6 \div \boxed{2}}{8 \div \boxed{2}} = \dfrac{3}{4}$

★ **ANSWER:** Either way, Lee uses $\frac{3}{4}$ of a stick of butter.

Adding Fractions with Unlike Denominators

To add fractions with unlike denominators, rewrite them with like denominators.

MORE HELP
See 220, 221

EXAMPLE: Ali made a pizza. He put only pepperoni on $\frac{1}{2}$ of the pizza and only green peppers on $\frac{1}{4}$ of the pizza. He left the rest plain. What fraction of Ali's pizza had topping?

To find the answer, add. $\frac{1}{2} + \frac{1}{4} = \blacksquare$

ONE WAY You can draw a picture.

❶ Draw a circle to stand for one whole pizza.	❷ Draw a line to show halves. Color $\frac{1}{2}$ to show the part with pepperoni.	❸ Draw another line to show fourths. Color $\frac{1}{4}$ to show the part with green peppers.

ANOTHER WAY You can also add without drawing a picture.

MORE HELP
See 222–223

❶ Rewrite the fractions so they have like denominators.	❷ Add the fractions.	❸ Write the sum in simplest form.
$\frac{1}{2} \rightarrow \frac{1 \times 2}{2 \times 2} = \frac{2}{4}$ $\frac{1}{4} = \frac{1}{4}$	$\frac{2}{4} + \frac{1}{4} = \frac{3}{4}$	$\frac{3}{4}$ is already in simplest form.

⭐ **ANSWER:** Either way, $\frac{3}{4}$ of Ali's pizza had topping.

Adding Mixed Numbers

MORE
HELP
See 217,
221

You can add mixed numbers by adding the fractions and then adding the whole numbers.

EXAMPLE 1: A fruit punch recipe calls for $2\frac{1}{8}$ quarts of orange juice and $1\frac{3}{8}$ quarts of pineapple juice. How many quarts of juice are needed?

To solve the problem, add. $2\frac{1}{8} + 1\frac{3}{8} = \blacksquare$

ONE WAY You can use models and act it out.

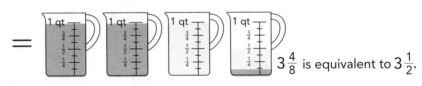

$2\frac{1}{8}$ $1\frac{3}{8}$

$3\frac{4}{8}$ is equivalent to $3\frac{1}{2}$.

ANOTHER WAY You can add without models.

❶ Add the fractions.	❷ Add the whole numbers.	❸ Write the sum in simplest form.
$2\frac{1}{8}$ $+ 1\frac{3}{8}$ $\overline{\frac{4}{8}}$	$2\frac{1}{8}$ $+ 1\frac{3}{8}$ $\overline{3\frac{4}{8}}$	$3\frac{4}{8} = 3\frac{1}{2}$ $\frac{4}{8}$ is equivalent to $\frac{1}{2}$.

★ **ANSWER:** Either way, $3\frac{1}{2}$ quarts of juice are needed.

EXAMPLE 2: $1\frac{1}{2} + 1\frac{3}{4} = \blacksquare$

ONE WAY You can draw a picture.

$1\frac{1}{2}$ $\longrightarrow$ $1\frac{2}{4}$

Change $\frac{1}{2}$ to $\frac{2}{4}$.

$1\frac{3}{4}$

$$1\frac{2}{4} + 1\frac{3}{4} = 3\frac{1}{4}$$

ANOTHER WAY You can add without drawing a picture.

MORE
HELP
See 218,
221

❶ If the fractions do not have like denominators, rewrite them so that they have like denominators.	$\frac{1}{2} \longrightarrow \frac{1 \times 2}{2 \times 2} = \frac{2}{4}$ $\frac{3}{4} = \frac{3}{4}$
❷ Add the fractions. Regroup, if needed, by writing the fraction as a mixed number.	$\begin{array}{r} 1 \\ 1\frac{2}{4} \\ + 1\frac{3}{4} \\ \hline \frac{1}{4} \end{array}$ $\frac{5}{4} = 1\frac{1}{4}$
❸ Add the whole numbers. Write the answer in simplest form.	$\begin{array}{r} 1 \\ 1\frac{2}{4} \\ + 1\frac{3}{4} \\ \hline 3\frac{1}{4} \end{array}$ $3\frac{1}{4}$ is already in simplest form.

⭐ **ANSWER:** Either way, $1\frac{1}{2} + 1\frac{3}{4} = 3\frac{1}{4}$.

Subtracting Fractions

You can use a lot of what you know about adding fractions to help you subtract fractions.

Subtracting Fractions with Like Denominators

If the fractions have like denominators, subtract the numerators and keep the denominator the same.

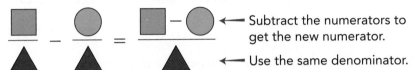

← Subtract the numerators to get the new numerator.

← Use the same denominator.

EXAMPLE: Jerry lives $\frac{5}{8}$ mile from school. Sharon lives $\frac{1}{8}$ mile from school. How much farther from school does Jerry live than Sharon?

To solve the problem, subtract. $\frac{5}{8} - \frac{1}{8} = \blacksquare$

ONE WAY You can use a number line as a model.

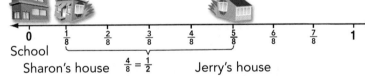

School
Sharon's house $\quad \frac{4}{8} = \frac{1}{2} \quad$ Jerry's house

ANOTHER WAY You can also subtract fractions without models.

MORE HELP
See 221

1 Write the denominator of the like fractions.	**2** Subtract the numerators.	**3** Write the difference in simplest form.
$\frac{5}{8} - \frac{1}{8} = \frac{}{8}$	$\frac{5}{8} - \frac{1}{8} = \frac{4}{8}$	$\frac{4}{8} \rightarrow \frac{4 \div \boxed{4}}{8 \div \boxed{4}} = \frac{1}{2}$

★ **ANSWER:** Either way, Jerry lives $\frac{1}{2}$ mile farther from school than Sharon.

Subtracting Fractions
with Unlike Denominators

To subtract fractions with unlike denominators, rewrite them with like denominators.

MORE
HELP
See 220,
221

EXAMPLE: Mindy buys $\frac{3}{4}$ yard of fuzzy fabric. She uses $\frac{5}{8}$ of a yard to make a stuffed animal. How much fabric does she have left?

To solve, subtract. $\frac{3}{4} - \frac{5}{8} = \blacksquare$

 You can draw a picture.

❶ Draw a rectangle to stand for one yard of fabric.	
❷ Draw lines to show fourths. Color $\frac{3}{4}$ to show how much fabric there is.	
❸ Draw lines to show eighths. Cross out 5 of the colored eighths to show how much fabric is used.	

ANOTHER WAY You can subtract without drawing a picture.

❶ Rewrite the fractions so that they have like denominators.	❷ Subtract the fractions.	❸ Write the difference in simplest form.
$\frac{3}{4} \longrightarrow \frac{3 \times 2}{4 \times 2} = \frac{6}{8}$ $\frac{5}{8} = \frac{5}{8}$	$\frac{6}{8} - \frac{5}{8} = \frac{1}{8}$	$\frac{1}{8}$ is already in simplest form.

★ **ANSWER:** Either way, $\frac{1}{8}$ of a yard of fabric is left.

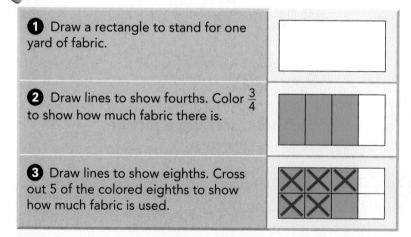

Subtracting Mixed Numbers

You can subtract mixed numbers by subtracting the fractions and then subtracting the whole numbers.

MORE HELP
See 217, 221 **EXAMPLE 1:** After the class party, there were $2\frac{7}{8}$ pizzas left. The teachers then ate $1\frac{5}{8}$ of the pizzas. How many pizzas were then left?

To solve the problem, subtract. $2\frac{7}{8} - 1\frac{5}{8} = \blacksquare$

ONE WAY You can draw a picture.

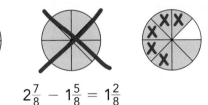

$$2\frac{7}{8} - 1\frac{5}{8} = 1\frac{2}{8}$$

$1\frac{2}{8}$ is equivalent to $1\frac{1}{4}$.

ANOTHER WAY You can add without drawing a picture.

❶ Subtract the fractions.	$\begin{array}{r} 2\frac{7}{8} \\ -1\frac{5}{8} \\ \hline \frac{2}{8} \end{array}$ The fractions already have like denominators. So, you don't have to rewrite.
❷ Subtract the whole numbers.	$\begin{array}{r} 2\frac{7}{8} \\ -1\frac{5}{8} \\ \hline 1\frac{2}{8} \end{array}$
❸ Write the difference in simplest form.	$1\frac{2}{8} = 1\frac{1}{4}$ $\frac{2}{8}$ is equivalent to $\frac{1}{4}$.

★ **ANSWER:** There were $1\frac{1}{4}$ pizzas left.

EXAMPLE 2: Lauren studied plant growth for a science project. At the beginning of one month, the plant was $2\frac{1}{2}$ feet tall. At the end of the month the plant was $3\frac{1}{4}$ feet tall. How much did the plant grow during one month?

To solve the problem, subtract. $3\frac{1}{4} - 2\frac{1}{2} = \blacksquare$

ONE WAY You can use models.

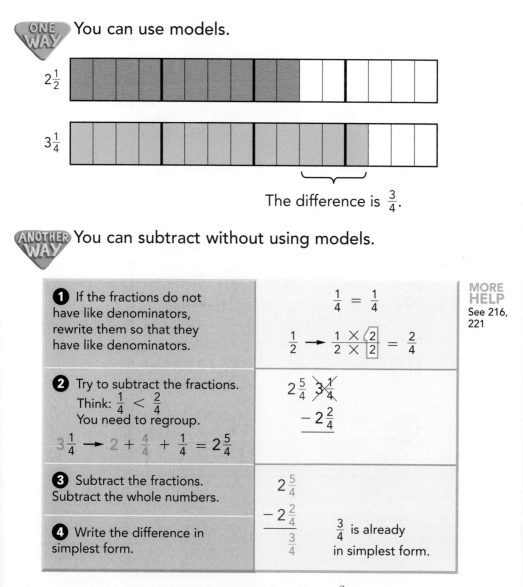

$2\frac{1}{2}$

$3\frac{1}{4}$

The difference is $\frac{3}{4}$.

ANOTHER WAY You can subtract without using models.

		MORE HELP
❶ If the fractions do not have like denominators, rewrite them so that they have like denominators.	$\frac{1}{4} = \frac{1}{4}$ $\frac{1}{2} \longrightarrow \frac{1 \times \boxed{2}}{2 \times \boxed{2}} = \frac{2}{4}$	See 216, 221
❷ Try to subtract the fractions. Think: $\frac{1}{4} < \frac{2}{4}$ You need to regroup. $3\frac{1}{4} \longrightarrow 2 + \frac{4}{4} + \frac{1}{4} = 2\frac{5}{4}$	$2\frac{5}{4} \; 3\frac{1}{4}$ $-\;2\frac{2}{4}$	
❸ Subtract the fractions. Subtract the whole numbers.	$2\frac{5}{4}$ $-\;2\frac{2}{4}$ $\overline{\frac{3}{4}}$	
❹ Write the difference in simplest form.		$\frac{3}{4}$ is already in simplest form.

⭐ **ANSWER:** Either way, the plant grew $\frac{3}{4}$ of a foot during the month.

Algebraic Thinking

Alligators enjoy algebra even more than spelling.

Let's say that you have a cousin who is 2 years younger than you are. When you're 12, she'll be 10. When you're 15, she'll be 13. Your age and your cousin's age will change, but something about your ages stays the same. Your cousin will always be 2 years younger than you are. When you look at things that change and think about how they are related, that's algebraic thinking.

When you look at numbers and operations in that same way, it's also algebraic thinking. For example, you might think about what kinds of things always happen, no matter what numbers you add.

Algebraic thinking may be a new challenge for you. Try it. It may make you (and your cousin, too) a more powerful thinker.

Positive and Negative Numbers

Positive numbers are numbers that are greater than zero.

Negative numbers are numbers that are less than zero.

Zero is neither positive nor negative.

You probably know a lot about positive and negative numbers already. You may have seen them used in these ways.

Distance above or below sea level   Temperature

Positive and negative numbers are sometimes called **signed numbers.**

The Number Line

You can show positive and negative numbers on a number line. Think of a street. You enter the street at zero. To your left are the negative numbers. To your right are the positive numbers.

Usually positive numbers are written without a sign. So, you're looking at a positive number unless the number is 0, or you see a negative sign.

Comparing Signed Numbers

EXAMPLE 1: Which temperature is greater, ⁻5°F or 4°F? Compare ⁻5 and 4. You can use a number line.

Some people describe ⁻5° as "five degrees below zero."

less than 0 | greater than 0

-6 -5 -4 -3 -2 -1 0 1 2 3 4 5 6

A positive number is greater than a negative number.

⭐ **ANSWER:** 4°F is greater than ⁻5°F.

EXAMPLE 2: Compare ⁻8 and ⁻2. Which is greater?

As you move to the right, the numbers get greater.

-10 -9 -8 -7 -6 -5 -4 -3 -2 -1 0 1 2

⭐ **ANSWER:** ⁻2 is greater than ⁻8.

Properties

When you compute, you discover some things about numbers that are always true. These things are called **properties**.

Order Properties

Sometimes it doesn't matter which of two things you do first, and sometimes it *does* matter.

Order Property of Addition

The **Order Property of Addition** tells you that changing the order of two addends does not change the sum.

EXAMPLE: Add. $35 + 17 + 5 =$ ■

The Order Property can make mental math easier.

MORE
HELP
See 41, 109

$$35 + 5 + 17$$

Think: $40 + 17 = 57$

> You can move compatible numbers like 35 and 5 together. Because of the Order Property, $35 + 5 + 17$ has the same sum as $35 + 17 + 5$.

⭐ **ANSWER:** $35 + 17 + 5 = 57$

Order Property of Multiplication

The **Order Property of Multiplication** tells you that changing the order of two factors does not change the product.

MORE
HELP
See 67, 138

$$\begin{array}{r} 4 \\ \times\ 2 \\ \hline 8 \end{array} \qquad \begin{array}{r} 2 \\ \times\ 4 \\ \hline 8 \end{array}$$

EXAMPLE: Multiply. $5 \times 27 \times 2 =$ ■

Use the Order Property and mental math.

$$5 \times 2 \times 27$$

Think: $10 \times 27 = 270$

> Because of the Order Property, $5 \times 2 \times 27$ has the same product as $5 \times 27 \times 2$.

⭐ **ANSWER:** $5 \times 27 \times 2 = 270$

> The **Order Properties** are also called the **Commutative Properties**. Commute means "to go back and forth." For example, people commute to work.

MATH ALERT

Subtraction and Division Do Not Have an Order Property

$8 - 4$ is not equal to $4 - 8$.

$8 - 4 = 4 \quad 4 - 8 = {}^{-}4$

$8 \div 4$ is not equal to $4 \div 8$.

$8 \div 4 = 2 \quad 4 \div 8 = \frac{4}{8}$, or $\frac{1}{2}$

Grouping Properties

Some things can be grouped in any way.

There are other things that should not be grouped in certain ways.

In mathematics, the **Grouping Properties** tell you that you can group addends or factors and not change the answer. These are also called the **Associative Properties.**

Grouping Property of Addition

The **Grouping Property of Addition** tells you that changing the grouping of three or more addends does not change the sum.

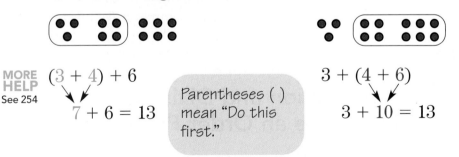

MORE HELP See 254

$(3 + 4) + 6$

$7 + 6 = 13$

Parentheses ( ) mean "Do this first."

$3 + (4 + 6)$

$3 + 10 = 13$

This property can help you add numbers mentally.

EXAMPLE: Add. $(27 + 5) + 65 = \blacksquare$

MORE
HELP
See 90,
109

Use the Grouping Property and mental math.

$(27 + 5) + 65$

$27 + (5 + 65)$

$27 + 70 = 97$

> 65 and 5 are compatible. They are both multiples of 5.

> When two numbers change position, you are using the Order Property. When three or more addends change position, you are using the Grouping Property.

★ **ANSWER:** $(27 + 5) + 65 = 97$

Grouping Property of Multiplication

The **Grouping Property of Multiplication** tells you that changing the grouping of three or more factors does not change the product.

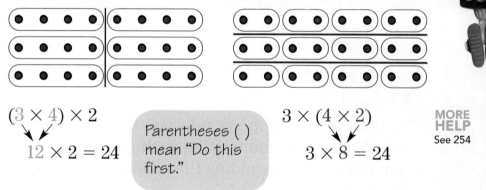

$(3 \times 4) \times 2$

$12 \times 2 = 24$

> Parentheses ( ) mean "Do this first."

$3 \times (4 \times 2)$

$3 \times 8 = 24$

MORE
HELP
See 254

This property can help you multiply numbers mentally.

EXAMPLE: Multiply. $(9 \times 2) \times 5 = \blacksquare$

MORE
HELP
See 120,
138

Use the Grouping Property and mental math.

$(9 \times 2) \times 5$

$9 \times (2 \times 5)$

$9 \times 10 = 90$

> It is easy to multiply by 10 in your head.

★ **ANSWER:** $(9 \times 2) \times 5 = 90$

Subtraction and Division Do Not Have a Grouping Property

MORE HELP

See 254

$(8 - 4) - 2$ $8 - (4 - 2)$ $(8 \div 2) \div 2$ $8 \div (2 \div 2)$

$4 - 2 = 2$ $8 - 2 = 6$ $4 \div 2 = 2$ $8 \div 1 = 8$

2 is not equal to 6.   2 is not equal to 8.

> If you can show even one case in which a property is not true, then that property does not work for that operation.

Distributive Property

When you distribute something, you separate it into parts. The **Distributive Property** lets you separate numbers into parts so that the numbers are easier to work with.

MORE HELP

See 123, 124

The Distributive Property tells you that you can multiply a sum by multiplying each addend separately and then adding the products.

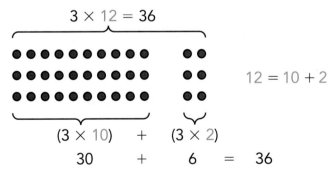

$3 \times 12 = 36$

$12 = 10 + 2$

(3×10) + (3×2)

30 + 6 = 36

EXAMPLE 1: How many weeks are there in 4 years?

To solve, you can find the product of 4 and 52.

To multiply in your head, you can use the Distributive Property.

> There are 52 weeks in a year.
> $52 = 50 + 2$

$4 \times 52 = 4 \times (50 + 2)$

$$(4 \times 50) + (4 \times 2)$$
$$200 + 8 = 208$$

⭐ **ANSWER:** There are 208 weeks in 4 years.

The Distributive Property also tells you that you can multiply a difference by multiplying each part separately and then subtracting the products.

EXAMPLE 2: Multiply mentally. $6 \times 19 = \blacksquare$

$6 \times 19 = 6 \times (20 - 1)$

$$(6 \times 20) - (6 \times 1)$$
$$120 - 6 = 114$$

> 20 is easier to work with than 19.

⭐ **ANSWER:** $6 \times 19 = 114$

Adding 0 Property

MORE HELP
See 40 This is an example of the **Adding 0 Property**. This property tells you that when you add 0 to any number, you end up with that same number.

There is a special name for numbers that don't change things. They are called **identity elements**.

The **identity element for addition** is 0.

Multiplying by 1 Property

MORE HELP
See 66 This is an example of the **Multiplying by 1 Property**. This property tells you that when you multiply any number by 1, you end up with that same number.

The **identity element for multiplication** is 1. If you multiply any number by 1, or multiply 1 by any number, the product will be that number.

Zero Property of Multiplication

The **Zero Property of Multiplication** tells you that the product of any number and 0 is 0.

For example, $4 \times 0 = 0$ and $0 \times 4 = 0$.

There are 0 hats on each table. So, there are 0 hats in all.

You can sometimes use this property to find the product of more than two factors mentally. If one of the factors is zero, the product will always be 0.

This makes sense. No matter how many groups you have, if each group has no things, you still have no things.

EXAMPLE: What is $45 \times 44 \times 43 \times 0$?

$45 \times 44 \times 43 \ \times 0$

Some big number! $\times 0$

0

MORE
HELP
See 67

⭐ **ANSWER:** $45 \times 44 \times 43 \times 0 = 0$

Equality Properties

MORE HELP
See 255, 424–425
The **Equality Properties** can help you solve equations. Think of an equation as a scale that is balanced.

The Addition Property of Equality

The **Addition Property of Equality** tells you that you can add the same number to both sides of an equation and it will still be true.

The scale is balanced.

$3 = 3$

If you add 1 on the left, the scale is **not** balanced.

$3 + 1 \neq 3$.

If you then add 1 on the right, the scale is balanced again.

$3 + 1 = 3 + 1$

The symbol $\neq$ means "is not equal to."

You can also subtract the same number from both sides of an equation and it will still be true.

The scale is balanced.

$3 = 3$

If you take 1 away from the left, the scale is **not** balanced.

$3 - 1 \neq 3$

If you then take 1 away from the right, the scale is balanced again.

$3 - 1 = 3 - 1$

The Multiplication Property of Equality

The **Multiplication Property of Equality** tells you that you can multiply both sides of an equation by the same number and it will still be true.

  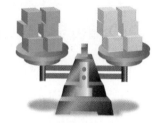

The scale is balanced. 2 = 2	If you multiply the amount in the left pan by 3, the scale is **not** balanced. 3 × 2 ≠ 2	If you then multiply the amount in the other pan by 3, the scale is balanced again. 3 × 2 = 3 × 2

You can also divide both sides of an equation by the same number and it will still be true.

The scale is balanced. 6 = 6	If you divide the amount in the left pan by 2, the scale is **not** balanced. 6 ÷ 2 ≠ 6	If you then divide the amount in the other pan by 2, the scale is balanced again. 6 ÷ 2 = 6 ÷ 2

Expressions

In language, an expression can be a short way to describe an idea or feeling. In mathematics, an **expression** is a short way to describe an amount.

Wipe that expression off your face!

$2+3$

Variables

If something varies, that means it changes. Most things, like your height and weight, do not stay the same. To describe things that change, or vary, you can use letters instead of numbers. When you use letters that way, they are called **variables**.

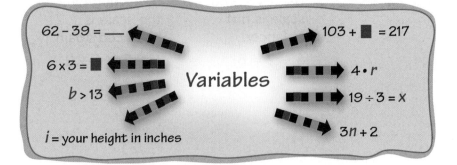

$62 - 39 = \underline{\quad}$

$6 \times 3 = \blacksquare$

$b > 13$

$i =$ your height in inches

Variables

$103 + \blacksquare = 217$

$4 \cdot r$

$19 \div 3 = x$

$3n + 2$

Writing Expressions

In mathematics, an **expression** names an amount.

- Sometimes an expression is just a number, like 5.
- Sometimes an expression is just a **variable**, like n.
- Sometimes an expression is a combination of numbers, variables, and operations, like 2×3 or $y - 6$.

Writing Addition and Subtraction Expressions

EXAMPLE 1: There are 3 more girls than boys in the class. Write an expression to show how many girls are in the class.

Think: The number of girls is 3 more than the number of boys.

b = number of **b**oys

Any letter of the alphabet can be used as a variable. Sometimes the first letter of the word that the variable stands for is used, such as **b** for the number of **b**oys.

⭐ ANSWER: **Write:** $b + 3$ **Say:** b *plus three*

EXAMPLE 2: A school bus carrying 8 students comes to a bus stop. No more students get on, but some of the students get off. Write an expression to show the number of students left on the bus.

Think: The number of students left on the bus is 8 minus the number of students who get off.

n = **n**umber of students who get off

⭐ ANSWER: **Write:** $8 - n$ **Say:** *eight minus* n

Writing Multiplication and Division Expressions

EXAMPLE 1: Kai has 3 times as many shirts as he has jackets. Write an expression for the number of shirts Kai has.

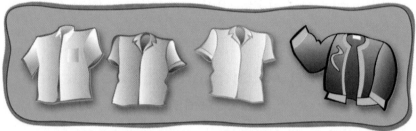

j = number of jackets

⭐ **ANSWER: Write:** $3 \times j$ **Say:** *three times j*

You can also write 3*j* or
3 · *j* to mean *three times j.*

EXAMPLE 2: Four people share a box of marbles equally. Write an expression to show how many marbles each person gets.

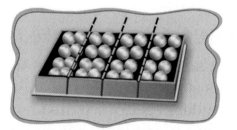

m = number of marbles in the box

⭐ **ANSWER: Write:** $m \div 4$ **Say:** m *divided by four*

You can also write $\frac{m}{4}$ to
mean *m* divided by 4.

Order of Operations

Order of operations is a set of rules. It tells you the order in which to compute so that you'll get the same answer that anyone else would get.

MORE
HELP
See 418

Rules for Order of Operations

When you have a problem with different operations, you must perform the operations in this order.

1. Multiply and divide in the order they appear.
2. Add and subtract in the order they appear.

EXAMPLE: $10 - 2 + 4 \times 3 \div 2 = \blacksquare$

❶ Multiply.	$10 - 2 + 4 \times 3 \div 2$ 12	$4 \times 3 = 12$ Replace 4×3 with 12.
❷ Divide.	$10 - 2 + 12 \div 2$ 6	$12 \div 2 = 6$ Replace $12 \div 2$ with 6.
❸ Subtract.	$10 - 2 + 6$ 8	$10 - 2 = 8$ Replace $10 - 2$ with 8.
❹ Add.	$8 + 6 = 14$	

Since the subtraction comes before the addition, subtract, then add.

⭐ ANSWER: $10 - 2 + 4 \times 3 \div 2 = 14$

If instead of following the Order of Operations, you do the operations from left to right, you will get 18, the wrong answer!

Order of Operations with Parentheses and Exponents

MORE HELP
See 98, 418 If a problem has parentheses or exponents, you need to follow these rules:

1. Compute inside the **parentheses** first.

2. Do the work with the **exponents**.

3. **M**ultiply and **d**ivide in the order they appear.

4. **A**dd and **s**ubtract in the order they appear.

EXAMPLE: $4 \div 2 + (3 \times 5) - 3^2 = \blacksquare$

1 Compute inside the parentheses.	$4 \div 2 + (3 \times 5) - 3^2$ 15
2 Do the work with the exponents.	$4 \div 2 + 15 - 3^2$ 9
3 Multiply and divide in the order they appear.	$4 \div 2 + 15 - 9$ 2
4 Add and subtract in the order they appear.	$2 + 15 - 9$ $17 - 9 = 8$

★ **ANSWER:** $4 \div 2 + (3 \times 5) - 3^2 = 8$

Equations

An **equation** is a mathematical sentence that tells you that two expressions are equal. It uses an equals sign.

MORE
HELP
See 250

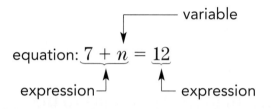

equation: $7 + n = 12$

expression ⌐   └ expression

Writing Equations

To write an equation, think about which two amounts are equal. Then write an expression for each amount.

EXAMPLE 1: A gift box weighs 5 ounces when empty. When a basketball is placed inside, the box weighs 28 ounces. How much does the ball weigh? Write an equation to find the weight of the ball.

MORE
HELP
See 251

Think: 5 ounces + weight of ball = 28 ounces

★ **ANSWER:** $5 + b = 28$

EXAMPLE 2: Caitlin gave away 5 of her stuffed animals. She has 34 animals left. Write an equation to find how many stuffed animals Caitlin had before she gave away 5.

Think: total animals − 5 animals = 34 animals

★ **ANSWER:** $a - 5 = 34$

Solving Equations

To **solve an equation**, find the value of the variable that makes the equation true.

Case 1 Sometimes you can use mental math.

MORE HELP See 49

EXAMPLE 1: Solve. $2 + n = 5$

Think: 2 plus *what number* is equal to 5?

Since $5 - 3 = 2$, then $2 + 3 = 5$.

★ ANSWER: $n = 3$

MORE HELP See 255, 376–377

Case 2 You can use the guess, check, and revise problem-solving strategy.

EXAMPLE 2: After Tunu fed 12 peanuts to the elephants, he still had 39 peanuts in the bag. Write and solve an equation to find how many peanuts Tunu had before he fed the elephants.

Think:

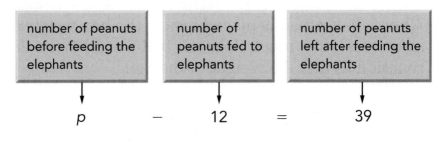

number of peanuts before feeding the elephants	number of peanuts fed to elephants	number of peanuts left after feeding the elephants
p	$-$ 12	$=$ 39

Guess: $p = 42$

Check: $42 - 12 = 30$ 30 is less than 39.

Try again. Make a higher guess.

Guess: $p = 51$

Check: $51 - 12 = 39$ $39 = 39$ It checks.

★ ANSWER: Tunu had 51 peanuts in the bag before he fed the elephants.

EXAMPLE 3: A person takes a breath about 1200 times every hour. Write and solve an equation that tells how about many times a person takes a breath in 1 minute. *Source: www.medhelp.org*

Think:

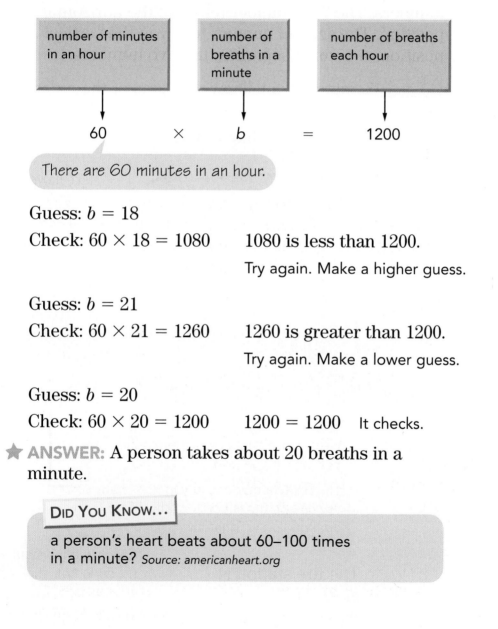

number of minutes in an hour		number of breaths in a minute		number of breaths each hour
60	×	b	=	1200

There are 60 minutes in an hour.

Guess: $b = 18$

Check: $60 \times 18 = 1080$ 1080 is less than 1200.

Try again. Make a higher guess.

Guess: $b = 21$

Check: $60 \times 21 = 1260$ 1260 is greater than 1200.

Try again. Make a lower guess.

Guess: $b = 20$

Check: $60 \times 20 = 1200$ $1200 = 1200$ It checks.

⭐ **ANSWER:** A person takes about 20 breaths in a minute.

DID YOU KNOW...

a person's heart beats about 60–100 times in a minute? *Source: americanheart.org*

Graphing Ordered Pairs

You can use an **ordered pair** of numbers to name a location on a grid. An ordered pair is made up of two numbers. The first number tells you the horizontal position. The second number tells you the vertical position. A comma separates the two numbers.

Case 1 Sometimes you know the name of the ordered pair and need to find what is at that point.

EXAMPLE 1: What building is at (2, 5)?

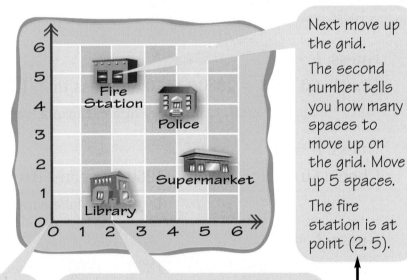

Next move up the grid.

The second number tells you how many spaces to move up on the grid. Move up 5 spaces.

The fire station is at point (2, 5).

Always start at (0, 0).

First move to the right along the bottom of the grid.

The first number tells you how many spaces to move horizontally. Move 2 spaces to the right from (0, 0).

★ **ANSWER:** The fire station is at (2, 5).

Order is important. (2, 5) is not the same as (5, 2). The supermarket is at (5, 2).

Case 2 Sometimes you know the point and need to name it.

EXAMPLE 2: Name the ordered pair of numbers that gives the location of the video store.

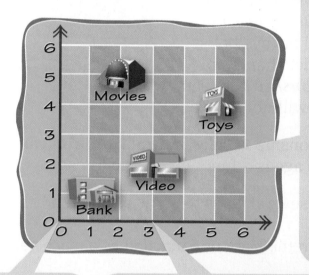

Next move up the grid.

Move up until you reach the video store. You moved 2 spaces so 2 is the second part of the name for the point.

Write the name as (3, 2) which stands for 3 spaces to the right and 2 spaces up.

Always start at (0, 0).

First move to the right along the bottom of the grid.

Move to the right from (0, 0) until you get to the place under where the video store is located. You moved 3 spaces so 3 is the first part of the name for the point.

Write: (3, 2)

Say: *point three two*

⭐ **ANSWER:** The video store is located at point (3, 2).

Functions

Arlene's brother Tom was born on her fourth birthday. She is exactly 4 years older than Tom. Her age *will change* and his age *will change*, but Arlene will always be 4 years older than Tom. The *relationship* between their ages will not change.

This relationship is called a **function**. You can say that Tom's age is a function of Arlene's age.

There are several ways to show a function.

ONE WAY You can think about a function as a machine.

For this machine, the rule is + 4. When the input changes, the output will change. But for any input there will be only one possible output.

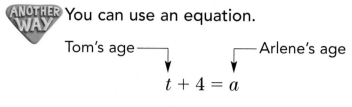 You can use an equation.

Tom's age ⟶ ⎤   ⎡ ⟵ Arlene's age

$$t + 4 = a$$

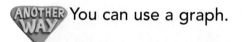 You can use a function table.

A **function table** lists pairs of numbers.

Rule: + 4	
Input	**Output**
0	4
1	5
2	6
3	7
4	8
5	9
6	10
7	11
8	12

Input is Tom's age.
Output is Arlene's age.

For any input, there is only one possible output.

You can use a graph.

Every point on the line represents a pair of numbers that have the same relationship. The second number is 4 more than the first number.

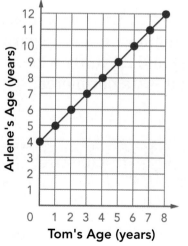

Arlene's Age (years)

Tom's Age (years)

MORE
HELP
See 258

Formulas

MORE HELP
See 255–257

A rule that is written as an equation is called a **formula**. When you use a formula, you can solve it just as you solve any equation.

Formula for Perimeter of a Rectangle

MORE HELP
See 174, 253, 348–349

The distance around a figure is called the **perimeter.** You can find the perimeter of any figure by adding the lengths of all the sides.

You can also use this formula to find the perimeter of a rectangle.

Perimeter of rectangle

$$P = 2l + 2w$$

2 times the length of the rectangle

2 times the width of the rectangle

EXAMPLE: An Olympic-size swimming pool is 55 yards long and 23 yards wide. What is its perimeter?

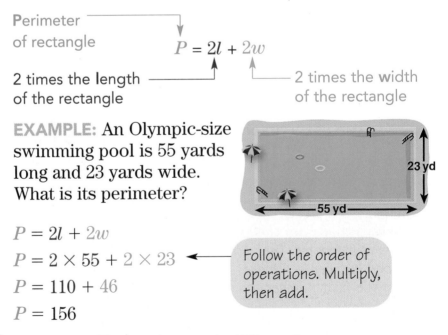

23 yd

55 yd

$P = 2l + 2w$

$P = 2 \times 55 + 2 \times 23$ ← Follow the order of operations. Multiply, then add.

$P = 110 + 46$

$P = 156$

⭐ **ANSWER:** The perimeter is 156 yards.

Formula for Area of a Rectangle

Area is the number of square units needed to cover a figure. You can find the area of a rectangle by using this formula:

MORE
HELP
See 350

Area of rectangle

$$A = l \times w$$

length of rectangle ⎯⎯⎯⎯⎯⎯⎯⎯ width of rectangle

EXAMPLE: If you are ever in Salt Lake City, Utah, you can visit the Great Salt Lake Desert. This is one of the world's largest deserts and is about 110 miles long and 50 miles wide. About what is its area?

Source: 1999 Time Almanac

$A = l \times w$

$A = 110 \times 50$

$A = 5500$

50 miles

110 miles

⭐ **ANSWER:** The area of the Great Salt Lake Desert is about 5500 square miles.

The area of the state of Rhode Island is only 1045 square miles. That means that the Great Salt Lake Desert is more than 5 times the size of Rhode Island!

Great
Salt
Lake

Rhode Island

Great
Salt Lake
Desert

0   20   40 miles

Graphing, Statistics, and Probability

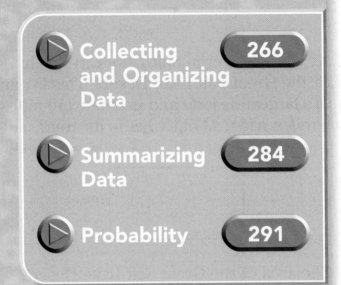

How healthy was your breakfast? Which sneakers are the best? Will it rain tomorrow? These questions sound simple, but finding useful answers is not so simple. That's why we have graphing, statistics, and probability. These tools help you gather information, organize it, study it, and make sense of it. They help you answer hard questions that sound simple. Then you are able to make better choices about what to eat, what to buy, and whether to bring an umbrella to school.

Collecting and Organizing Data

In a **survey**, you ask lots of people the same question. The answers you get are pieces of **data** that you organize and study to see whether there are some answers that occur more often than others.

What did you buy at the refreshment stand?

Other ways to collect data include counting, sampling, and experimenting.

The mathematics used for collecting, organizing, and studying data is called **statistics**.

Tally Charts

When you collect data, you need a way to keep track of the information as you collect it.

One simple way to keep track of things that you are counting is to make **tally marks**.

EXAMPLE: Your music teacher is forming a school band. The tally chart shows which musical instruments your classmates can play.

Instrument	Tally	Number of Students
Piano	卌 |||	8
Guitar	卌		6
Flute	|||	3
Trumpet	卌	5

Make a tally mark for each student who plays that instrument. Instead of every fifth tally mark, draw a slash through four marks. This makes it easier to count the tally marks by fives.

After you've surveyed everyone, write the number of tally marks for each item.

It helps to collect information in an organized way. For example, looking at the tally chart, you can see that more of your classmates play the piano than play other instruments.

1, 2, 3, 4, 5, 6, 7, 8, 9, oops! Did I count this twice?

5, 10, 15, 20, 21, 22

Tables

When you have lots of data, a **table** can make it easy to find and compare the data. Just open a newspaper or read a magazine, and you're sure to find many tables filled with data.

EXAMPLE: In which year was the Navajo Jewelry stamp issued? How much did one Navajo Jewelry stamp cost when it was issued?

U.S. Post Office Stamps		
Stamp	Year Issued	Denomination
Circus Wagon	1998	5¢
Navajo Jewelry	2004	2¢
Special Olympics	2003	80¢
First Powered Flight	2003	37¢

Source: United States Postal Service

- Find the row for Navajo Jewelry.
- Move across the row to the column titled *Year Issued*. The year is 2004.
- Continue moving across the row to the column titled *Denomination*. The cost when issued was 2¢.

⭐ ANSWER: The Navajo Jewelry stamp was issued in 2004. It cost 2¢ when it was issued.

Venn Diagrams

A **Venn diagram** can show how data can belong in more than one group. It is made up of circles or rings, which sometimes overlap, or **intersect.**

Each circle or ring is named for the data found inside. Data that belong in more than one group are placed inside the section where the circles or rings intersect.

EXAMPLE 1: Which of Amy's friends own dogs? Which ride bicycles to school?

Think: Which names are in each circle?

★ **ANSWER:** Lamar, Joy, and Erin own dogs. Erin, Luís, and Bua ride bicycles to school.

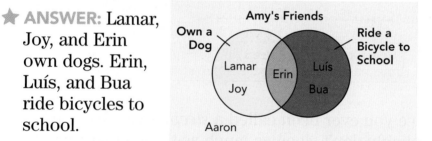

EXAMPLE 2: Which of Amy's friends own a dog *and* ride a bicycle to school?

Think: Are there any names in the section where *both circles overlap?*

★ **ANSWER:** Erin has a dog *and* rides a bicycle to school.

EXAMPLE 3: Which of Amy's friends *doesn't* own a dog *and doesn't* ride a bicycle to school?

Think: Are there any names that are *not inside a circle?*

★ **ANSWER:** Aaron *doesn't* own a dog *and doesn't* ride his bicycle to school.

Pictographs

A **pictograph** uses pictures or symbols to show data. It's a good way to present data that will be compared. The pictures help make the graph interesting and help people remember what the graph is about.

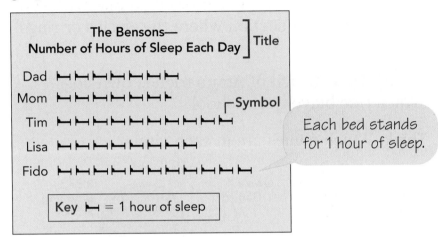

The Bensons—
Number of Hours of Sleep Each Day] Title

Dad ⊢⊣ ⊢⊣ ⊢⊣ ⊢⊣ ⊢⊣ ⊢⊣ ⊢⊣

Mom ⊢⊣ ⊢⊣ ⊢⊣ ⊢⊣ ⊢⊣ ⊢⊣ ⊢⊢

Tim ⊢⊣ ⊢⊣ ⊢⊣ ⊢⊣ ⊢⊣ ⊢⊣ ⊢⊣ ⊢⊣ ⊢⊣ ⊢⊣ ⌐Symbol

Lisa ⊢⊣ ⊢⊣ ⊢⊣ ⊢⊣ ⊢⊣ ⊢⊣ ⊢⊣ ⊢⊣

Fido ⊢⊣ ⊢⊣ ⊢⊣ ⊢⊣ ⊢⊣ ⊢⊣ ⊢⊣ ⊢⊣ ⊢⊣ ⊢⊣

Key ⊢⊣ = 1 hour of sleep

Each bed stands for 1 hour of sleep.

Have you ever been called a *sleepyhead*? Well, you probably don't sleep as much as these creatures.

Sleepiest Animals	
Animals	**Number of Hours of Sleep Each Day**
Armadillo	19 hours
Koala	22 hours
Lemur	16 hours
Opossum	19 hours
Sloth	20 hours

Source: The Top Ten of Everything, 1999 by Russell Ash

EXAMPLE: Make a pictograph that shows the data for the five sleepiest animals.

1 Title your graph.	**2** Choose a symbol to use for time spent sleeping. Include a key to tell what the symbol stands for.	**3** Next to the name of each animal, draw the number of symbols needed to show the amount of time spent sleeping for that animal. Sometimes you may need to draw only part of a symbol.

Each bed stands for 2 hours, so half a bed stands for 1 hour. To show 19 hours, you need $9\frac{1}{2}$ beds.

Sleepiest Animals— Number of Hours of Sleep Each Day

Armadillo ⊢⊣⊢⊣⊢⊣⊢⊣⊢⊣⊢⊣⊢⊣⊢⊣⊢⊣⊢

Koala ⊢⊣⊢⊣⊢⊣⊢⊣⊢⊣⊢⊣⊢⊣⊢⊣⊢⊣⊢⊣⊢⊣

Lemur ⊢⊣⊢⊣⊢⊣⊢⊣⊢⊣⊢⊣⊢⊣

Opossum ⊢⊣⊢⊣⊢⊣⊢⊣⊢⊣⊢⊣⊢⊣⊢⊣⊢⊣⊢

Sloth ⊢⊣⊢⊣⊢⊣⊢⊣⊢⊣⊢⊣⊢⊣⊢⊣⊢⊣⊢⊣

Key ⊢⊣ = 2 hours of sleep

If you change the value of a symbol, remember to change the number of symbols for each item. For example, the bed could stand for 3 hours. Then you would need $6\frac{1}{3}$ beds to show 19 hours.

Line Plots

A **line plot** is a useful tool. It makes it easy to see how the data is grouped, or **clustered**.

EXAMPLE: A survey of 12 students shows how many videotapes they rented during the past month. Make a line plot of the data.

Number of Videos Rented Last Month	Number of Students
2	1
3	1
4	3
5	4
6	2
10	1

1 Draw a number line. It must include all the numbers in the first column of the table.

```
 ┌─┬─┬─┬─┬─┬─┬─┬─┬─┬─┬─┬─┐
 0 1 2 3 4 5 6 7 8 9 10 11 12
     ↑                ↑
 least number     greatest number
 of videos         of videos
```

2 Draw an X for each student answer in the table.

Since one student answered 2 and one student answered 3, make an X for each. Since three students answered 4, make three Xs above 4.

```
            X
            X
        X X X
 ┌─┬─┬─┬─┬─┬─┬─┬─┬─┬─┬─┬─┐
 0 1 2 3 4 5 6 7 8 9 10 11 12
```

3 When all the Xs are recorded, title the line plot.

Number of Videos Rented Last Month
```
            X
        X X
        X X X
      X X X X X         X
 ┌─┬─┬─┬─┬─┬─┬─┬─┬─┬─┬─┬─┐
 0 1 2 3 4 5 6 7 8 9 10 11 12
```

Bar Graphs

A **bar graph** can show how data compare.

Case 1 Some bar graphs have vertical bars. The *height* of each bar represents a number.

EXAMPLE 1: The graph shows the most popular countries to visit for vacation. Each bar represents the number of tourists that visit that country.

Source: World Tourism Organization

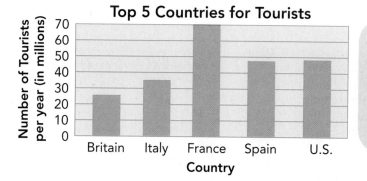

Top 5 Countries for Tourists

You can see that the United States is a more popular country to visit than Italy, but it is not as popular as France.

Case 2 Some bar graphs have horizontal bars. The length of each bar represents a number.

EXAMPLE 2: What's your favorite thing to do when you are not in school? This bar graph shows how children from around the world, ages 7 through 12, answered. *Source: A.B.C. Global Kids Study 1996, Just Kid Inc.*

Children's Most Popular Pastime

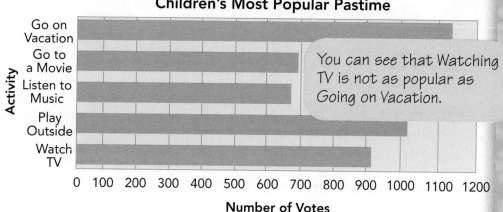

You can see that Watching TV is not as popular as Going on Vacation.

Making a Bar Graph

When you want to show data for others to compare and read quickly, make a **bar graph**.

MORE HELP
See 303

EXAMPLE: Make a bar graph that shows the data in the Veggies table.

America's Favorite Veggies	
Vegetable	Pounds Eaten per Person per Year
Lettuce	25
Onions	16
Potatoes	49

Source: U.S. Dept. of Agriculture and The Produce Marketing Association

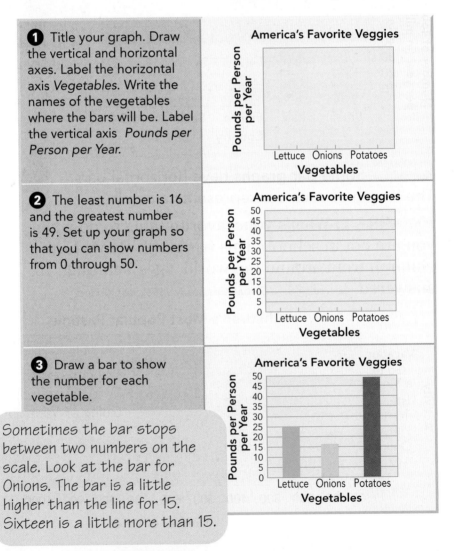

1 Title your graph. Draw the vertical and horizontal axes. Label the horizontal axis *Vegetables*. Write the names of the vegetables where the bars will be. Label the vertical axis *Pounds per Person per Year.*

2 The least number is 16 and the greatest number is 49. Set up your graph so that you can show numbers from 0 through 50.

3 Draw a bar to show the number for each vegetable.

Sometimes the bar stops between two numbers on the scale. Look at the bar for Onions. The bar is a little higher than the line for 15. Sixteen is a little more than 15.

How Graphs Can Fool You

The scale used on a bar graph can give you the wrong idea about the data.

These two graphs show the number of animal species found at some popular zoos in the United States.

Source: World Almanac and Book of Facts 2005

> *Species means kind of animal.*

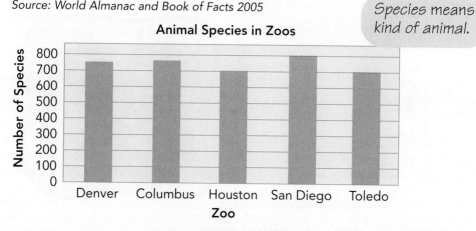

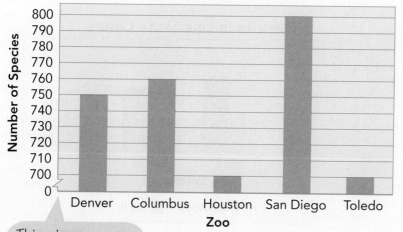

> This zigzag symbol means that the numbers between 0 and 700 are not shown.

The bar for the Columbus Zoo is about 7 times as long as the bar for the Houston Zoo. But the Columbus Zoo doesn't have 7 times as many species.

Double-Bar Graphs

Sometimes you will have two groups of data to compare. You can use a **double-bar graph**.

MORE HELP See 273 **EXAMPLE 1:** Ace Sporting Goods took a survey. They asked 75 boys and 75 girls what color they liked best for in-line skates. Use a double-bar graph to show this data.

Favorite In-Line Skate Colors		
Color	Boys	Girls
Black	25	15
Lime	12	24
Purple	20	20
Other	18	16

ONE WAY You can use vertical bars.

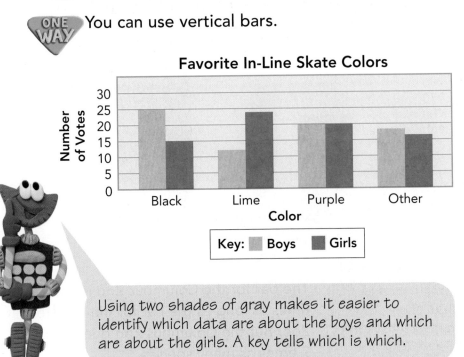

Favorite In-Line Skate Colors

Using two shades of gray makes it easier to identify which data are about the boys and which are about the girls. A key tells which is which.

ANOTHER WAY You can use horizontal bars.

Here's how the same data would look with horizontal bars.

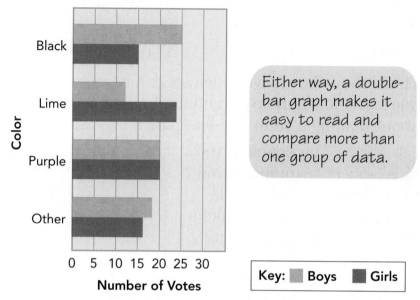

Favorite In-Line Skate Colors

Either way, a double-bar graph makes it easy to read and compare more than one group of data.

Key: Boys ▮ Girls

EXAMPLE 2: Use the graph. What was the most popular skate color for boys? What was the most popular skate color for girls?

- Look at all the light bars for the boys. The longest light bar is next to the color black.

- Look at the dark bars for the girls. The longest dark bar is next to the color lime.

★ **ANSWER:** Black is the most popular color for the boys. Lime is the most popular color for the girls.

EXAMPLE 3: Which color was chosen by an equal number of boys and girls?

Look for a pair of bars that have the same length.

★ **ANSWER:** An equal number of boys and girls chose purple as their favorite color.

Stem-and-Leaf Plots

Stem-and-leaf plots can also show data. The numbers themselves make the display, so the plot shows each piece of data.

Think about how several leaves can be attached to one stem. It will help you understand how to go about making a stem-and-leaf plot.

EXAMPLE: The coach of the girls' soccer team measured the heights of the ten girls who are on the team. Make a stem-and-leaf plot showing the heights of all the members of the girls' soccer team.

Heights of Soccer Players	
Girl	Height (in inches)
Flora	51
Zoe	49
Aurelia	43
Lauren	39
Mia	49
Suki	45
Bethany	45
Karima	49
Alison	38
Mariah	48

❶ Write the data in order from least to greatest.	38 39 43 45 45 48 49 49 49 51
❷ Find the greatest and the least values.	38 is the least value. 51 is the greatest value.
❸ Choose the stems. Use the three different digits in the tens place as the stems.	3, 4, and 5 will be the stems.
❹ Write the stems in a vertical list. Go from least to greatest. Draw a vertical line.	3 4 5 *This row shows 38 and 39.*
❺ Show each piece of data by writing its ones digit next to its tens digit. (The ones digits are the leaves.)	3|8 9 4|3 5 5 8 9 9 9 5|1
❻ Write a key that explains how to read the stems and leaves.	3|8 9 4|3 5 5 8 9 9 9 5|1 Key: 3|8 means a height of 38 inches.
❼ Title your plot.	**Heights of Soccer Players** 3|8 9 4|3 5 5 8 9 9 9 5|1 Key: 3|8 means a height of 38 inches.

Line Graphs

A **line graph** is a good way to show how data change over time. Line graphs usually show minutes, hours, days, months, or years on the horizontal, or bottom, axis.

EXAMPLE 1: Susan drives from Boston to Albany to visit her friends. Use the data in this table to make a line graph.

Trip from Boston to Albany	
Time	Total Miles Traveled
9:00 A.M.	0
10:00 A.M.	42
11:00 A.M.	60
12:00 noon	118
1:00 P.M.	142
2:00 P.M.	172

1 Title your graph. Draw and label both axes.

2 List each of the times along the horizontal axis.

3 The least number of miles is 0 and the greatest is 172. Set up the vertical scale so that you can show numbers from 0 to 200.

4 Mark points to show each amount. Connect the points.

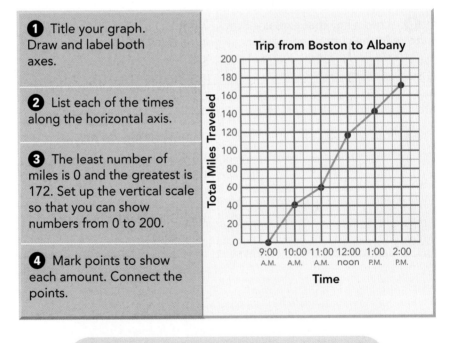

Sometimes you need to estimate where to place a point. 172 is a little more than halfway between 160 and 180 on the scale. Just like bar graphs, you can't always read the data *exactly* from a line graph.

EXAMPLE 2: During which hour did Susan travel the most miles?

Look for the line segment with the steepest upward rise.

> The line segment between 11:00 and 12:00 has the steepest rise.

Trip from Boston to Albany

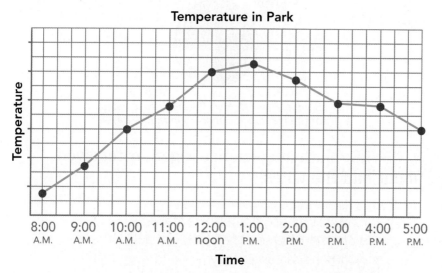

⭐ **ANSWER:** Susan traveled the most miles during the hour from 11:00 A.M. to 12:00 noon.

A line graph can show how something changes even if the graph has no numbers.

This line graph shows how the temperature in a park changed during the day. It is missing the temperatures on the vertical scale.

Temperature in Park

You can't tell what the temperature was at any time, but you can see how it changed. The temperature rose until 1 P.M. and then fell until at least 5 P.M.

Circle Graphs

A **circle graph** is helpful in showing how parts make up a whole.

They wouldn't let me vote for recess.

FAVORITE SUBJECT

EXAMPLE: The circle graph shows the results of a survey taken across the United States. Students were asked to name their favorite school subject. Which two subjects together received about half the votes?

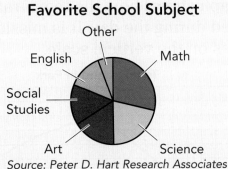

Favorite School Subject

Other

English

Social Studies

Math

Art

Science

Source: Peter D. Hart Research Associates for the National Science Foundation, Bayer

⭐ **ANSWER:** Math and science together received about half the votes.

Circle graphs are sometimes called pie charts because they look like a pie that has been cut up.

Making a Circle Graph

Sometimes you want to make a circle graph to show the size of each part of a whole.

EXAMPLE: A bag of 12 star erasers has 5 red, 4 purple, 2 yellow, and 1 green. Make a circle graph to show this data.

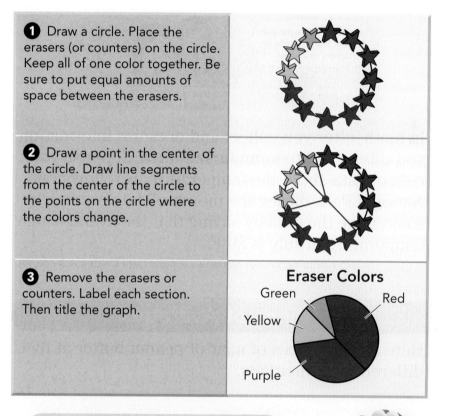

1 Draw a circle. Place the erasers (or counters) on the circle. Keep all of one color together. Be sure to put equal amounts of space between the erasers.

2 Draw a point in the center of the circle. Draw line segments from the center of the circle to the points on the circle where the colors change.

3 Remove the erasers or counters. Label each section. Then title the graph.

Eraser Colors

Green
Red
Yellow
Purple

By just looking at the circle graph, you can see that a little less than half of the erasers are red.

Summarizing Data

In math, after you collect and organize information, you often need to **summarize data**. Suppose you collect data about the temperature in Yellowstone National Park during the month of July. You might summarize the data by saying that the average high temperature in July is 80°F.

Source: NOAA National Climatic Data Center, Ashville, NC

Kinds of Averages

Here are the prices of a jar of peanut butter at five different supermarkets.

Suppose someone asked, "What is the price of a jar of peanut butter? You might say: "The **average** price is $3.29 because that price occurs most often." You would be using the **mode**, one kind of average. Other kinds of averages are the **mean** and the **median**. Each is useful in different ways.

Mean

The **mean** is the kind of average that is most often used. If the numbers for a group of data could be *evened out* so that all of the numbers are the same, that evened-out number would be the mean.

EXAMPLE: The table shows the number of hours Alan practiced the piano during the week. What was the mean number of hours Alan practiced each day?

The mean is very useful when there aren't one or two numbers far away from the rest of the data.

Day	Hours Practicing the Piano
Monday	3
Tuesday	1
Wednesday	4
Thursday	2
Friday	5

ONE WAY You can use counters to even out the numbers.

MORE HELP See 78

❶ Use counters to show each number in a separate stack.	❷ Move the counters until each stack has the same number of counters.
3 1 4 2 5	3 3 3 3 3

ANOTHER WAY You can add and then divide.

❶ Find the sum of all the numbers.	❷ Divide the sum by the number of addends.
3 + 1 + 4 + 2 + 5 = 15	15 ÷ 5 = 3

This is the same as "evening out the stacks."

★ **ANSWER:** Either way, Alan practiced a mean of 3 hours per day.

Median

If you put a group of data in order from least to greatest, the **median** is the number in the middle.

If your group of data doesn't have big gaps in the middle, then the median may be the best kind of average to use.

> **Median** is also the name of the strip that runs down the middle of a highway.

Case 1 When there is an odd number of pieces of data, the median is the middle number.

MORE HELP
See 14

EXAMPLE 1: When this survey was taken, there were 634 roller coasters in the United States. The table shows the number of roller coasters in five states. What was the median number of roller coasters for these states?

States with the Most Roller Coasters	
State	Number of Roller Coasters
California	73
New York	39
Pennsylvania	49
Ohio	48
Texas	43

Source: www.aceonline.org

❶ Order the numbers from least to greatest.	❷ Find the middle number.
39, 43, 48, 49, 73	39, 43, 48, 49, 73

★ **ANSWER:** The median number of roller coasters for these five states was 48.

Case 2 When there is an even number of pieces of data, there are two middle numbers. Find the mean of these two numbers.

EXAMPLE 2: Taylor Elementary School held a school carnival that lasted six days. What was the median daily attendance at the school carnival?

Taylor School Carnival	
Day	Attendance
1	375
2	400
3	300
4	350
5	275
6	75

1 Order the numbers from least to greatest. Then find the two middle numbers.	**2** Find the mean of the two middle numbers.	MORE HELP See 285
75, 275, 300, 350, 375, 400	300 + 350 = 650 650 ÷ 2 = 325	

⭐ **ANSWER:** The median daily attendance was 325 people.

Rain on Day 6 of the school carnival made the attendance much lower than on the other days. If you used the mean to describe the "average" attendance, Day 6 would make the average much lower. That one low number affects the mean, but not the median.

Mode

Sometimes the best way to describe what is typical about a group of data is to use the value that occurs most often. This value is called the **mode**.

Case 1 Sometimes there is one value that occurs most often.

MORE HELP
See 267

EXAMPLE 1: The table below shows the results of a survey taken by Ms. Engel's class. Students with pets at home were asked how many pets they have. What is the mode of the data?

Student	Number of Pets
Sarah	2
Kazuo	1
Jacob	1
Bian	3
Diego	6
Paul	1
Maria	4

The value 1 occurs most often in this group of data.

⭐ **ANSWER:** The mode is 1.

DID YOU KNOW...

that nearly 6 million households have pet birds? The typical bird owner has 2 or 3 birds. The most popular bird is the parakeet.

Source: American Pet Products Manufacturers Assoc., Inc.

Case 2 Sometimes there is more than one value that occurs most often.

EXAMPLE 2: The table below shows the shoe sizes of all the third-grade students at Eastbrook School. What is the mode of the shoe sizes?

Shoe Size	Number of Students
$3\frac{1}{2}$	13
4	11
$4\frac{1}{2}$	13
5	12
$5\frac{1}{2}$	9
6	9

No one value occurs most often. The sizes $3\frac{1}{2}$ and $4\frac{1}{2}$ each occur 13 times.

★ **ANSWER:** There are two modes, $3\frac{1}{2}$ and $4\frac{1}{2}$.

Case 3 Sometimes there is no value that occurs more often than any other value. In this case, there is no mode.

EXAMPLE 3: The 5 third-grade classes in Andrew Jackson Elementary School have the following class sizes: 27, 29, 30, 31, and 33 students. What is the mode?

★ **ANSWER:** No number occurs more than once. There is no mode.

Statistics Can Fool You

You can't always believe what you see. That's especially true with statistics. They can be used to mislead you.

The mean is $200, but no new bicycle actually sells for that price or less. Including the $50 price for a beat-up wreck makes the mean price misleading.

Range

The **range** of a group of data is the difference between the greatest and least numbers in the group. If the range is a small number, the data are close together.

EXAMPLE: What is the range of the heights of the boys on the basketball team?

Find the difference between the greatest and the least numbers.

$68 - 63 = 5$

★ **ANSWER:** The range is 5 inches.

Heights of Boys on Basketball Team	
Height (in inches)	Number of Players
63	3
64	1
65	3
66	2
68	1

Probability

Do you ever listen to or watch weather reports? Many people do. They want to know how warm or cold it will be and whether it may rain or snow.

Are weather reports always correct? Well, most are. Weather **predictions** are made after studying statistics and determining the likelihood, or **probability**, of an event happening.

Probability can help you decide how often something is likely to happen. But it can't guarantee that something will definitely happen, unless the probability of that event is certain.

Today should be sunny and warm with no chance of showers.

Likelihood of an Event

An **event** is something that may or may not happen.

Some events are **certain** and you know that they *must happen*. For example, it is certain that the sun will rise in the morning.

Some events are **impossible** and you know that they *can never happen*. For example, it is impossible that a pig will fly like a bird.

When you talk about the likelihood of an event, you are talking about the **probability** that the event will occur.

Think of **impossible** as 0. Think of **certain** as 1. Other events fall in between. The more unlikely an event is, the closer its probability is to 0. The more likely an event is, the closer its probability is to 1.

Probability

Less often than not ← → More often than not

0	unlikely	$\frac{1}{2}$	likely	1
impossible		equally likely		certain

If an event has a probability of $\frac{1}{2}$, some people say that there is a 50-50 chance that the event will happen. For example, when you flip a penny there is a 50-50 chance that it will land heads up and a 50-50 chance that it will land tails up.

You know this bag has 4 marbles in it. How likely is it that without looking in the bag, you will reach in and pick a green marble?

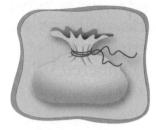

Without knowing the colors of the marbles in the bag, you would have to guess. However, if you know how many marbles in the bag are green, you can describe the likelihood of picking a green marble.

EXAMPLE: Describe the likelihood of picking a green marble from each bag without looking.

⭐ **ANSWER:**

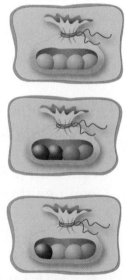

- Since all the marbles are green, any marble you choose will be green. You are *certain* to pick a green marble.

- Since no marbles are green, whichever marble you choose will not be green. It is *impossible* to pick a green marble.

- 2 of the 4 marbles, or $\frac{1}{2}$ of the marbles, are green. You have an *equally likely* chance of picking a green marble as not picking a green marble.

- It is *unlikely*, but not impossible, that you will pick a green marble from the bag that has only 1 green marble.

- It is *likely*, but not certain, that you will pick a green marble from the bag that has 3 green marbles.

Equally Likely Outcomes

The six faces of a number cube are usually numbered 1 through 6. Suppose you want to find out how likely it would be to roll a 3.

There are six things that can happen if you roll the number cube. In other words, there are 6 **possible outcomes**. All are *equally likely*. There is only 1 **favorable outcome,** rolling a 3.

> Favorable outcomes are the ones we want to find the probability for.

1 favorable outcome ⟶ rolling a 3

6 possible outcomes ⟶ rolling 1, 2, 3, 4, 5, or 6

Since all possible outcomes are equally likely, you can use this rule to write the probability.

1 ⟶ Use the number of favorable outcomes for the numerator.

---

6 ⟶ Use the number of possible outcomes for the denominator.

The probability of rolling a 3 is $\frac{1}{6}$.

> You can read the fraction as one sixth or one out of six.

EXAMPLE 1: What is the probability of flipping a penny and having it land heads up?

Heads Up   Tails Up

Think:

1 favorable outcome → heads up

2 possible outcomes → heads up, tails up

⭐ **ANSWER:** The probability of flipping a penny and getting heads is $\frac{1}{2}$.

EXAMPLE 2: What is the probability of picking a card with a circle?

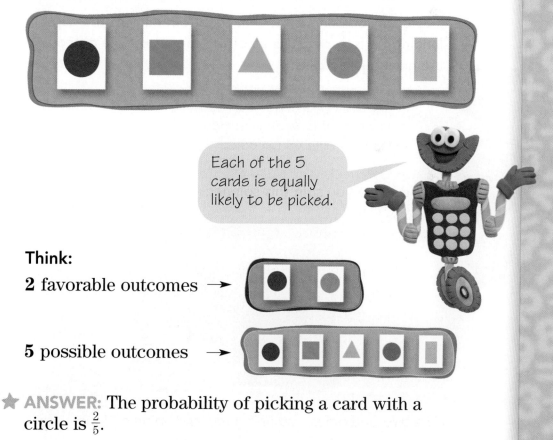

Each of the 5 cards is equally likely to be picked.

Think:

2 favorable outcomes →

5 possible outcomes →

⭐ **ANSWER:** The probability of picking a card with a circle is $\frac{2}{5}$.

Outcomes Are Not Always Equally Likely

Not all outcomes are equally likely. Suppose you toss a paper cup. It can land in three ways.

It can land up. It can land down. It can land on its side.

However, you *cannot* say that the probability of the cup landing up is $\frac{1}{3}$, because all of the three possible outcomes are not equally likely.

> Try tossing a paper cup. You'll probably find that it is most likely to land on its side.

Or, suppose you spin this spinner.

The two outcomes—spinning red and spinning blue—are not equally likely. The probablity of spinning blue is greater than the probability of spinning red.

Making Predictions

Suppose you flip a coin 20 times. How many times will it land heads up?

When you know the probability of an event, you can use this probability to make a **prediction**.

Since the probability of a coin landing heads up is $\frac{1}{2}$, you can predict that if you flip a coin 20 times, it will probably land heads up $\frac{1}{2}$ of 20, or 10 times.

There is no guarantee that this will actually happen, but it is a reasonable prediction.

EXAMPLE: How many times do you predict that you will spin a 2, if you spin this spinner 100 times?

The probability of spinning a 2 is $\frac{1}{4}$.

MORE
HELP
See 215

Think: $\frac{1}{4}$ of $100 = 100 \div 4$
$$= 25$$

⭐ **ANSWER:** If you spin the spinner 100 times, you will probably get a 2 about 25 times.

I predict that you will be going to school tomorrow.

Counting Possible Outcomes

Counting possible outcomes can be tricky. You may need to find an organized way to list them so you don't miss any or count one twice.

EXAMPLE: Suppose you are getting dressed in the morning and have the following shirts and shorts to choose from.

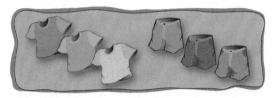

What are all the possible combinations of a shirt and a pair of shorts?

 You can draw pictures showing each combination of a shirt and a pair of shorts.

The first row is for combinations with orange shirts.

The second row is for green shirts.

The third row is for yellow shirts.

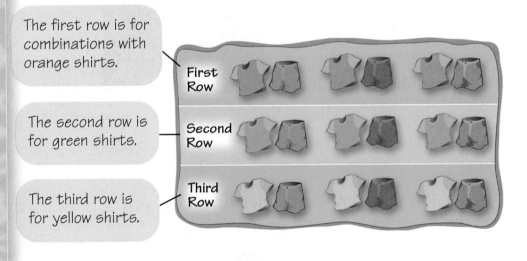

First Row

Second Row

Third Row

Organizing the picture makes it easier to keep track.

ANOTHER WAY You can use a tree diagram to list all possible combinations.

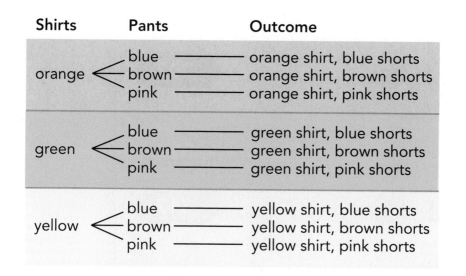

Shirts	Pants	Outcome
orange	blue	orange shirt, blue shorts
	brown	orange shirt, brown shorts
	pink	orange shirt, pink shorts
green	blue	green shirt, blue shorts
	brown	green shirt, brown shorts
	pink	green shirt, pink shorts
yellow	blue	yellow shirt, blue shorts
	brown	yellow shirt, brown shorts
	pink	yellow shirt, pink shorts

⭐ **ANSWER:** Either way, there are 9 possible shirt and shorts combinations you can wear.

You can multiply the number of shirt choices (3) by the number of choices of shorts (3) to find the total number of possible combinations. 3 × 3 = 9

There may be 9 different combinations, but I'm not sure I'd want to wear some of these!

Geometry

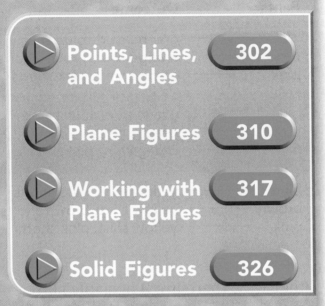

The shortest distance between two points is a straight line—unless of course, there's a dinosaur in the way.

The world can be perfect in your imagination and in geometry. Geometry has words for things we can only imagine.

Imagine a speck so small that it has no size. Imagine a ball so smooth that you can't find a scratch on it. Imagine something so long that it goes on forever.

Even though we can only imagine these things, they help us talk about the world we live in. With geometry, you can describe the path to a friend's house even though the path is not perfectly straight. You can describe the wheels on the bicycle you ride there even though the wheels wobble a little.

The world may not be perfect, but it sure can be fun. In this section you'll find just the right words to describe it. Imagine that!

Points, Lines, and Angles

If you look up in the sky on a clear night you'll see lots of stars. Each appears as a separate point of light. Some sailors still use the location of these points of light to help them navigate their ships.

You can form figures by connecting these points with imaginary line segments. This group of stars is called the Big Dipper.

Points

A **point** is an exact location in space. A point has no length or width. You cannot measure its size, but you can describe where it is. To identify a point, you can use a dot and name it with a capital letter.

Write: *P*

Say: *point P*

Lines

A **line** is a straight path of points that never ends. It goes on forever in two directions. You cannot measure the length of a line.

When you draw a picture of a line, you can name it by using any two points on the line. Another way to name a line is to use a single small letter.

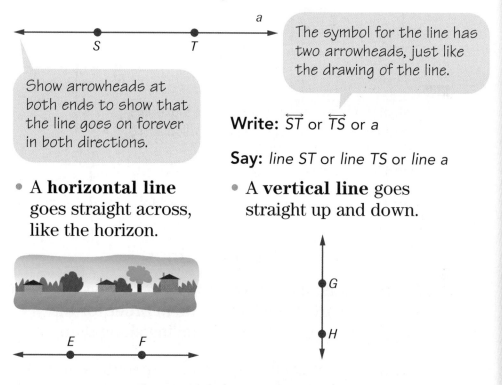

a

S   *T*

The symbol for the line has two arrowheads, just like the drawing of the line.

Show arrowheads at both ends to show that the line goes on forever in both directions.

Write: $\overleftrightarrow{ST}$ or $\overleftrightarrow{TS}$ or *a*

Say: *line ST* or *line TS* or *line a*

- A **horizontal line** goes straight across, like the horizon.

- A **vertical line** goes straight up and down.

G

H

E   *F*

Intersecting Lines

Intersecting lines are lines that cross. They cross at a point. For example, think about streets that meet and cross at intersections.

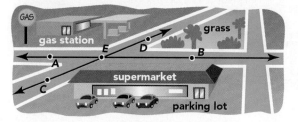

Write: $\overrightarrow{AB}$ intersects $\overrightarrow{CD}$ at *E*.

Say: *Line AB intersects line CD at point E.*

Perpendicular Lines

When two intersecting lines meet to form square corners, they are called **perpendicular lines**.

MORE
HELP
See 308

You can fold a piece of paper in half and in half again to make perpendicular lines.

A square corner is a right angle.

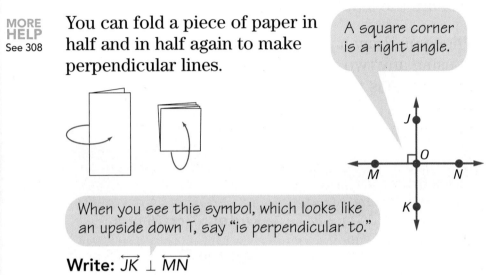

When you see this symbol, which looks like an upside down T, say "is perpendicular to."

Write: $\overleftrightarrow{JK} \perp \overleftrightarrow{MN}$

Say: *Line JK is perpendicular to line MN.*

Parallel Lines

The two rails of a railroad track are always the same distance apart. They have to be in order for the wheels of the train to keep moving along them.

If you think of each rail as a line, then the two rails represent a pair of **parallel lines**. Parallel lines are always the same distance apart. They will never cross, or intersect, one another.

When you see this symbol, say "is parallel to."

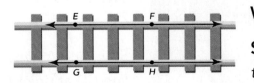

Write: $\overleftrightarrow{EF} \parallel \overleftrightarrow{GH}$

Say: *Line EF is parallel to line GH.*

Line Segments

Think of a line as a rope that never ends. You can cut the rope into pieces. Each piece is a segment of the rope.

MORE HELP See 302

A **line segment** is a part of a line. It has two **endpoints**. You can measure the length of a line segment.

You can name a line segment by using its two endpoints.

C   D

Write: $\overline{CD}$ or $\overline{DC}$

> When you see this symbol over the letters that name the endpoints, say "line segment."

Say: *line segment CD* or *line segment DC*

Rays

A **ray** is part of a line. It has one endpoint and goes on forever in one direction. Think of a ray of light coming from a flashlight.

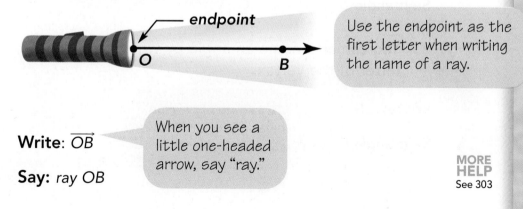

endpoint

O   B

> Use the endpoint as the first letter when writing the name of a ray.

Write: $\overrightarrow{OB}$

> When you see a little one-headed arrow, say "ray."

Say: *ray OB*

MORE HELP See 303

Angles

An **angle** is formed when two rays meet at an endpoint. The endpoint is called the **vertex** of the angle. Look at this ski jumper. His body and his skis form an angle.

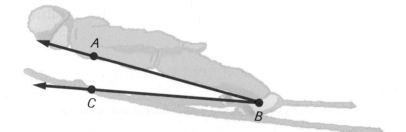

You can name this angle in two ways.

 ONE WAY You can name an angle by writing the point on one ray, the vertex, and the point on the other ray.

> When you see a sharp corner symbol say "angle."

> The vertex is always written in the middle.

Write: ∠ABC or ∠CBA

Say: *angle ABC or angle CBA*

ANOTHER WAY You can also name an angle by writing just the letter of the vertex.

Write: ∠B

Say: *angle B*

> You can do this when there is only one angle with the vertex B.

Measuring Angles

The measure of an angle tells how far one side is turned from the other side—0° is no turn and 360° is one full turn. Look at how this stamp makes one full turn.

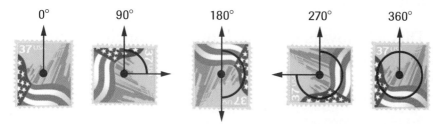

When the stamp turns $\frac{1}{4}$ of the way, it turns 90°.
$\frac{1}{4}$ of 360° = 90°

When it turns $\frac{1}{2}$ of the way, it turns 180°.
$\frac{1}{2}$ of 360° = 180°

When it turns $\frac{3}{4}$ of the way, it turns 270°.
$\frac{3}{4}$ of 360° = 270°

When it turns all the way around so that it is back to the start position, it turns 360°.

MATH ALERT

Sides of an Angle Don't Have Length

The sides of an angle are rays. The length of the sides in a drawing does not affect the measure of the angle.

is not greater than

Each of these angles measures 90°.

Kinds of Angles

You can name angles by how their measures compare to 90° or 180°.

An **acute angle** is an angle that measures less than 90°.

This window is opened at an acute angle to the building.

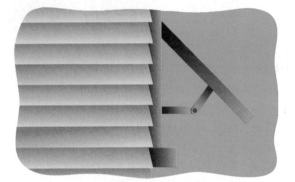

acute angle

A **right angle** is an angle that measures exactly 90°.

The back of the chair makes a right angle with the seat of the chair.

right angle

An **obtuse angle** is an angle with a measure greater than 90° and less than 180°. A **straight angle** measures exactly 180°.

The back of this chair can be moved to change the angle to an obtuse angle or to a straight angle.

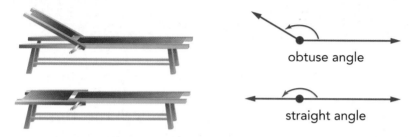

obtuse angle

straight angle

You can use the corner of an index card to identify the kind of angle. Line up the corner so that it touches the vertex of the angle and one side of the angle.

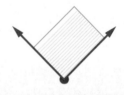

It's an acute angle if you can't see all of the other side.

It's a right angle if the other side goes along the edge of the index card.

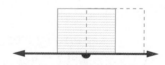

It's an obtuse angle if the other side opens past the edge of the index card.

It's a straight angle if you can move the card so that one edge of the card can touch both sides of the angle.

Plane Figures

Have you ever watched a cartoon in which a character gets run over by a steamroller? The character becomes an example of a **plane figure**. A plane figure lies flat on a plane, or flat surface.

Open and Closed Figures

Plane figures are either open or closed. If you place your pencil outside a closed figure, you cannot move it inside without touching part of the figure or lifting your pencil. Think of being outside a closed room. You cannot enter the room without opening the door.

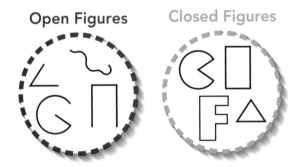

Open Figures   Closed Figures

Polygons

A **polygon** is a closed figure whose sides are all line segments.

MORE
HELP
See 305

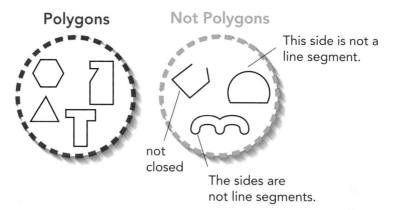

Polygons   Not Polygons

This side is not a line segment.

not closed

The sides are not line segments.

Naming Polygons
by the Number of Sides

You will come across different types of polygons as you walk down a street. Just look at traffic signs. All these signs are polygons, but they don't all have the same number of sides.

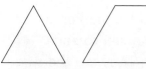

The name of a polygon depends on the number of sides it has.

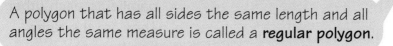

| triangle | quadrilateral | pentagon | hexagon | octagon |
| 3 sides | 4 sides | 5 sides | 6 sides | 8 sides |

A polygon that has all sides the same length and all angles the same measure is called a **regular polygon**.

Naming Quadrilaterals

All of these polygons are **quadrilaterals**. A quadrilateral has 4 sides.

Some quadrilaterals have more than one name. Look at the quadrilaterals again.

MORE
HELP
See 304

This quadrilateral is also called a **trapezoid**.

These quadrilaterals are also called **parallelograms**.

- A **trapezoid** has exactly one pair of parallel sides.

The sides marked in red are parallel.

- A **parallelogram** has two pairs of sides that are the same length and are parallel.

The sides marked in red are parallel to each other. They are the same length. The sides marked in blue are parallel to each other. They are the same length.

Look again at just the parallelograms.

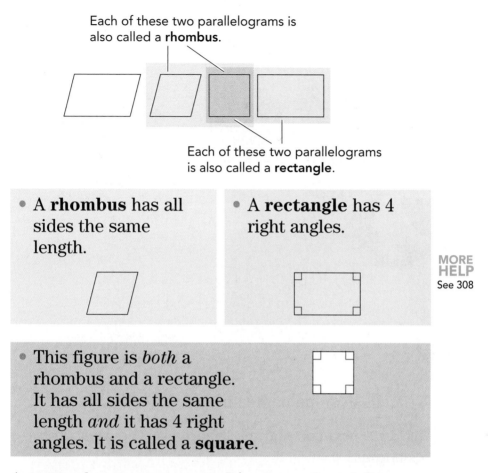

Each of these two parallelograms is also called a **rhombus**.

Each of these two parallelograms is also called a **rectangle**.

- A **rhombus** has all sides the same length.

- A **rectangle** has 4 right angles.

MORE
HELP
See 308

- This figure is *both* a rhombus and a rectangle. It has all sides the same length *and* it has 4 right angles. It is called a **square**.

A square has many names. It's also a closed figure, a polygon, a quadrilateral, a parallelogram, a rectangle, and a rhombus.

And I thought my friend Michael Samuel Carson Jones had a lot of names!

Naming Triangles

A triangle is a polygon with 3 sides. You see triangles all over.

Triangles hold their shape very well. That's why they are used a lot in bridges and buildings.

Triangles can be named in two different ways.

Case 1 You can name a triangle by the measure of its angles.

MORE HELP
See 306, 307

You can use rubber bands and geoboards to make triangles with angles of different measures.

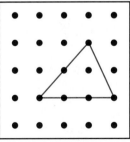 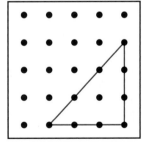 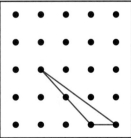

Acute triangle
All angles measure less than 90°.

Right triangle
One angle measures exactly 90°.

Obtuse triangle
One angle measures more than 90°.

If you cut out and then paste together the angles of a triangle, you will form a straight line, or a **straight angle**.

 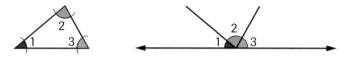

This shows you that if you add the measures of the three angles of a triangle, you will always get 180°.

Case 2 You can name a triangle based on the lengths of its sides.

Equilateral triangle
All sides are the same length.

Isosceles triangle
Two sides are the same length.

Scalene triangle
Each side is a different length.

An equilateral triangle is also **equiangular**. All angles have the same measure.

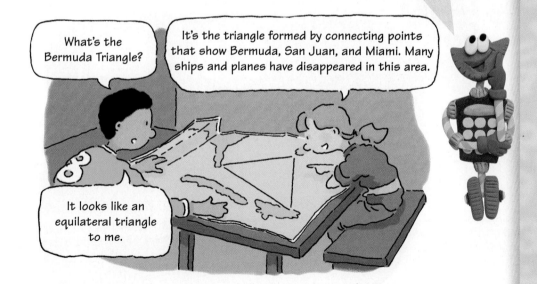

What's the Bermuda Triangle?

It's the triangle formed by connecting points that show Bermuda, San Juan, and Miami. Many ships and planes have disappeared in this area.

It looks like an equilateral triangle to me.

Circles

A **circle** is a set of points that are all the same distance from the point at its **center**.

- A **radius** is a line segment from the center of a circle to any point on the circle.

- A **diameter** is a line segment that passes through the center of the circle and has endpoints on the circle.

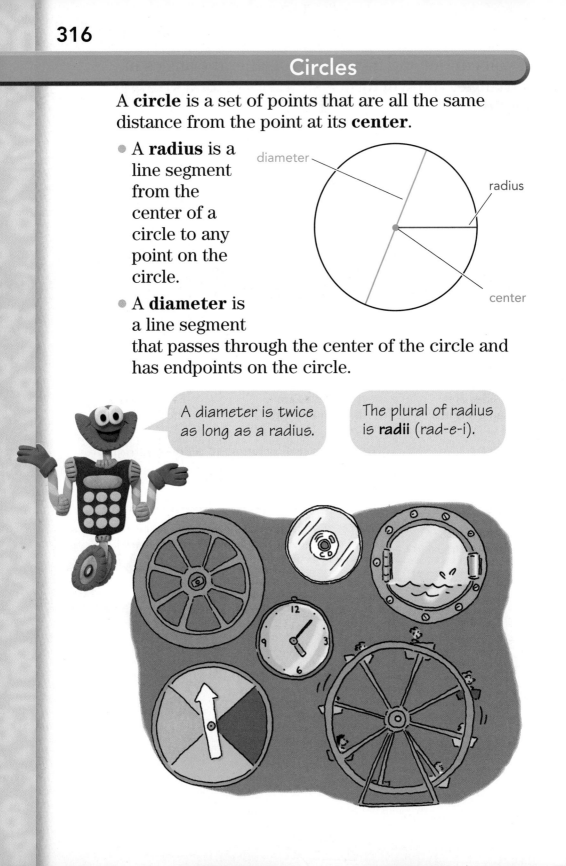

A diameter is twice as long as a radius.

The plural of radius is **radii** (rad-e-i).

Working with Plane Figures

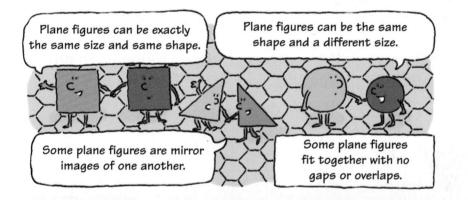

Plane figures can be exactly the same size and same shape.

Plane figures can be the same shape and a different size.

Some plane figures are mirror images of one another.

Some plane figures fit together with no gaps or overlaps.

Congruent Figures

Figures that have the same shape and size are **congruent**. When two figures are congruent, you can place one on top of the other and they will match exactly.

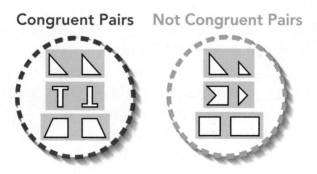

Congruent Pairs   Not Congruent Pairs

Slides, Flips, and Turns

In geometry, there are three different ways to move a figure from one place to another without changing its shape or size.

Case 1 You can slide a figure.

Think of sliding on ice. Imagine gliding smoothly from one spot to another without turning.

When you **slide** a figure, it doesn't change in any way except that it is now in a different place.

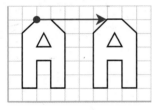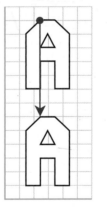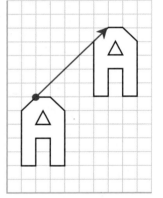

Another name for a **slide** is a **translation**.

Case 2 You can flip a figure across a line.

Think of standing with a line drawn in front of you. Then you flip yourself around the line so that you are now standing on the other side facing in the opposite direction. It's as though you were looking at yourself in a mirror.

When you **flip** a figure across a line, the new figure looks like a reflection of the original figure. Another name for a **flip** is a **reflection**.

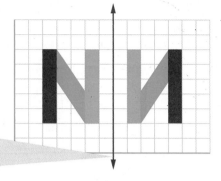

The line is called a **line of reflection**. The two figures are mirror images of one another.

Case 3 You can turn a figure.

Think of turning a door knob. Look at where your fingers grip the knob before you start turning. Then notice where your fingers are after you have turned the knob.

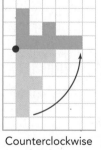

When you **turn** a figure, it spins around a point. It looks different, but it is still congruent to the original figure.

Clockwise   Counterclockwise

A figure can turn **clockwise**. That's the direction clock hands move. A figure can also turn **counterclockwise**, or the opposite of clock hands.

Another name for a **turn** is a **rotation**.

Slides, flips, and turns are also called **transformations**.

Similar Figures

In geometry, **similar figures** have the same shape. Sometimes they are the same size. Sometimes they are different sizes.

MORE
HELP
See 317

All circles are similar. They all have the same shape.

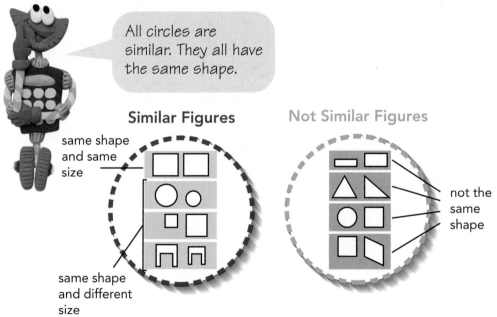

Similar Figures

same shape and same size

same shape and different size

Not Similar Figures

not the same shape

Making Similar Figures

Animators draw the characters and scenes for cartoons and animated movies. They need to know how to make similar figures.

You can use grid paper to make similar figures.

To enlarge the cartoon, you can draw the figures on grid paper with larger squares. Copy one square at a time.

To reduce the cartoon, you can draw it on grid paper with smaller squares. Copy one square at a time.

The mouse is still the same shape. Only the size changed.

DID YOU KNOW...

that it takes 24 pictures, or cells, to make one second of animated film?

Source: www.pixar.com

Symmetry

Some figures can be folded, or turned, in such a way that the parts of the figures match. We say they have **symmetry**.

Line Symmetry

If you can fold a figure so that it has two parts that match exactly, the figure has **line symmetry**. The line where you fold is called a **line of symmetry**.

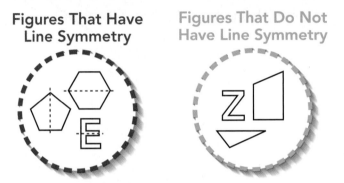

Figures That Have Line Symmetry

Figures That Do Not Have Line Symmetry

A figure may have more than one line of symmetry.

EXAMPLE: How many lines of symmetry does a square have?

- Fold a square vertically. The parts match.

- Fold it horizontally. The parts match.

- Fold it along either diagonal. The parts match.

A **diagonal** is a line segment that joins two vertices that are not next to each other.

★ ANSWER: A square has 4 lines of symmetry.

Making a Figure that Has Line Symmetry

You can make a figure with line symmetry by folding and cutting a piece of paper.

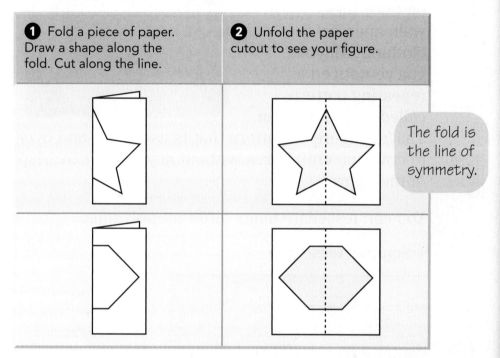

| **1** Fold a piece of paper. Draw a shape along the fold. Cut along the line. | **2** Unfold the paper cutout to see your figure. |

The fold is the line of symmetry.

Turn Symmetry

If you can turn a figure less than a complete turn and it doesn't look like it was turned, then this figure has **turn symmetry**.

This faucet handle has turn symmetry. If you turn it $\frac{1}{4}$ of the way, it looks the same.

This faucet handle does not have turn symmetry.

Did you ever look carefully at designs on floor tiles, wallpaper, or clothing? Maybe you've noticed a repeating pattern called a **tessellation**.

MORE
HELP
See 311,
313
That's a figure or pattern that is used over and over to cover an entire area without any gaps or overlaps of the figure.

You can tessellate many different polygons.

- Squares tessellate.

The squares fit together. There are no gaps and no overlaps.

- Equilateral triangles tessellate.

MORE
HELP
See 315

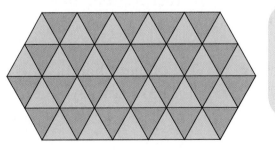

The equilateral triangles fit together. There are no gaps and no overlaps.

You cannot tessellate every polygon.

For example, regular pentagons do not tessellate.

MORE
HELP
See 311

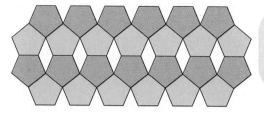

The regular pentagons do not fit together. There are gaps.

You can tessellate more than one shape.

You can make your own tessellation shapes.

❶ Cut out a square.	❷ Cut a part out of one side of the square.	❸ Slide the part to the opposite side and tape the pieces together.

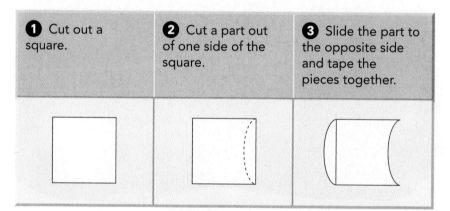

You can now trace around this new shape over and over to make a tessellation.

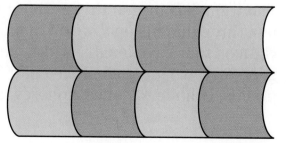

Solid Figures

Have you ever seen a 3-D movie? To watch the movie you need special glasses that make things seem to pop out of the flat movie screen.

The term **3-D** means **three-dimensional**. You live in a three-dimensional world. It's filled with **solid figures** that have length, width, and height. In geometry, we look at simple solid figures like prisms, cylinders, cones, spheres, and pyramids.

You can sort solid figures by how they look and how they act. For example, some solid figures roll and some don't.

Figures That Roll   Figures That Do Not Roll

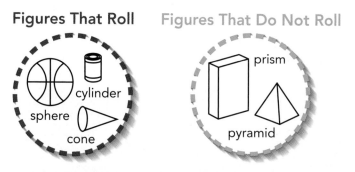

Parts of Solid Figures

A **face** of a solid figure is a flat surface. An **edge** is a line segment where two faces meet. A **vertex** is a point where two edges meet, or the tip of a cone.

MORE
HELP
See 302,
305, 310

This figure has 6 faces, 12 edges, and 8 vertices.

an edge

a face

a vertex

The plural of vertex is **vertices** (ver-tuh-sees).

Some faces are called **bases**. Prisms have two bases.

a base

a base

A cylinder has 2 circular faces which are bases. The bases are connected by a curved surface.

a base

a base

curved surface

A pyramid has 1 base and a face for each side of the base.

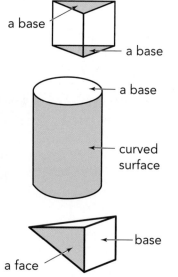

base

a face

Names for Solid Figures

If you look around you can spot different types of solid figures that are named according to the number and shape of their faces.

prisms

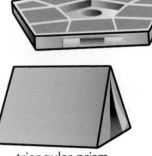
pentagonal prism

rectangular prism

cube

triangular prism

cylinders

Check the glossary to see how each solid figure is defined.

cones

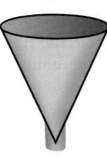

spheres

pyramids

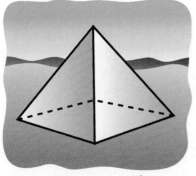

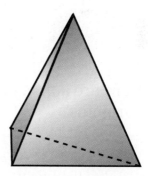

square pyramid

triangular pyramid

Nets of Solid Figures

If you could cut a prism or pyramid along some edges, you could unfold the figure into a flat shape. This is a pattern for the figure and it is called a **net**. Prisms or pyramids may have more than one net.

- Here are some, but not all, nets for some prisms.

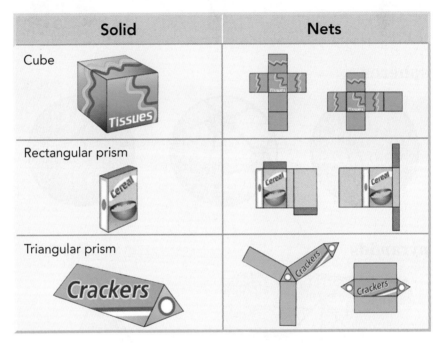

Solid	Nets
Cube	
Rectangular prism	
Triangular prism	

- Here are some, but not all, nets for some pyramids.

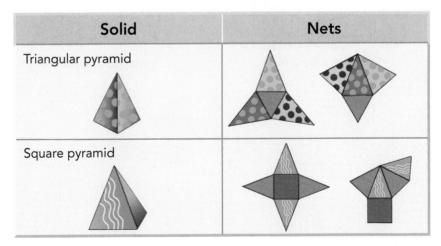

Solid	Nets
Triangular pyramid	
Square pyramid	

- You can also make nets for cylinders or cones.

You can cut around the circular bases and down the face to unroll a cylinder.

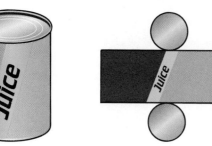

> If you peel the label from any cylinder-shaped can, you'll see that the face unrolls to become a rectangle.

Unfolding a cone to find its net is tricky. You can make a cut around the base and up to the vertex.

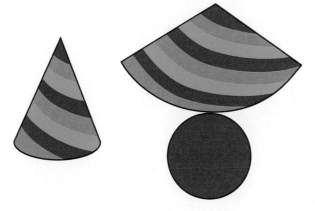

- To think about a possible net for a sphere, think about a baseball.

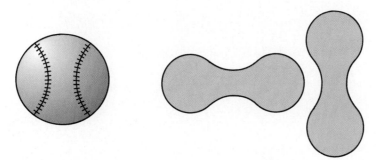

Measurement

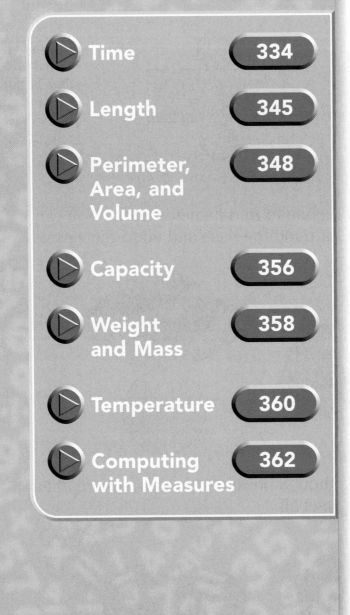

It would not be easy to walk if your shoes were the size of backpacks or if your pants were as long as a telephone pole. Your clothing fits a lot better than that because it's measured.

If you say, "I need a big uniform" or "I need a small uniform," you may not get the size you want. But if you say things like, "I need the sleeves to be 24 inches long," you can get just what you order.

Lots of other things besides clothing are measured. Your weight is measured. The amount of orange juice in a carton and the size of your playground are also measured. Without measurement, everything would be a lot more difficult, not just walking.

Time

You and your friends plan to have a picnic at the neighborhood park. You know where to meet. Now what you need to decide is when to meet. What day? What hour? To answer these questions, you need to know about **time**.

Clocks and Watches

There are many different kinds of watches and clocks. Here are just a few.

This is an **analog clock**. It has a minute hand and an hour hand. Sometimes it has a second hand.

This is a **digital** clock. The left side shows the hours from 1 through 12. The right side shows the minutes after the hour from 00 through 59.

All of these can be used to help you tell time—if they are set to the correct time.

Using Quarter Hours to Tell Time

Think of a clock face. As the minute hand goes around once, it marks 60 minutes, or 1 hour. Now think of a clock face divided into 4 equal sections, or fourths. As the minute hand goes one fourth of the way around the clock, it marks 15 minutes, or a **quarter hour**.

MORE HELP

See 214

1 hour = 60 minutes   1 quarter hour

1 quarter hour = 15 minutes
1 half hour = 30 minutes
3 quarters of an hour =
    45 minutes

1 half hour

> Each mark equals one minute.

> One half is the same as 2 quarters.

EXAMPLE: What time is shown on each clock?

1:15   7:30   10:45

> As the minute hand moves around the clock, the hour hand moves from one hour to the next.

> At **half past** 7, the hour hand is halfway between 7 and 8.

> At **quarter to** 11, the hour hand is closer to 11 than to 10.

⭐ **ANSWER:**

Say:

quarter after one,   half past seven, or   quarter to eleven,
or one fifteen   seven thirty   or ten forty-five

Telling Time to the Minute

MORE
HELP
See 90 It takes 60 seconds, or 1 minute, for the minute hand on a clock to move from one little mark to the next. Sometimes you have to tell time to the nearest minute, so those little marks are important.

EXAMPLE: What time does the clock show?

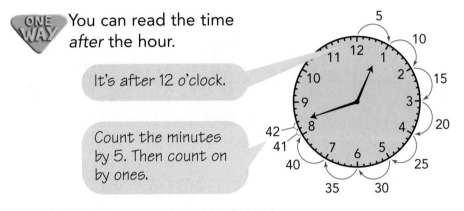

ONE WAY You can read the time *after* the hour.

> It's after 12 o'clock.

> Count the minutes by 5. Then count on by ones.

It's 42 minutes after 12 o'clock.

Write: *12:42*   **Say:** *twelve forty-two*

ANOTHER WAY You can read the time *to* the hour.

MORE
HELP
See 334 When the time is more than 30 minutes *after* an hour, people will sometimes read the time on an analog clock as the number of minutes *to* the next hour. That means the number of minutes *before* the next hour.

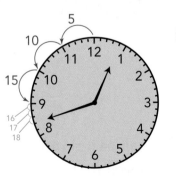

> Count the minutes by 5. Then count on by ones.

> It's before 1 o'clock.

It's 18 minutes to 1 o'clock.

Say: *eighteen minutes to one*

A.M. and P.M.

All times between midnight and noon are labeled **A.M.**

For example, some students go to school at 8:30 A.M.

All times between noon and midnight are labeled **P.M.**

For example, some students go to sleep at 8:30 P.M.

Noon (12:00) and midnight (12:00) are neither A.M. or P.M. But one minute after noon is 12:01 P.M. and one minute after midnight is 12:01 A.M.

Some people use a 24-hour clock. Instead of starting at 1:00 again after 12:00 noon, the clock continues to 1300, 1400, and so on.

5:00 A.M. is 0500   **Say:** *oh five hundred hours*

2:00 P.M. is 1400   **Say:** *fourteen hundred hours*

Seconds

It takes about 1 second to jump up in the air or to snap your fingers. A **second** is a very short period of time.

1 minute = 60 seconds

A second hand goes around the clock face once every minute.

Believe it or not, as short as a second is, you sometimes need to measure time to the nearest tenth or hundredth of a second.

MORE HELP
See 22–25

Elapsed Time

The time that went by between 8:00 A.M. and 9:00 A.M. is the time that passed, or the **elapsed time**. You can find elapsed time by counting on from the starting time to the finishing time.

Train number	6639	6641
Port City	3:23 P.M.	4:10 P.M.
Newton	3:39 P.M.	4:26 P.M.
Summit	4:02 P.M.	4:50 P.M.
Morristown	4:18 P.M.	5:07 P.M.
Dover	4:38 P.M.	5:27 P.M.

EXAMPLE 1: It is 1:23 P.M. How many hours is it until the 6639 train leaves the Port City station?

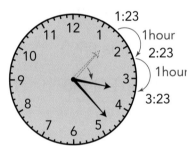

Count the hours from 1:23 to 3:23.

⭐ **ANSWER:** It is 2 hours until the 6639 train leaves.

EXAMPLE 2: How long does it take to travel from Port City to Summit on train 6641?

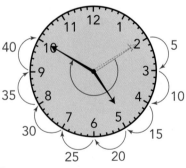

Count the minutes from 4:10 to 4:50.

⭐ **ANSWER:** It takes 40 minutes.

EXAMPLE 3: How long does it take to travel from Port City to Dover on train 6639?

Train leaves: 3:23 P.M.   Train arrives: 4:38 P.M.

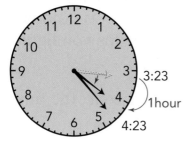

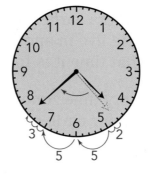

Count the hours.

From 3:23 P.M. to 4:23 P.M., 1 hour passes.

Then count the minutes.

From 4:23 P.M. to 4:38 P.M. 15 minutes pass.

★ ANSWER: It takes 1 hour and 15 minutes.

Sometimes you know the elapsed time and have to find the finishing or starting time.

EXAMPLE 4: You take the 4:10 train out of Port City and get off at your station 57 minutes later. Which station are you at?

Think: 57 minutes is 3 minutes less than 1 hour. 1 hour (60 minutes) after 4:10 is 5:10. Three minutes earlier is 5:07.

★ ANSWER: You are at the station in Morristown.

Time Zones

If you have lunch at 12 noon in Florida, your friends in California might have just finished breakfast. It is three hours earlier in California—9:00 A.M. Knowing if people live in another time zone helps you figure out what time it is for them.

For every time zone *west* of another zone, the time is one hour earlier.

west
1 hour earlier

For every time zone *east* of another zone, the time is one hour later.

east
1 hour later

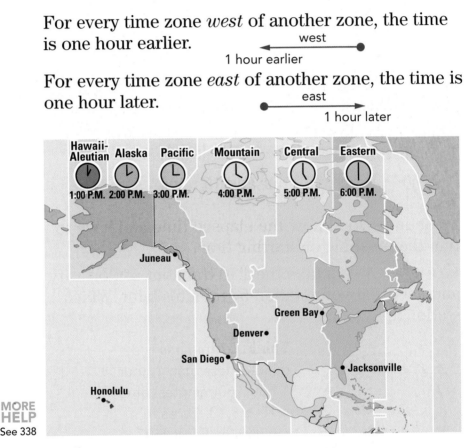

Hawaii-Aleutian	Alaska	Pacific	Mountain	Central	Eastern
1:00 P.M.	2:00 P.M.	3:00 P.M.	4:00 P.M.	5:00 P.M.	6:00 P.M.

Juneau

Green Bay

Denver

San Diego

Jacksonville

Honolulu

MORE HELP
See 338

When Super Bowl XXXIX was played in Jacksonville, Florida in 2005, the game began at 6:00 P.M. Eastern Standard Time (EST). People in Green Bay, Wisconsin saw the game begin at 5:00 P.M. Central Standard Time (CST).

Calendar

A **calendar** is used to keep track of days, weeks, and months of a **year**.

Each box with a number on a calendar page shows a date. A **date** is the month, day of the month, and sometimes the year.

Days and Weeks

There are 24 hours in one day and 7 days in one week. The days of the week in order are:

Sunday	Monday	Tuesday	Wednesday	Thursday	Friday	Saturday

When people make plans to do something together, they can choose a day and a date.

EXAMPLE: On July 5, Al and Yong-Soo made plans to go to the beach together on Saturday in two weeks. On what date are they planning to go to the beach?

ONE WAY You can look at a calendar and find the date.

Count two rows down from July 5.

July

S	M	T	W	T	F	S
		1	2	3	4	5
6	7	8	9	10	11	12
13	14	15	16	17	18	19
20	21	22	23	24	25	26
27	28	29	30	31		

ANOTHER WAY You can begin with 5 and add on the number of days in 2 weeks.

1 week = 7 days
2 weeks = 14 days

$$5 + 14 = 19$$

Start at 2 weeks is The date 2 weeks
July 5. 14 days. from the 5th.

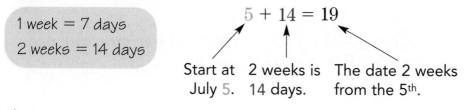

★ **ANSWER:** Either way, the date is July 19.

Months

A year is divided into 12 **months**. Here are the names of the months and their abbreviations.

January (Jan.)	May	September (Sept.)
February (Feb.)	June	October (Oct.)
March (Mar.)	July	November (Nov.)
April (Apr.)	August (Aug.)	December (Dec.)

Months are also identified by their position in the year. January is the first month, February is second, and so on.

EXAMPLE: Thanksgiving Day is on the fourth Thursday of November. What is the date of Thanksgiving in 2001?

November 2001						
S	M	T	W	T	F	S
				1	2	3
4	5	6	7	8	9	10
11	12	13	14	15	16	17
18	19	20	21	(22)	23	24
25	26	27	28	29	30	

⭐ **ANSWER:**

ONE WAY **Write:** *November 22, 2001*
Say: *November twenty-second, two thousand one*

ANOTHER WAY **Write:** *11/22/01*

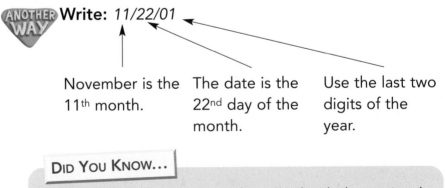

November is the 11th month.   The date is the 22nd day of the month.   Use the last two digits of the year.

DID YOU KNOW...

that in some countries, such as England, they write the day first, then the month, and the year? They would write 22/11/01.

Do you know how many days are in each month?
Some months are longer than others.

EXAMPLE: Which has more days, April or July?

 You can use this poem to help you remember the number of days in each month.

> Thirty days has September,
> April, June, and November;
> All the rest have thirty-one,
> Except for February alone,
> It has just twenty-eight we hear,
> And twenty-nine in each leap year.

ANOTHER WAY You can also use the knuckles on your hand.

Make two fists. The first knuckle is January, then the space between that and the next knuckle is February, the next knuckle is March, and so on. Every month that lands on a knuckle has 31 days, all the others have 30 days, except February.

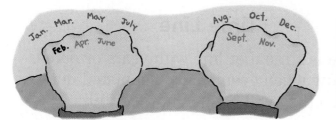

The months in red have 31 days. The months in blue have 30 days. February has 28 or 29 days.

ANOTHER WAY You can use a calendar.

April						
S	M	T	W	T	F	S
1	2	3	4	5	6	7
8	9	10	11	12	13	14
15	16	17	18	19	20	21
22	23	24	25	26	27	28
29	30					

April has 30 days.

July						
S	M	T	W	T	F	S
1	2	3	4	5	6	7
8	9	10	11	12	13	14
15	16	17	18	19	20	21
22	23	24	25	26	27	28
29	30	31				

July has 31 days.

⭐ **ANSWER:** July has more days than April.

Years

Did you ever notice that your birthday is not on the same day of the week each year? This is because a regular year is 365 days long, or 52 weeks + 1 day. That one extra day causes every date in the following year to move ahead one day.

MORE
HELP
See 454 If that's not enough to confuse you, a year is actually a little more than 365 days. To make up for lost time, every 4 years we have a **leap year**, which has 366 days.

In any leap year, we add the extra day at the end of February, which then has 29 days. The years 1992, 1996, 2000, and 2004 are leap years.

> Here are some names for times longer than a year.
> A **decade** is 10 years. A **century** is 100 years.
> A **score** is 20 years. A **millennium** is 1000 years.

Time Line

A **time line** is a number line with years or dates. You can show when events have happened in the past or when they will happen in the future.

This time line shows when some very familiar items were invented.

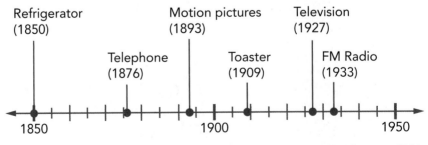

Source: Time For Kids Almanac, 2006

Length

How tall are you? How high does the roller coaster go? How far can you throw a softball? How deep is the swimming pool? How far do you live from the park? These questions can all be answered by measuring length and distance.

People did not always measure the way we measure today. Long ago, some people measured length with units such as the *cubit*, *palm*, and *span*.

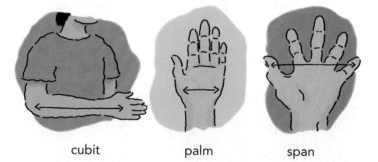

cubit   palm   span

The trouble with using units like these is that everyone is not the same size. That's why these units are called **nonstandard** units. What you might measure as 20 cubits long, someone else might measure as 25 cubits.

> **DID YOU KNOW...**
>
> The Mars Climate Orbiter crashed in 1999 because scientists used different units? One group of scientists used feet and the other group used meters. The $125 million satellite was lost because scientists did not communicate their system and units of measure.
>
> *Source: Philadelphia Inquirer Oct 15, 1999*

Customary Units of Length

One set of units for measuring is the **customary system**. Here are some customary units of **length**.

MORE HELP
See 220, 362, 420–421

Customary Units of Length	
inch (in.)	
foot (ft)	12 inches
yard (yd)	3 feet
mile (mi)	5280 feet

You can find your own benchmarks or use the following ones to help you understand the size of each unit.

The diameter of a quarter is about **1 inch**.

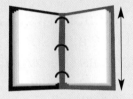

The length of the binder is about **1 foot**.

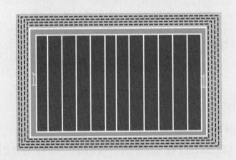

Four times around a football field is about **1 mile**.

The width of a doorway is about **1 yard**.

Metric Units of Length

One set of units for measuring is the **metric system**. This system uses numbers that are multiples of ten. Here are some metric units of length.

MORE HELP
See 90, 212, 362, 420

Metric Units of Length	
meter (m)	
millimeter (mm)	$\frac{1}{1000}$ of a meter
centimeter (cm)	$\frac{1}{100}$ of a meter
decimeter (dm)	$\frac{1}{10}$ of a meter
kilometer	1000 meters

Decimeter is used less often than the other units.

Each unit has the root word, *meter*. The prefix shows how big a unit is compared to a meter.

You can find your own benchmarks or use the following ones to help you understand the size of each unit.

The thickness of a dime is about **1 millimeter**.

The diameter of a crayon is about **1 centimeter**.

The length of a new crayon is about **1 decimeter**.

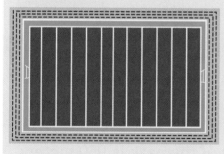

Three times around a football field is about **1 kilometer**.

The height from the floor to the doorknob is about **1 meter**.

Perimeter, Area, and Volume

Perimeter

The distance around a figure is called the **perimeter**. To find the perimeter of any figure, you can add the lengths of its sides.

> Did you know that two Greek words join together to form the word "perimeter"? *Peri* means *around* and *metron* means *measure*. An easy way to remember what perimeter means is to look for the word "rim" in perimeter.

Perimeter of Polygons

MORE HELP
See 347 **EXAMPLE:** What is the perimeter of the park?

To find the perimeter of the triangle, add the lengths of the three sides.

250 meters + 300 meters + 400 meters = 950 meters

⭐ **ANSWER:** The perimeter of the park is 950 meters.

> 950 meters! That's almost 1 kilometer.

Perimeter of Rectangles

EXAMPLE: Jasmin decides to sew red trim around the edge of a rectangular quilt she's making. How many feet of trim does she need to go around her quilt?

MORE HELP
See 311–312

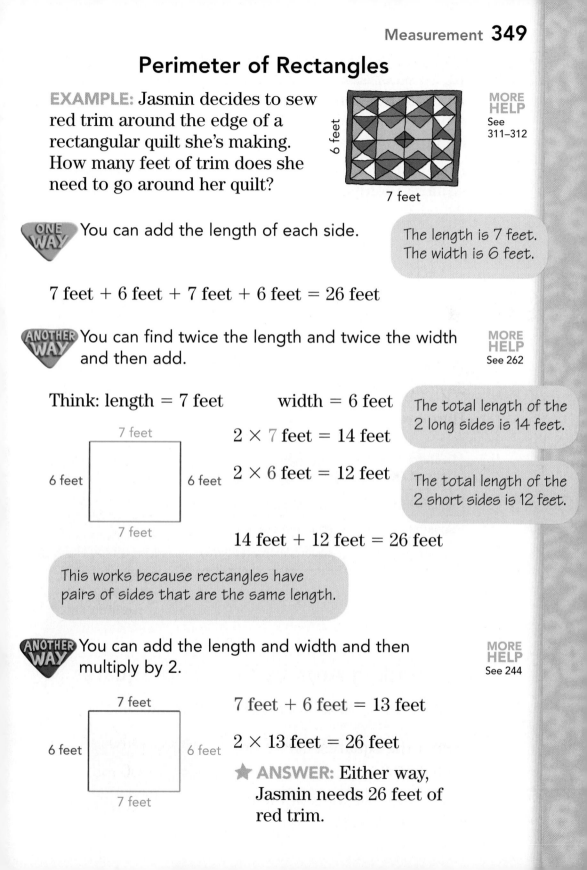

6 feet

7 feet

ONE WAY You can add the length of each side.

The length is 7 feet.
The width is 6 feet.

7 feet + 6 feet + 7 feet + 6 feet = 26 feet

ANOTHER WAY You can find twice the length and twice the width and then add.

MORE HELP
See 262

Think: length = 7 feet   width = 6 feet

7 feet

6 feet   6 feet

7 feet

2 × 7 feet = 14 feet

The total length of the 2 long sides is 14 feet.

2 × 6 feet = 12 feet

The total length of the 2 short sides is 12 feet.

14 feet + 12 feet = 26 feet

This works because rectangles have pairs of sides that are the same length.

ANOTHER WAY You can add the length and width and then multiply by 2.

MORE HELP
See 244

7 feet

6 feet   6 feet

7 feet

7 feet + 6 feet = 13 feet

2 × 13 feet = 26 feet

★ **ANSWER:** Either way, Jasmin needs 26 feet of red trim.

Area

Area is the number of square units needed to cover a figure. The units used to measure area are based on units of length, but they are very different.

Area can be measured in **square inches**.

Area can be measured in **square centimeters**.

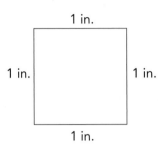

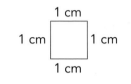

Write: *1 in.²*

Say: *one square inch*

Write: *1 cm²*

Say: *one square centimeter*

Here are some units for measuring area.

Customary Units of Area	Metric Units of Area
square inch (in.²)	square centimeter (cm²)
square foot (ft²)	square meter (m²)
square yard (yd²)	square kilometer (km²)

You can't use units of length for an area measurement, and you can't use units of area (square units) for a length measurement.

Finding Area by Counting Squares

EXAMPLE 1: What is the area of this patio?

Count the squares. There are 34 squares.

★ ANSWER: The area of the patio is 34 square feet.

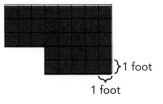

Sometimes the area of a figure is made up of half squares as well as whole squares.

EXAMPLE 2: What is the area of this rug?

} 1 meter

1 meter

1 Count the whole squares.	12 whole squares } 1 meter 1 meter
2 Count the half squares.	4 half squares = 2 squares
3 Add to find the area.	12 + 2 = 14 square meters

⭐ **ANSWER:** The area of the rug is 14 square meters.

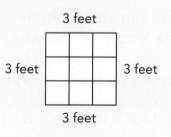

MATH ALERT

A 3-Foot Square Is Not 3 Square Feet

A square that is
3 feet on each side is
sometimes called a
3-foot square.
It has an area of 3 × 3,
or 9, square feet.

3 feet

3 feet   3 feet

3 feet

Area of Rectangles

You can find the area of a rectangle by counting squares or by multiplying.

EXAMPLE: Here is a standard-sized trampoline used in trampoline competitions.

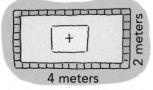

4 meters

2 meters

Source: Official World
Encyclopedia of Sports and Games

What is the area of the standard-sized trampoline?

ONE WAY You can find the area by counting the number of square units that cover the rectangle.

There are 8 squares.
Each is 1 square meter.

4 meters

2 meters   2 meters

4 meters

ANOTHER WAY You can also multiply the length by the width.

length = 4 meters   width = 2 meters

When you multiply meters by meters, you get square meters.

MORE HELP
See 263

4 meters × 2 meters = 8 square meters

⭐ **ANSWER:** Either way, the area of a standard-sized trampoline is 8 square meters.

MATH
ALERT

Rectangles with the Same Perimeter Can Have Different Areas

Suppose you have 16 feet of fencing and want to use it around a rectangular garden.

You can make the following rectangles. Each has a perimeter of 16 feet.

MORE
HELP
See
348–349,
352

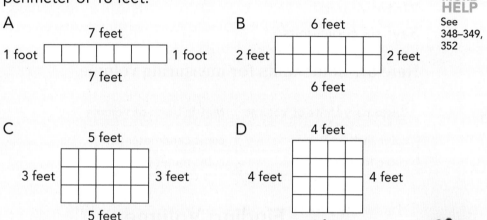

A
7 feet
1 foot ☐☐☐☐☐☐☐ 1 foot
7 feet

B
6 feet
2 feet ⊞⊞⊞⊞ 2 feet
6 feet

C
5 feet
3 feet ⊞⊞⊞ 3 feet
5 feet

D
4 feet
4 feet ⊞⊞ 4 feet
4 feet

Find the area of the rectangles.

Area of Rectangle A: 7 feet × 1 foot = 7 square feet

Area of Rectangle B: 6 feet × 2 feet = 12 square feet

Area of Rectangle C: 5 feet × 3 feet = 15 square feet

Area of Rectangle D: 4 feet × 4 feet = 16 square feet

To find the area of a square, you can multiply a side by itself. This is because all 4 sides of a square are the same length.

A square will give you the largest rectangular area for a given perimeter.

Volume

Volume is the amount a solid figure holds.

Volume is measured in cubic units.

MORE
HELP
See 326

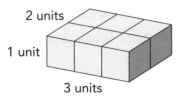

2 units

1 unit

3 units

Write: *6 units³*

Say: *six cubic units*

Here are some units for measuring volume.

Customary Units of Volume	Metric Units of Volume
cubic inch (in.³)	cubic centimeter (cm³)
cubic foot (ft³)	cubic meter (m³)

Finding Volume

You can find the volume of a rectangular prism by counting cubes or by multiplying.

EXAMPLE: How many centimeter cubes will this box hold?

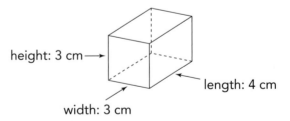

height: 3 cm

length: 4 cm

width: 3 cm

ONE WAY Fill the box with centimeter cubes.

1 Make the bottom layer. There are 4 rows of 3 cubes.	$4 \times 3 = 12$ There are 12 cubes in the bottom layer.
2 Keep building layers until the box is filled. Then count the layers.	There are 3 layers of 12.
3 Find the total by multiplying the number of layers by the number of cubes in each layer.	number of cubes in each layer $\downarrow$ $3 \times 12 = 36$ $\uparrow$ number of layers

ANOTHER WAY You can also find the volume by multiplying.

When you multiply centimeters by centimeters by centimeters, you get cubic centimeters.

Volume = length × width × height

length   width   height

$(4 \times 3) \times 3$

$12 \times 3 = 36$

number of cubes in each layer   number of layers   number of cubes in all

⭐ **ANSWER:** Either way, you can fill the box with 36 centimeter cubes. Its volume is 36 cubic centimeters.

Capacity

What size milk container does your family buy? How much orange juice does your family use each day? These questions can all be answered by measuring capacity. The amount of liquid a container holds is called its **capacity**.

Customary Units of Capacity

Here are some customary units of capacity.

teaspoon (tsp)	tablespoon (tbsp)	fluid ounce (fl oz)	cup (c)
	1 tbsp = 3 tsp	1 fl oz = 2 tbsp	1 c = 8 fl oz
pint (pt)	quart (qt)	half gallon ($\frac{1}{2}$ gal)	gallon (gal)
1 pt = 2 c	1 qt = 2 pt	$\frac{1}{2}$ gal = 2 qt	1 gal = 4 qt

EXAMPLE: Which is a more reasonable estimate of the capacity of a soup bowl—2 cups or 2 quarts?

Two quarts is the same as a half gallon. Think about the amount of liquid in a half-gallon container. That's too much for a bowl of soup.

★ **ANSWER:** A more reasonable estimate of the capacity of a soup bowl is 2 cups.

Metric Units of Capacity

Here are some metric units of capacity.

Metric Units of Capacity	
liter (L)	
milliliter (mL)	$\frac{1}{1000}$ of a liter

These benchmarks will help you understand the size of units in the metric system.

| A milliliter is about 10 drops. | A liter bottle of water is just a little more than 1 quart. | A teaspoon holds about 5 milliliters. | A soupspoon holds about 15 milliliters. | A fishbowl holds about 5 liters. |

EXAMPLE: Suppose you need a small bottle of glue. Will you buy a 59-milliliter or a 59-liter bottle?

Since one milliliter is about 10 drops, 59 milliliters is about 590 drops. Since one liter is about one quart, 59 liters is about 59 quarts.

59 × 10 = 590

★ **ANSWER:** You will likely buy a 59-milliliter bottle of glue.

Weight and Mass

Mass and weight are similar, but they are not the same. **Weight** measures how heavy an object is. **Mass** measures the amount of matter in an object.

Suppose you took a trip to the moon. If you got on a scale, you'd be quite surprised. The moon has less gravity than Earth, and the amount of gravity affects weight. The moon pulls down on your body less than Earth does, so your weight would be less on the moon.

There is still the same amount of you no matter where you are. Your mass on the moon would be the same as on Earth.

Customary Units of Weight

MORE HELP
See 424–425
Here are some customary units used to measure weight.

Customary Units of Weight	
ounce (oz)	
pound (lb)	16 ounces
ton (T)	2000 pounds

Find your own benchmarks or use these to help you understand customary units of weight.

A slice of cheese weighs about **1 ounce**.

A loaf of bread weighs about **1 pound**.

A Clydesdale horse weighs about **1 ton**.

Metric Units of Mass

Here are some metric units used to measure mass.

Metric Units of Mass	
gram (g)	
kilogram (kg)	1000 grams
metric ton	1000 kilograms

MORE HELP
See 424–425

Find your own benchmarks or use these to help you understand metric units of mass.

A dollar bill has a mass of about **1 gram**.

A nickel has a mass of about **5 grams**.

A textbook has a mass of about **1 kilogram**.

A really small car has a mass of about **1 metric ton**.

EXAMPLE: Which seems like a more reasonable estimate for the mass of a cat—6 kilograms or 6 grams?

Since the mass of a nickel is about 5 grams, 6 grams doesn't make sense.

It makes more sense that a cat would have a mass equal to that of 6 math books.

★ **ANSWER:** The more reasonable estimate for the mass of a cat is 6 kilograms.

Temperature

You can measure temperature to describe how hot or how cold something is.

You can use a thermometer to measure **temperature**. The colored liquid expands as it gets warmer, so it moves up the thin tube. As it gets colder, the liquid takes up less space, so it moves back down the tube.

Fahrenheit

In the customary system, temperature is measured on the **Fahrenheit** (Fare-in-hite) scale. The Fahrenheit scale is used in the United States to measure temperature.

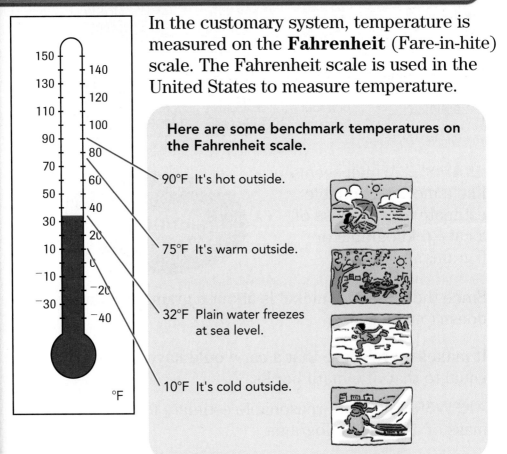

Here are some benchmark temperatures on the Fahrenheit scale.

90°F It's hot outside.

75°F It's warm outside.

32°F Plain water freezes at sea level.

10°F It's cold outside.

Write: 32°F   **Say:** thirty-two degrees Fahrenheit

Celsius

In the metric system, the scale for measuring temperature is based on 100. It is called the **Celsius** (Sel-see-us) scale. On this scale, water boils at 100°C and the freezing point of water is 0°C.

Write: *0°C*

Say: *zero degrees Celsius*

Celsius is sometimes called Centigrade.

Most countries, other than the U.S., measure temperature using the Celsius scale.

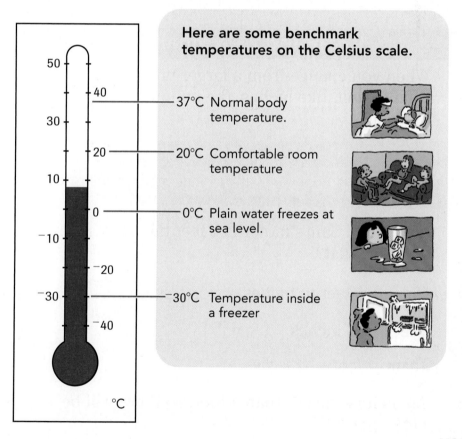

Here are some benchmark temperatures on the Celsius scale.

37°C Normal body temperature.

20°C Comfortable room temperature

0°C Plain water freezes at sea level.

⁻30°C Temperature inside a freezer

MORE HELP
See
238–239

Computing with Measures

Sometimes you need to compare measurements that are not in the same units. When you change from one unit to another, you need to know the relationship between the two units. If you don't remember the relationship, you can use the tables of measures in the Almanac.

Changing to a Smaller Unit

MORE HELP
See 431–432

When you change from a larger unit, like feet, to a smaller unit, like inches, the number of units will be greater.

Knowing that the number of units will be *greater* can help you remember to *multiply* rather than divide.

EXAMPLE: Sam's father is 6 feet tall. How many inches is that?

Change 6 feet to inches.

1 foot

12 inches

6 feet = ■ inches

Think: *1 foot = 12 inches*

An inch is smaller than a foot, so there will be *more* inches.

Multiply. 6×12 inches = 72 inches

⭐ ANSWER: 6 feet = 72 inches

Changing to a Larger Unit

When you change from a smaller unit to a larger unit, the number of units will be smaller.

MORE
HELP
See
431–432

> Knowing that the number of units will be *smaller* can help you remember to *divide* rather than multiply.

EXAMPLE: How many meters long is a fishing pole that is 400 centimeters long?

400 centimeters = ■ meters

Think: *1 meter = 100 centimeters*

1 meter

100 centimeters

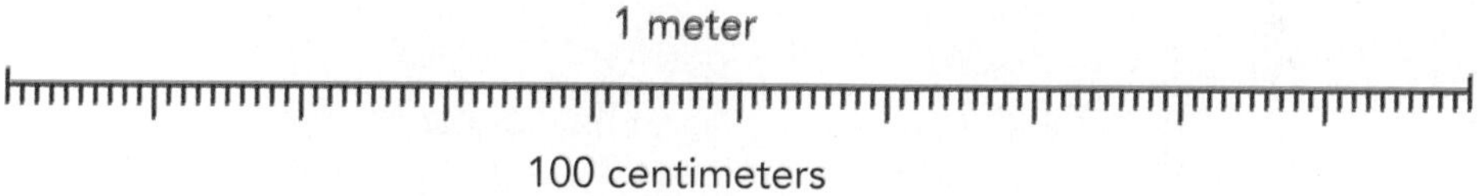

A meter is larger than a centimeter so there will be *fewer* meters.

Divide. 400 centimeters ÷ 100 centimeters = 4

400 centimeters = 4 meters

★ **ANSWER:** A 400-centimeter fishing pole is 4 meters long.

Problem Solving

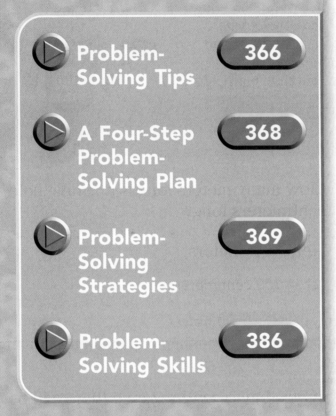

Mmm, where did I leave my notebook? What should I bring when I sleep at Paul's house tonight? How should we choose sides for our game of tag?

You solve problems every day. You're probably very good at figuring things out. Well, you can figure out math problems, too.

Many ideas that help you solve problems in your daily life can also help you solve math problems.

* Know what's going on.
* Remember things that have worked before.
* Really care about finding a solution.

You shouldn't be surprised if you find that you already know a lot about solving math problems. After all, problem solving is a big part of your life.

Problem-Solving Tips

Keep trying.

You and your dad are making
pancakes. The first one sticks to
the pan. Should you quit right
there? You should not. Even the
best pancake makers have to

throw out a bad pancake once in a while. It's a good
thing they don't give up. Successful problem solvers
don't give up either. When you work on a problem,
your first try may not work out. Don't worry. Just
look at what you've done and give it another try.

Practice.

Do you believe the saying that
practice makes perfect? If you play
the piano, basketball, chess, or do
any other activity, you know that
practice may not make you
perfect, but it makes you better.

It's the same with problem solving. Each time you
work on a problem, you learn something new. You
become a better problem solver.

Use what you know.

You are on a camping trip and
it starts to rain. You forgot to
pack a raincoat! You get
soaked. If this has happened
to you, you'll probably always

remember to pack a raincoat on future trips.
Experience is a very good teacher. When you solve
problems, use your experience. Think about
problems you have solved before.

Take chances.

A radio station calls and says that you can win a new bicycle. All you have to do is name the last song that was played. You don't know the name. But you take a chance and guess  because you've got nothing to lose — and you might win a bicycle. Problem solving is like that. It makes sense to take chances because you've got nothing to lose and a lot to gain. Better still, in a contest, you may get only one chance. But when you solve problems, you get as many tries as you want.

Watch what you do.

As you work on a problem, think about the method that you're using. Is it getting you closer to a solution? Are you just doing lots of calculations that won't help? If you think you're on the right track, stay on it. If you think you're not getting anywhere, stop and look around. You may find a different path.

Take a break.

Sometimes you're working on a really tough problem. You're getting nowhere. You feel like you've tried everything. It  may be time to get away from the problem for a while. Give your brain a chance to refresh itself. Throughout history, people have come up with great solutions after taking a rest.

A Four-Step Problem-Solving Plan

Getting stuck on a problem is like being lost. In both cases, a map certainly would help. Here is a problem-solving plan that can act like a map.

 Imagine playing a game but you don't know the object of the game. You won't have much chance of winning. It's like that in problem solving. If you don't understand what's going on, you won't have much chance of solving the problem. When you begin a problem, ask yourself questions such as, "What do I know? What do I need to find out?"

If you don't understand the problem, use these hints.
* Read the problem again slowly. Take notes or draw pictures to help.
* If there are charts or drawings, study them.
* Look up any words or symbols you don't know.

PLAN
2 When you're not sure how to solve a problem, take time to think. Try one or more strategies.

TRY
3 Go ahead with the method you picked. Work carefully. If your first try doesn't work, try something else.

 After you find an answer, don't stop. Ask yourself:
* Does your answer make sense?
* Did you answer the question that was asked?
* Did you compute correctly?

Problem-Solving Strategies

You might walk or skate to your friend's house. You might ride your bike or skateboard. You might ride in a bus or a car. There are many ways to get from one place to another. Solving a problem is like going somewhere. There are lots of different ways to get an answer. These methods are called **problem-solving strategies**.

Keep in mind a few things about strategies.

* You can use more than one strategy on a problem.
* You can use a strategy that's not on the list. You might even use one that you make up.
* You can use whatever strategy works for you. Your friend might make a table to solve a problem. You might write a number sentence to solve the same problem. Everyone doesn't have to solve a problem the same way.

Act It Out

Sometimes you can use objects to act out a problem. Acting out a problem with coins, counters, paper, connecting cubes, or other handy items can help you see what's going on.

EXAMPLE: Three boys shovel snow to earn money. They work together for three days and keep track of the amount they earn each day. To share the money equally, how much should each get?

MONEY EARNED
SHOVELING
SNOW
FRIDAY $4.⁰⁰
SATURDAY $9.⁰⁰
SUNDAY $8.⁰⁰

- Three boys earn money and want to share it.
- They earn $4.00, then $9.00, then $8.00.
- How much should each boy get?

PLAN
2

It would help to be able to see the amounts of money. Try using cubes to stand for dollars.

TRY
3

1 Show how much they earned each day.

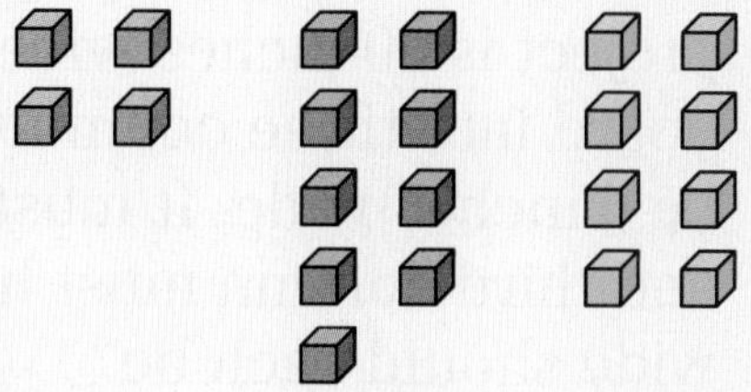

2 Put all the amounts together.

3 Make three equal groups.

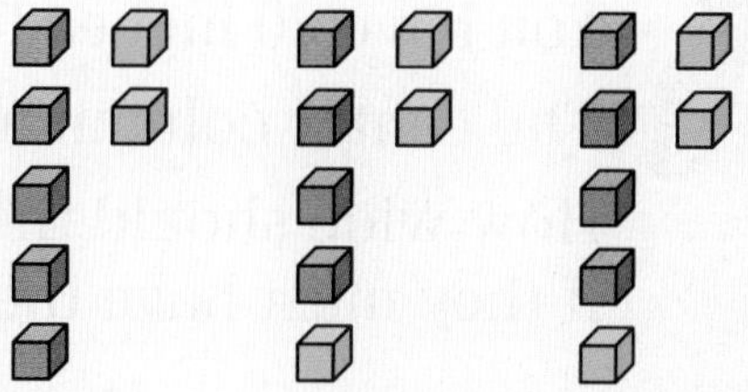

4 Count the number of cubes in each group.

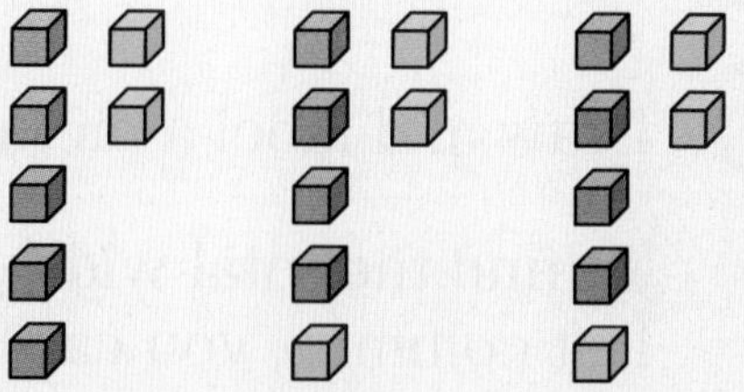

There are 7 cubes in each group.
Each boy should get $7.00.

LOOK BACK
4

- Does each boy get the same amount? Yes.
- Is all the money shared? Yes.

★ ANSWER: Each boy should get $7.00.

Draw a Picture

You don't have to be an artist to draw pictures that can help you solve problems.

EXAMPLE 1: The display board for your science fair project is 20 inches wide. You want to divide the board into three columns. The middle column must be 6 inches wide. It must be centered. So, the first and third column must have the same width. How wide should each be?

 UNDERSTAND 1
- You have 20 inches for 3 columns.
  - The center column must be 6 inches wide.
  - How wide should the first and third columns be if they must have the same width?

PLAN 2 A picture would help show what is going on.

TRY 3 Draw and label a picture.

To find the total width of the first and last columns, you can subtract.
20 − 6 = 14

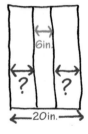

If you divide the total 14 inches into two equal groups, there are 7 inches in each group.

LOOK BACK 4 Make sure that your picture matches the problem.

★ **ANSWER:** The first and last columns should each be 7 inches wide.

Sometimes your drawing doesn't have to look like the problem, as long as it helps you see what's going on.

EXAMPLE 2: Dina's class had a race. Dina finished in second place. Carlos finished in seventh place. How many children finished between Dina and Jason?

UNDERSTAND 1

- Dina was second.
- Carlos was seventh.
- How many children finished behind Dina and ahead of Carlos?

PLAN 2

A picture can help you see and count the children.

TRY 3

- Use Xs (or any symbol that's easy to draw) to show children in the race. You don't have to show all of them. (In fact, the problem doesn't even tell you how many children were in the race.)
- Label Dina and Carlos. You can use the letters *D* and *C* instead of writing their whole names.

There are 4 Xs between Dina and Carlos.

LOOK BACK 4

- Did you put Dina and Carlos in the correct places?
- Did you count correctly?

⭐ **ANSWER:** Four children finished between Dina and Carlos.

Look for a Pattern

Imagine that on some days you get very tired around ten o'clock in the morning. You realize that this happens on days when you have a lot of sugar in your breakfast. You are noticing a pattern. You can use the pattern to solve the problem. Don't eat a lot of sweets for breakfast! Patterns help you act smarter when you eat and they can help you solve math problems, too.

EXAMPLE: Francisco used 15 cards to build this 3-story house of cards. Now he wants to build another one like it, but 8 stories high. How many cards does he need?

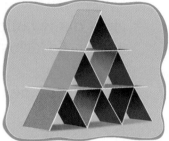

UNDERSTAND
1
- It takes 15 cards to make a 3-story house.
  - How many cards are needed for an 8-story house?

PLAN
2
The same shape is used over and over, so maybe there's a pattern that can help you.

TRY
3
Find out how many cards are needed for each of the first few stories. Since the upper stories are simpler, start at the top.

MORE
HELP
See 372,
378

	Story	Tilted Cards	Horizontal Cards	Total
	top	2	0	2
	2nd from top	4	1	5
	3rd from top	6	2	8
	4th from top	8	3	11

Notice the pattern. For each new story you add 3 cards (2 tilted and 1 horizontal). So, each story uses 3 more cards than the story above it.

You can use more than one strategy at a time. Draw a Picture and Make a Table were used with Look for a Pattern to solve this problem.

To find the total number of cards for 8 stories, add.
$2 + 5 + 8 + 11 + 14 + 17 + 20 + 23 = 100$

4 Make sure the pattern you used will really continue. In this case, it will continue until the house is too high to stay up.

★ ANSWER: Francisco needs 100 cards to build his 8-story house of cards.

Not All Patterns Continue

Just because you see a pattern doesn't mean it will continue.

			May			
Sun.	Mon.	Tues.	Wed.	Thur.	Fri.	Sat.
					1	2
3	4	5	6	7	8	9
10	11	12	13	14	15	16
17	18	19	20	21	22	23
24	25	26	27	28	29	30
31						

Suppose you sign up for six Monday tennis lessons. You have a class on May 4, May 11, May 18, and May 25. You notice the pattern in the numbers. Each number is 7 more than the number before. Does that mean your next lesson will be on May 32?

It will not be on May 32 because there are only 31 days in May. So, the pattern will not continue.

Whenever you use a pattern to solve a problem, ask yourself: Is there a reason for the pattern to continue?

Guess, Check, and Revise

Even as a baby you solved problems by trying things out. Now you are older and need to solve more complicated problems. But you can still use a strategy based on trying things. It's called Guess, Check, and Revise. The key is to think after each try and change (or revise) your guess when necessary.

EXAMPLE: Tanya had 12 coins, all nickels and dimes. She used them all to buy a notebook for 80¢. How many of each type of coin did Tanya have?

UNDERSTAND
1
- Tanya had a total of 12 nickels and dimes.
  - The coins were worth 80¢.
  - How many nickels did she have?
  - How many dimes did she have?

PLAN
2
Make a guess and check it. If it's right, great. If not, see if it's too high or too low. Think about how to make your next guess closer.

TRY
3

MORE
HELP
See 253

Guess (Sum must be 12.)	Check (Is the total 80¢?)	Think and Revise
dimes: 6 nickels: 6 (6 + 6 = 12)	(6 × 10¢) + (6 × 5¢) = 60¢ + 30¢ = 90¢	Too high! Make a guess that lowers the total. Try fewer dimes and more nickels.
dimes: 3 nickels: 9 (3 + 9 = 12)	(3 × 10¢) + (9 × 5¢) = 30¢ + 45¢ = 75¢	Too low! Make a guess that raises the total. Try more dimes and fewer nickels.
dimes: 4 nickels: 8 (4 + 8 = 12)	(4 × 10¢) + (8 × 5¢) = 40¢ + 40¢ = 80¢	Just right!

LOOK BACK
4
- Is the total 80¢? Yes.
  - Are there 12 coins in all? Yes.

★ **ANSWER:** Tanya had 4 dimes and 8 nickels.

Make a Table

When you play Concentration, you put cards in rows and columns. That makes it easier to keep track of the cards.

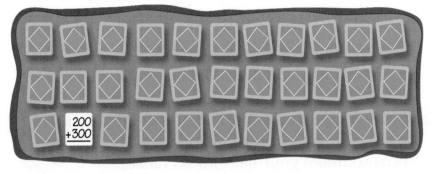

When you solve a math problem, you can put numbers in rows and columns. That can help you keep track of the numbers.

EXAMPLE: You want to buy a bird cage that costs $57. You have only $35, but you can save $4 every week. When will you have enough to buy the bird cage?

- You have $35.
  - You save $4 each week.
  - How many weeks will it take to have at least $57?

PLAN
2 Keep adding $4 to the $35 you have. Stop when the total reaches or goes over $57. A table will help you keep track.

TRY
3
- Make a table. Label it. Fill in the first column to show that you start with $35.

MORE HELP
See 268

Weeks	Now
Money	$35

- Fill in the second column to show that after 1 week you will have $4 more, or $39 in all.

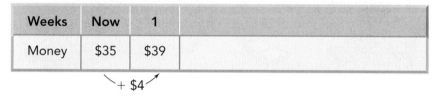

Weeks	Now	1
Money	$35	$39

+ $4

- Keep filling in the table until you reach or go over $57.

Weeks	Now	1	2	3	4	5	6
Money	$35	$39	$43	$47	$51	$55	$59

It looks like you will have enough money in 6 weeks.

LOOK BACK
4
- In 6 weeks, you will have $59. That's more than enough to buy the cage.
- In 5 weeks, you will have only $55. So, 6 weeks makes sense.

★ **ANSWER:** In 6 weeks you will have enough money to buy the bird cage.

You'll have $2 left over to buy bird food, bird toys, . . .

Make a List

Organizing makes it easier to know where things are. So, if you make a list to solve a math problem, you should organize the list.

EXAMPLE: You are setting up a basketball tournament in your class. There are 5 teams. Every team will play each of the other teams one time. How many games will be played?

- There are 5 teams.
- Each team plays every other team once.
- How many games will there be?

Try making an organized list. Use the letters A, B, C, D, and E to stand for the 5 teams.

TRY
3 First, list all the games for Team A. Then list the games for Team B, and so on.

Don't list AA, BB, and so on, because a team doesn't play against itself.

A Games	B Games	C Games	D Games	E Games
■	BA	CA	DA	EA
AB	■	CB	DB	EB
AC	BC	■	DC	EC
AD	BD	CD	■	ED
AE	BE	CE	DE	■

It looks like there are 20 different pairs.

LOOK BACK
4 • Are games AB and BA the same or different? They are the same. Teams play each other only once.

You need to cross out one of each pair that is listed twice.

A Games	B Games	C Games	D Games	E Games
■	~~BA~~	~~CA~~	~~DA~~	~~EA~~
AB	■	~~CB~~	~~DB~~	~~EB~~
AC	BC	■	~~DC~~	~~EC~~
AD	BD	CD	■	~~ED~~
AE	BE	CE	DE	■

same

★ **ANSWER:** 10 games will be played.

Work Backward

When you wrap a gift, you put on the bow last.
When you unwrap a gift, you take off the bow first.
You do things in reverse order. Each action is the
opposite. Putting on is the opposite of taking off.

You can work backward to solve some math
problems.

EXAMPLE: Your friend's party starts at 1:45 P.M. She
wants you there 15 minutes early. It will take you
30 minutes to get ready and 10 minutes to get there.
When should you start getting ready?

UNDERSTAND
1
- It takes you 30 minutes to get ready and
  10 minutes to get there.

- You need to be there 15 minutes before 1:45 P.M.

- At what time should you start to get ready?

PLAN
2
You know the end (when the party starts). You
know the steps and how much time each step
takes. You can work backward to find the
beginning (when you should start).

TRY
3

- First write out the steps to show all the things that will take time.

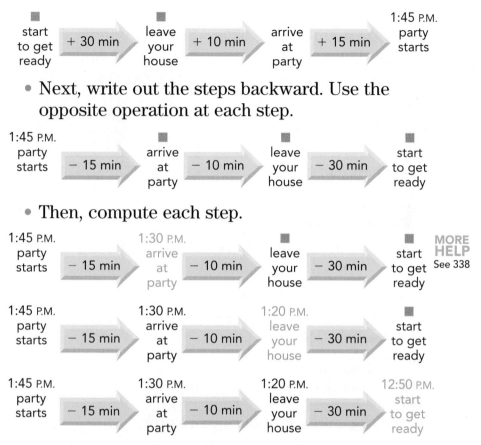

- Next, write out the steps backward. Use the opposite operation at each step.

- Then, compute each step.

It looks like you'll get there just in time if you start to get ready at 12:50 P.M.

Check by working forward.

- If you start to get ready at 12:50 P.M., you will be ready 30 minutes later, at 1:20 P.M.

- You will get there 10 minutes later, at 1:30 P.M.

- The party will start 15 minutes later, at 1:45 P.M. The answer checks.

★ **ANSWER:** You should start getting ready no later than 12:50 P.M.

Write a Number Sentence

You can use number sentences with missing numbers to solve math problems.

EXAMPLE 1: Hsu has 3 cans and 5 boxes of Sun-Ray Fruit Punch. How many ounces of punch is that?

- Each can holds 12 ounces.

- Each box holds 8 ounces.

- How many ounces are in 3 cans and 5 boxes?

PLAN
2 You can write and solve a number sentence.

- Write a number sentence with words to describe the problem.

$$\text{total number of ounces} = \text{number of cans} \times 12 + \text{number of boxes} \times 8$$

TRY
3 • Write in the numbers you know.

$$\text{total number of ounces} = 3 \times 12 + 5 \times 8$$

MORE HELP
See 253

- Solve the number sentence.

$$\text{total number of ounces} = 36 + 40$$
$$= 76$$

> Use the Order of Operations. Multiply first, then add.

Make sure that you correctly wrote and solved the number sentence.

★ **ANSWER:** Hsu has 76 ounces of fruit punch.

EXAMPLE 2: Hsu had $1.25 in her bank yesterday. This morning she put in some more money and now she has $2.00 in her bank. How much money did she put in this morning?

UNDERSTAND 1

- Hsu had $1.25.
- She added some money.
- Now she has $2.00.
- How much did she add?

PLAN 2

You can write a number sentence for the problem. Then you can solve the number sentence.

MORE
HELP
See 49

TRY 3

1 Write a number sentence with words to show how things are related.	amount she had $+$ amount she put in $=$ total
2 Write in the numbers you know.	$1.25 + amount she put in = $2.00
3 Find the missing amount to solve the number sentence.	$1.25 + ■ = $2.00 You can subtract to find the missing addend. $2.00 − $1.25 = $0.75 $1.25 + $0.75 = $2.00

It looks like she put in 75 cents.

LOOK BACK 4

- Make sure your number sentence matches the problem.
- Check your calculations.

★ **ANSWER:** Hsu put $0.75 into her bank this morning.

Problem-Solving Skills

It takes more than one skill to play a sport. In soccer, for example, you need to know how to pass, dribble, trap, shoot, and play defense. In problem solving, too, you need many skills. The more skills you have, the better all-around problem-solver you'll be.

More Than One Answer

Suppose you need 75¢ in exact change to buy a bag of peanuts from a vending machine. You could use 3 quarters, or you could use 7 dimes and a nickel, or you could use other combinations. You can usually make exact change in more than one way. Some math problems are like exact change. There may be more than one answer.

EXAMPLE 1: How can you fold a sheet of paper to form 4 rectangles that have the same size and shape?

⭐ **ANSWER:** This problem has several answers:

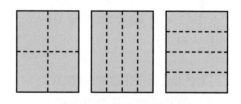

EXAMPLE 2: You throw three darts. Show how you can get a score of 90.

⭐ **ANSWER:** This problem has three correct answers.

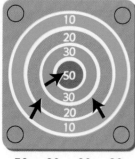 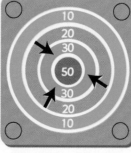

50 + 20 + 20 = 90   30 + 30 + 30 = 90   50 + 30 + 10 = 90

Choose an Operation

MORE
HELP
See
34–35,
46–47,
60–61,
74–75

You can solve some math problems simply by adding, subtracting, multiplying, or dividing. Of course, you have to think about which operation to use and which numbers to use.

EXAMPLE 1: On average, how much trash is produced by a person in France in 1 week?

Average Amount of Trash Produced By 1 Person in 1 Day	
Country	**Pounds**
Germany	2
Spain	2
France	2
United Kingdom	$2\frac{1}{2}$
Sweden	$2\frac{1}{2}$
Japan	$2\frac{1}{2}$
Netherlands	3
Canada	$3\frac{1}{2}$
United States	$4\frac{1}{4}$

Source: United States Environmental Protection Agency

The table shows that, on average, a person in France produces 2 pounds of trash each day.

You know there are 7 days in a week.

So you need to think about 7 groups of 2 pounds.

You can multiply 7 times 2 to find the answer.

$7 \times 2 = 14$

★ **ANSWER:** A person in France produces about 14 pounds of trash each week on average.

EXAMPLE 2: On average, how much more trash does a person in the Netherlands produce each day than a person in Spain?

The table shows that a person in the Netherlands produces about 3 pounds of trash each day and a person in Spain produces about 2 pounds.

You can subtract to compare. $3 - 2 = 1$

★ ANSWER: On average, a person in the Netherlands produces 1 more pound of trash each day than a person in Spain.

Sometimes you don't need any operation to solve a problem.

EXAMPLE 3: In which country does the average person produce the most trash?

Of the countries listed, the number for the United States is highest. You don't need to do any computation. You only need to compare numbers.

★ ANSWER: In the United States, a person produces the most trash on average.

Choose an Estimate or Exact Amount

Sometimes estimating makes things easier.

Sometimes estimating doesn't make sense.

I'll estimate to see if I have enough money. 79¢ is less than a dollar. So, $2 is enough.

Two pens, 79 cents each. Hmmm, 79 cents is about a dollar. So you owe me about $2.00.

We need an exact answer, $0.79 × 2 = $1.58. I can't afford to estimate this time.

Think before deciding whether you can estimate or whether you need an exact amount.

Case 1 You can often estimate when you are finding whether one amount is greater than or less than another amount.

EXAMPLE 1: The chart shows how J.J. the baby whale grew while her rescuers took care of her. Did J.J.'s length double from the time she was 5 days old to when she was 6 months old?

Age	Weight	Length
5 days	1670 pounds	13 feet 10 inches
6 months	9060 pounds	24 feet
15–16 months	20,000 pounds	30 feet
adult	70,000 pounds	48 feet

Source: Sea World

You are trying to find out whether J.J.'s length at age 6 months was about two times her length at age 5 days. So, maybe you can estimate.

Since $13 \times 2 = 26$, if you multiply 13 feet 10 inches by 2 the result will be more than 26 feet. J.J. was only 24 feet long at age 6 months.

★ ANSWER: J.J.'s length almost doubled from 5 days old to 6 months old.

Case 2 You can estimate when you just need to know about how many or about how much.

EXAMPLE 2: About how many pounds did J.J. gain from the time she was 6 months old to when she was about 15 months old?

MORE HELP
See 132–133

You just need to know *about* how much weight J.J. gained. Besides, the chart doesn't show J.J.'s weight at exactly 15 months. So you can't be exact.

9060 is about 9000.

$20,000 - 9000 = 11,000$

★ ANSWER: J.J. gained about 11,000 pounds from the time she was 6 months old to when she was about 15 months old.

Case 3 Sometimes you need to find an exact amount.

EXAMPLE 3: How many pounds did J.J. gain from age 5 days to age 6 months?

This problem asks for an exact answer.

To solve this problem, subtract. $9060 - 1670 = 7390$

MORE HELP
See 166

★ ANSWER: J.J. gained 7390 pounds from the time she was 5 days to age 6 months.

Solve Multi-Step Problems

When you get ready for school, you do it step-by-step. You get up. You wash. You get dressed. You eat breakfast. You brush your teeth. To solve math problems, too, you often need to do more than one step. You can make a plan to help you keep track of the steps.

EXAMPLE 1: How much will it cost for 2 adults and 3 children to enter the science museum?

ADMISSION
Adult: $5   Child: $3

Science Museum

Make a plan by thinking of the steps you will use.

Here is one plan.

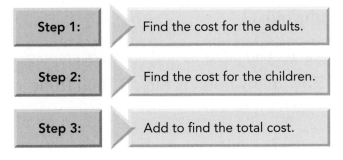

Step 1: Find the cost for the adults.

Step 2: Find the cost for the children.

Step 3: Add to find the total cost.

Then go through your plan step by step.

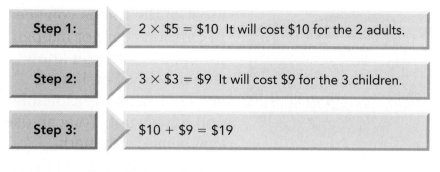

Step 1:	2 × $5 = $10 It will cost $10 for the 2 adults.
Step 2:	3 × $3 = $9 It will cost $9 for the 3 children.
Step 3:	$10 + $9 = $19

★ **ANSWER:** It will cost $19 for 2 adults and
3 children to enter the science museum.

EXAMPLE 2: How much longer
is the Mummy Show than the
Dinosaur Show?

MUMMY SHOW
9:45 a.m. to 10:30 a.m.

DINOSAUR SHOW
11:30 a.m. to 12 noon

Here is a plan you could use.

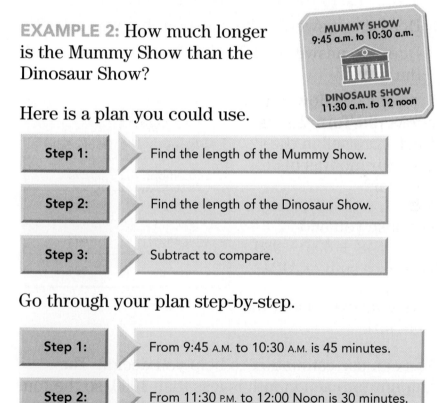

Step 1:	Find the length of the Mummy Show.
Step 2:	Find the length of the Dinosaur Show.
Step 3:	Subtract to compare.

Go through your plan step-by-step.

Step 1:	From 9:45 A.M. to 10:30 A.M. is 45 minutes.
Step 2:	From 11:30 P.M. to 12:00 Noon is 30 minutes.
Step 3:	45 min − 30 min = 15 min

★ **ANSWER:** The Mummy Show is 15 minutes longer
than the Dinosaur Show.

MORE
HELP
See 338

Is the Answer Reasonable?

Most of the things you see in cartoons cannot happen in real life. But you know that already. You have a sense of what's reasonable and what's not. You can use that sense with math problems. After you have solved a problem, look over your solution. Ask yourself:

- Is the size of the answer about right?
- Does the answer fit the question that was asked?
- Does the answer match what I know about the world?

EXAMPLE 1: How many books did Turn-the-Page Bookstore sell in the last four months of the year?

Turn-the-Page Bookstore	
Month	Books Sold
September	894
October	548
November	693
December	989

Suppose you add 894 + 548 + 693 + 989 and get a sum of 4124.

Is that answer about the right size?

MORE HELP
See 132

You can use estimation to help you decide. The amount for each month is less than 1000, so the four months together must be less than 4000.

Since 4124 is greater than 4000, the sum is not reasonable.

⭐ **ANSWER:** The bookstore sold 3124 books in the last four months of the year.

EXAMPLE 2: At Turn-the-Page Bookstore, how many more books were sold in November and December than in September and October?

Suppose you answered that 1682 books were sold in November and December and 1442 books were sold in September and October. That's true, but it doesn't answer the question about how many more.

To solve the problem, you need to subtract. $1682 - 1442 = 240$

⭐ **ANSWER:** At Turn-the-Page Bookstore, 240 more books were sold in November and December than in September and October.

EXAMPLE 3: When Andrew stands with both legs on the scale, he weighs 80 pounds. How much will he weigh when he stands on the scale balancing on one leg?

Suppose someone solved this by finding half of 80. That would give an answer of 40 pounds.

Does 40 pounds make sense? Is that the way the world works? No, your weight doesn't change when you stand on one leg. (If you're not sure about that, try it.)

⭐ **ANSWER:** Andrew will still weigh 80 pounds.

Use Logical Reasoning

Do you ever figure things out, like where your mom left her keys or who ate the last cookie? You probably think like a detective to solve these mysteries. You can do that to solve math problems, too.

EXAMPLE: Arlo, Briana, and Ricardo had a race. Briana is taller than the winner. Arlo finished 5 seconds after Briana. In what order did the 3 children finish?

To solve this problem, you can use logical reasoning to eliminate possible answers. Make a chart to keep track.

	1st	2nd	3rd
Arlo			
Briana			
Ricardo			

Since Briana is taller than the winner, Briana did not come in first. Write an *X* to show that.

	1st	2nd	3rd
Arlo			
Briana	X		
Ricardo			

Since Arlo finished after Briana, he did not come in first. Make an *X* to show that.

	1st	2nd	3rd
Arlo	X		
Briana	X		
Ricardo			

Since Arlo and Briana did not win, Ricardo must have won. Show that with a ✓.

	1st	2nd	3rd
Arlo	X		
Briana	X		
Ricardo	✓		

Since Ricardo is first, Ricardo cannot be second or third. Make two *X*s to show that.

	1st	2nd	3rd
Arlo	X		
Briana	X		
Ricardo	✓	X	X

Since Arlo finished after Briana, he could not be second. So, Briana was second and Arlo was third.

	1st	2nd	3rd
Arlo	X	X	✓
Briana	X	✓	
Ricardo	✓	X	X

⭐ **ANSWER:** Ricardo came in first, Briana came in second, and Arlo came in third.

Find Information You Need

Your friend invites you to a party. You want to go. You need to know when it is and where it is. So, you look at the invitation. Knowing what information you need and how to find it can come in handy when you solve math problems, too.

- What information could help solve the problem?
- Can I look up the information? What resources could I use?
- Can I ask someone?
- Can I take a measurement?
- Can I use an estimate?

EXAMPLE: You are going to use 28 inches of ribbon for your project. If you buy 1 yard of ribbon, how many inches will you have left?

MORE HELP
See 362 You need to know how many inches are in a yard.

If you don't know, you can ask someone, you can look at a yardstick, or you can look at a table (like the one on page 431 of this book).

1 yard = 36 inches

$$
\begin{array}{rcl}
1 \text{ yd} & \rightarrow & 36 \text{ in.} \\
- 28 \text{ in.} & \rightarrow & - 28 \text{ in.} \\
\hline
 & & 8 \text{ in.}
\end{array}
$$

★ **ANSWER:** You will have 8 inches of ribbon left.

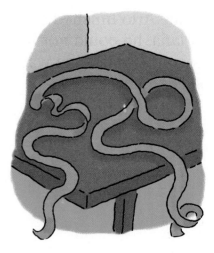

Ignore Information You Don't Need

Sometimes reading a math problem can be like walking through a store — there's a lot more information than you need. Try to look at the information you need and ignore the rest.

EXAMPLE: Every year in Alaska there is a dogsled race called the Iditarod that is more than 1000 miles long. In the 2005 Iditarod, how many more dogs did Ed Iten use than Robert Sorley used?

Place	Name	Time		Number of Dogs
1	Robert Sorley	9 days 18 hours	39 minutes 31 seconds	8
2	Ed Iten	9 days 19 hours	13 minutes 33 seconds	9
3	Mitch Seavey	9 days 19 hours	20 minutes 58 seconds	9

Source: www.cabelaiditarod.com

You need to compare the number of dogs used by the top two racers. Find out how many dogs they each used. You can ignore the rest of the information.

Robert Sorley used 8 dogs.

Ed Iten used 9 dogs.

Subtract to compare. $9 - 8 = 1$

⭐ **ANSWER:** Ed Iten used 1 more dog than Robert Sorley used.

That problem was a lot easier than it looked!

Whenever you play, your brain is busy thinking about the space around you: How do these parts fit together? Where is the ball going? How should I move my body? That kind of thinking is called **spatial reasoning**. It helps you play and it can help you solve math problems, too.

EXAMPLE: Each link in a chain is 5 inches long. The chain has 10 links. Will the chain be 50 inches long?

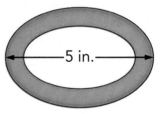

Use what you know about how things go together.

- The links of a chain do not go end-to-end like this:

- They go through each other, like this:

⭐ **ANSWER:** No, the chain will be a little shorter than 50 inches.

Almanac

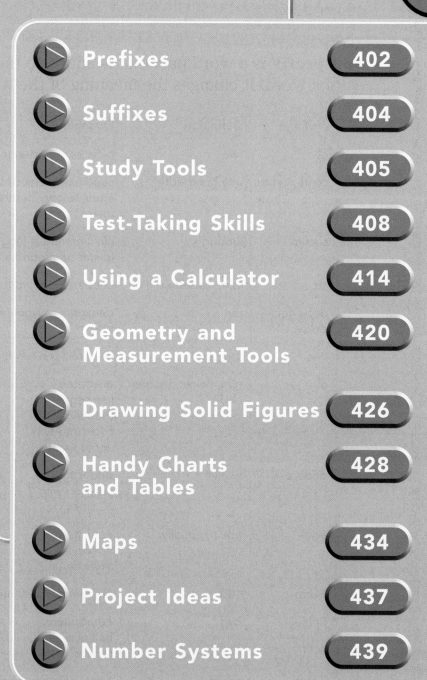

This almanac includes very useful tables and lists. It has tips on how to best use your class time and how to study for and take tests. It shows how to use a calculator and even how to read a map.

Prefixes

A **prefix** is a word part that is added to the beginning of a word. It changes the meaning of the word.

Prefix	Definition	Example
bi-	two	*bicycle:* two-wheeled vehicle
centi-, cent-	one hundredth	*centimeter:* unit of length equal to one hundredth of a meter
circum-	around	*circumference:* length (distance) around a circle
co-	joint, together	*cooperate:* to work together
dec-, deca-, deka-	ten	*decagon:* polygon with ten sides
deci-	one tenth	*deciliter:* one tenth of a liter
di-	two, twice, double	*diameter:* line segment that divides a circle into two equal parts
dodeca-	twelve	*dodecagon:* polygon with 12 sides
equi-	equal, equally	*equilateral:* having all sides equal
hecto-	100	*hectometer:* 100 meters
hemi-	half	*hemisphere:* half of a sphere
hepta-	seven	*heptagon:* polygon with seven sides

Prefix	Definition	Example
hex-, hexa-	six	*hexagon:* polygon with six sides
inter-	between, mutual	*intersecting lines:* lines that cross or meet
kilo-	1000	*kilogram:* 1000 grams
mid-	middle	*midpoint:* point on a line segment that cuts it into two congruent segments midpoint 3 ft 3 ft
milli-	one thousandth	*millimeter:* one thousandth of a meter
nona-	nine	*nonagon:* polygon with nine sides
octa-, octo-, oct-	eight	*octagon:* polygon with eight sides
penta-, pent-	five	*pentagon:* polygon with five sides
per-	for each	*percent:* per hundred
poly-	many	*polygon:* a closed figure made of three or more line segments
quad-	four	*quadrilateral:* a four-sided polygon
semi-	half	*semicircle:* half of a circle
tri-	three	*triangle:* polygon with three sides

Suffixes

A **suffix** is a word part added to the end of a word. It changes the meaning of the word.

Suffix	Definition	Examples
-centenary	refers to a 100-year period	*bicentenary:* referring to two centuries
-gon	figure with angles	*polygon:* a figure with many angles *hexagon:* a polygon with six angles and six sides
-hedron	figure with faces or surfaces	*polyhedron:* a solid with faces that are polygons *heptahedron:* polyhedron with seven faces
-lateral	relating to sides	*equilateral:* having all sides equal
-metry	measuring	*geometry:* mathematics of properties, measurement, and relationships of points, lines, angles, surfaces, and solids
-sect	cut or divide	*bisect:* cut into two equal parts

Study Tools

Listening Skills

When the teacher first shows you something new, it may seem clear and easy, or it may seem totally confusing. In either case, listen carefully. Try to focus on the big picture as well as on each detail.

Listen actively. That means think about what the teacher is saying. Ask yourself, "Do I understand what the teacher is trying to do?" If the answer is no, ask the teacher to explain. Don't be afraid to ask questions. Your classmates often have the same question in mind. When you listen carefully, you are also ready to answer questions or help to solve a part of a problem.

People can combine their skills and solve problems. Here are some ways to help your groups succeed.

- **Cooperate.** "Cooperate" means "work together." Encourage everyone in the group to take part. You can disagree with group members but don't put them down or tease them.

- **Be responsible.** Chip in and do your part. Then if other group members need help, give them a hand.

- **Listen.** Listen to what others have to say. Someone may look at the problem differently than you do. Even if one idea doesn't work, it may lead to another idea.

- **Encourage others.** Be sure to offer help and to ask for help. When someone does a good job or has a good idea, say so. People who feel appreciated will want to do more.

- **Make group decisions.** Don't feel you have to have everything exactly your own way. Work together to develop and follow a good group plan.

- **Share the work fairly.** Try to make sure that each person has the same amount of work. If one part of a topic is longer than another part, break it up and share the load.

Managing Your Time

Is it hard for you to get things done on time or sometimes to even get things done at all? Try planning your time. You will probably find you have more free time than you thought.

- **Keep a weekly planner.**
Use the planner to write your homework assignments and reminders to prepare for tests and projects. Write questions about things you don't understand. Then set a time with your teacher to talk about your questions.

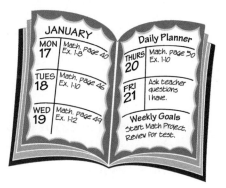

- **Make a daily list.** Write down things you need to do today and tomorrow. Number them in order of importance. Check off items as you complete them.

- **Have a homework schedule.** Do your homework at your planned time for each day. Give yourself short breaks. Make the breaks 5 minutes or less.

- **Set goals.** Be realistic. Give yourself enough time to do a good job. Do not be too hard on yourself. If you don't quite achieve a goal, try to figure out how you can do better next time. Reward yourself for goals that you do reach.

- **Get it done and turn it in on time.** Read directions carefully. Start with something easy first. After you're finished, check the directions again to make sure your homework is really complete. Put your completed homework in a place where you won't forget to take it to school.

Test-Taking Skills

Success in school depends on you! Give yourself time to prepare before a test. The last minute is only for a quick review.

Taking the Test

- **Try to relax before the test.** Breathe deeply. Think of the problems on the test as puzzles or mysteries that you want to solve.

- **Check that you have all the materials you need for the test.** You may need a ruler, sharp pencils, paper, and so on.

- **Know the rules of the test.** You should know how much time you have to complete the test. Ask if some questions count more than others and if you need to give explanations for your answers.

- **Look over the entire test quickly.** Then begin the test. Check the time once in a while.

- **Read the directions carefully.** If you don't understand something, ask your teacher. It is very important to follow the directions.

- **Answer the questions you are sure of first.** If you're stuck, don't waste time on that problem. Skip it. If you have time, you can come back to it.

- **Double-check.** Make sure that you have answered all the questions that you can. Recheck your work if you have time. Estimate to see if your answers make sense. Make sure you copied problems accurately. When possible, do each computation again in a different way. If you just look at the computation, you may not catch your errors.

- **Only change your answers if you are sure they are wrong.** Do not rush through a problem a second time and quickly change your answer. You are often right the first time!

- **Check that all your answers are readable.**

- **Check that your name is on the test.**

Tips for Taking Multiple-Choice Tests

In a multiple-choice problem, usually only one answer is correct. If you can tell which choices are wrong, you have a better chance of finding the right one.

MORE HELP
See 67

• Use number sense to save time and work.

1. $85 \times 2 \times 0 = \blacksquare$

   (A) 0   (B) 85   (C) 87   (D) 170

Remember that any number times 0 is 0.

★ ANSWER: **A**

MORE HELP
See 132–133

• Estimate when you can. Check for reasonableness.

2. $3.72 + 12.8 = \blacksquare$

   (A) 5.00   (B) 9.08   (C) 15.52   (D) 16.52

First, estimate the sum. Round each number to the nearest whole number: 4 + 13. The sum is about 17. You know the answer must be either C or D.

★ ANSWER: **D**

3. If you have $2.80, what is the greatest number of quarters you could have?

   (A) 8   (B) 11   (C) 12   (D) 14

There are 4 quarters in a dollar, so A is too small and C and D are too large. The only reasonable choice is B.

★ ANSWER: **B**

• Eliminate obviously wrong choices.

MORE
HELP

See 75,
185, 205

4.   9 R ■
     7)68

(A) 2   (B) 5   (C) 7   (D) 8

Both C and D are obviously wrong since the
remainder must be less than the divisor (7). So the
answer is either A or B. Since A is an easier number,
try it first ($9 \times 7 + 2 = 65$).
It doesn't work.

⭐ **ANSWER: B**

5. Find the area of a rectangular floor that is 3 feet
     long and 4 feet wide.

MORE
HELP

See 263

(A) 12 ft   (B) 12 ft²   (C) 14 ft   (D) 14 ft²

The answer must be a unit of area like square
inches (in.²) or square feet (ft²). Choices A and C
cannot be correct because feet (ft) is a unit of
length. Multiply 3 ft × 4 ft to get 12 ft².

⭐ **ANSWER: B**

Tips for "Explain-Your-Thinking" Tests

When you have to explain your answer, include everything you think will help the teacher understand your thinking.

PROBLEM: A clerk has made a display of cans. The display has 1 can on the top, 2 cans in the next row, 3 cans in the third row, and so on. The display has 10 rows. How many cans are in the display?

1. First, you can draw a diagram to help you understand what the problem looks like. You may discover a pattern.

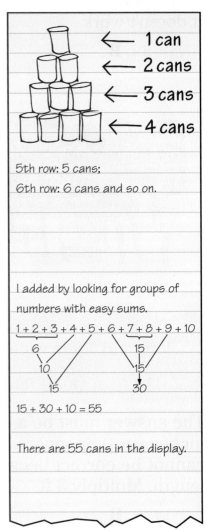

← 1 can
← 2 cans
← 3 cans
←4 cans

2. Each row has 1 more can than the row on top of it. The fifth row will have 5 cans. The sixth row will have 6 cans.

5th row: 5 cans;
6th row: 6 cans and so on.

3. So, for 10 rows, you can add:
$1 + 2 + 3 + 4 + 5 + 6 + 7 + 8 + 9 + 10$.

I added by looking for groups of numbers with easy sums.

$1 + 2 + 3 + 4 + 5 + 6 + 7 + 8 + 9 + 10$

6
10
15
15
15
30

$15 + 30 + 10 = 55$

4. After solving the problem, use the original question to write your answer.

There are 55 cans in the display.

Tips for Short-Answer or Fill-In Problems

- Do exactly what the directions tell you to do.

- Be very careful with your computation. You may not get any credit even if you are just a little off.

- If you are asked for a diagram, make sure you draw the diagram.

- Be sure to label your answer, if necessary (in., ft, and so on).

MORE
HELP
See 176,
77, 82,
220, 27,
433, 262

Problem	Solution	Answer
A. $9 \times 346 =$ _____	$\begin{array}{r} 346 \\ \times\ \ 9 \\ \hline 3114 \end{array}$	3114
B. $72 \div \blacksquare = 12$	$\blacksquare = 6$ because $12 \times 6 = 72$	6
C. Draw two diagrams to show that $\frac{3}{4}$ and $\frac{6}{8}$ are equivalent fractions.	Draw a circle and divide it into fourths. Shade to show $\frac{3}{4}$. Draw another circle the same size and divide it into eighths. Shade to show $\frac{6}{8}$.	
D. Compare. Write $>$ or $<$. 2.23 _____ 2.3	$2.3 = 2.30$, and $2.23 < 2.30$	$<$
E. Complete. 15 ft = $\blacksquare$ yd	Think: 3 ft = 1 yd So, $15 \div 3 = 5$.	5
F. Find the perimeter. 4 in. 6 in. 6 in. 9 in.	Add to find the perimeter. $6 + 4 + 6 + 9 = 25$ Include the unit of measurement in your answer.	25 in.

Using a Calculator

Using a Calculator to Compute

Calculators can compute, but they can't think. The calculator doesn't know if you pressed a wrong key. It will give an answer anyway!

Use your calculator as a tool to help you solve problems. But you have to decide when to use it. And you have to decide whether the answer it shows makes sense.

The keys you use to add ☐+☐, subtract ☐-☐, multiply ☐×☐, or divide ☐÷☐ are often placed together along the right side of a calculator. The equal sign ☐=☐ is usually near these keys.

The number keys are usually in the center of the calculator.

Using a Calculator to Compute with Whole Numbers and Decimals

EXAMPLE 1: Add. $73 + 96 =$ ■

| 7 | 3 | + | 9 | 6 | = | *169.* |

⭐ **ANSWER:** $73 + 96 = 169$

EXAMPLE 2: Subtract. $8 - 2.65 =$ ■

| 8 | − | 2 | . | 6 | 5 | = | *5.35* |

⭐ **ANSWER:** $8 - 2.65 = 5.35$

EXAMPLE 3: Multiply. $9 \times 216 =$ ■

| 9 | × | 2 | 1 | 6 | = | *1944.* |

⭐ **ANSWER:** $9 \times 216 = 1944$

EXAMPLE 4: Divide. $21 \div 4 =$ ■

ONE WAY Use your calculator to get a decimal quotient.

| 2 | 1 | ÷ | 4 | = | *5.25* |

If you need to find the answer with a remainder, use the whole number part of the quotient: 5. Think $5 \times 4 = 20$, so the remainder is 1. The answer with a remainder is 5 R1.

ANOTHER WAY Some calculators have a key that shows the remainder as a whole number instead of as a decimal. The key may look like INT÷ .

| 2 | 1 | INT÷ | 4 | = | *Q5 R1* |

The Q shows that the whole number part of the quotient is 5. The R shows that the remainder is 1.

⭐ **ANSWER:** The quotient can be written as 5.25 or 5 R1.

Using a Calculator to Compute with Money

You can use a calculator to compute with money amounts. Just think of the money amounts as decimals on your calculator. If you are recording your answer, remember to write the dollar sign.

MORE HELP
See 26

EXAMPLE 1: Add. $10.84 + $6.26 = ■

| 1 | 0 | . | 8 | 4 | + | 6 | . | 2 | 6 | = | *17.1* |

Notice that the answer does not look like a money amount because it doesn't have a hundredths place. But remember, 17.1 = 17.10. So, write the answer as $17.10.

★ **ANSWER:** $10.84 + $6.26 = $17.10

EXAMPLE 2: Subtract. $5.00 − $0.98 = ■

| 5 | − | . | 9 | 8 | = | *4.02* |

For $5.00, you only have to press 5 . However, if you press 5 . 0 0 instead, that is all right.

Also you do not have to press 0 for $0.98. However, pressing that key is all right, too.

★ **ANSWER:** $5.00 − $0.98 = $4.02

MATH ALERT

What Happens When a Number Won't Fit on the Display?

Sometimes a number has more digits than the calculator display will hold. Your calculator might handle this problem in different ways. Don't be alarmed. You have not broken your calculator!

Another Use for the Equals Key

You can use the $=$ key to add or subtract the same number. Just press $=$ as many times as you want to add or subtract the number. The display will change by the same amount each time you press the key.

> Some calculators have a constant key to do this. Check your calculator.

EXAMPLE 1: Find $7 + 4 + 4 + 4$.

| 7 | + | 4 | = | = | = | 19 |

★ ANSWER: $7 + 4 + 4 + 4 = 19$

EXAMPLE 2: Find $58 - 6 - 6 - 6 - 6$.

| 5 | 8 | − | 6 | = | = | = | = | 34 |

★ ANSWER: $58 - 6 - 6 - 6 - 6 = 34$

You can also use the $=$ key to divide by the same number.

EXAMPLE 3: Find $400 \div 2 \div 2 \div 2 \div 2$.

| 4 | 0 | 0 | ÷ | 2 | = | = | = | = | 25 |

★ ANSWER: $400 \div 2 \div 2 \div 2 \div 2 = 25$

The rule is a little different for multiplication. When the same number is used as a factor several times, you must enter that number first.

EXAMPLE 4: Find $25 \times 2 \times 2 \times 2 \times 2$.

| 2 | × | 2 | 5 | = | = | = | = | 400 |

★ ANSWER: $25 \times 2 \times 2 \times 2 \times 2 = 400$

Order of Operations on the Calculator

MORE
HELP
See 253

Some calculators automatically follow the rules for order of operations. Other calculators carry out operations in the order that you enter them, even if that order is different from the rules.

You can check your calculator for order of operations by using $6 + 3 \times 2$.

Press 6 + 3 × 2 =

If your display shows [12.], your calculator uses order of operations. If it shows [18.], it doesn't.

It is important to know whether your calculator uses the order of operations. If it does not, you have to enter the calculations in the correct order.

EXAMPLE: Calculate $6 + 3 \times 2$ using a calculator that does not use the order of operations.

 ONE WAY Enter the operations according to the order of operations.

3 × 2 + 6 = 12.

ANOTHER WAY Use grouping symbols.

6 + (3 × 2) = 12.

When you enter (, the calculator waits until you enter) before calculating what's between those grouping symbols.

★ **ANSWER:** $6 + 3 \times 2 = 12$

Fractions on the Calculator

ONE WAY Some calculators have special keys for fractions.

MORE HELP See 221, 218

To show $\frac{2}{3}$, press $\boxed{2}$ $\boxed{/}$ $\boxed{3}$ $\boxed{2/3}$

To simplify $\frac{3}{6}$, press $\boxed{3}$ $\boxed{/}$ $\boxed{6}$ $\boxed{\text{simp}}$ $\boxed{=}$ $\boxed{1/2.}$

To show $\frac{5}{4}$ as a mixed number, press

$\boxed{5}$ $\boxed{/}$ $\boxed{4}$ $\boxed{\text{Ab/c}}$ $\boxed{1u1/4.}$

To show $1\frac{2}{5}$, press $\boxed{1}$ $\boxed{\text{Unit}}$ $\boxed{2}$ $\boxed{/}$ $\boxed{5}$ $\boxed{1u2/5.}$

> The u separates the whole number part from the fraction part of the number.

EXAMPLE 1: Subtract. $2\frac{3}{4} - 1\frac{1}{8} = \blacksquare$

$\boxed{2}$ $\boxed{\text{Unit}}$ $\boxed{3}$ $\boxed{/}$ $\boxed{4}$ $\boxed{-}$ $\boxed{1}$ $\boxed{\text{Unit}}$ $\boxed{1}$ $\boxed{/}$ $\boxed{8}$ $\boxed{=}$ $\boxed{1u5/8.}$

⭐ **ANSWER:** $2\frac{3}{4} - 1\frac{1}{8} = 1\frac{5}{8}$

ANOTHER WAY Even if your calculator doesn't have special keys for fractions, you can still use it to compute with fractions. Just enter each fraction as the numerator divided by the denominator. And don't forget to use grouping symbols. Your answer will be a decimal.

> If your answer must be a fraction, you may not want to use your calculator in this way.

EXAMPLE 2: Add. $\frac{2}{5} + \frac{3}{8} = \blacksquare$

$\boxed{(}$ $\boxed{2}$ $\boxed{\div}$ $\boxed{5}$ $\boxed{)}$ $\boxed{+}$ $\boxed{(}$ $\boxed{3}$ $\boxed{\div}$ $\boxed{8}$ $\boxed{)}$ $\boxed{=}$ $\boxed{0.775}$

⭐ **ANSWER:** $\frac{2}{5} + \frac{3}{8} = 0.775$

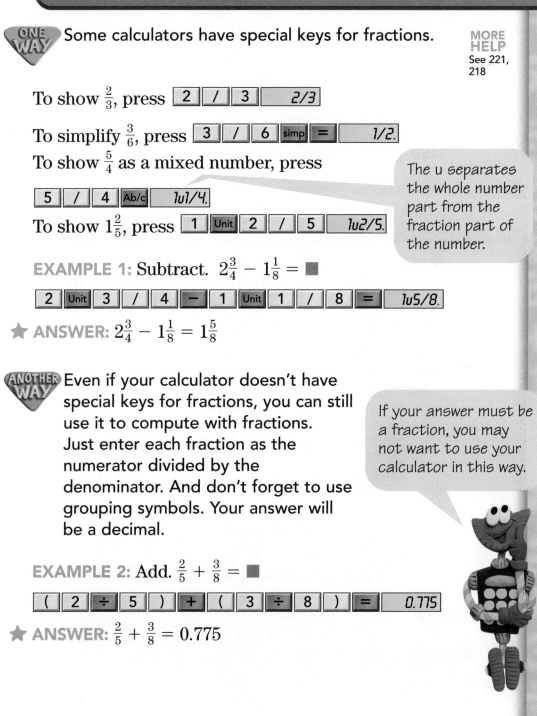

Geometry and Measurement Tools

Using Rulers

A **ruler** is a strip of wood, metal, or plastic with a straight edge. It is used to measure lengths in customary units or metric units. You can also use a ruler's edge to draw lines.

Some rulers show inches on one side and centimeters on the other side

Customary Units

This is 1 in.

Metric Units

This is 1 mm.

This is 1 cm.

Sometimes a ruler for measuring millimeters and centimeters will have mm written in the corner. Don't be confused—the numbers are for counting cm!

You can measure an object to the nearest inch, $\frac{1}{2}$-inch, $\frac{1}{4}$-inch, or $\frac{1}{8}$-inch. It depends on how close you need to be.

MORE
HELP
See 220

Line up the zero mark of the ruler with the left edge of the object. The zero mark may not be labeled. It's the first mark, or the left edge of the ruler.

Read the length at the right-edge of the object.

- You can say the leaf is 4 in. long, measured to the nearest inch.
- You can say the leaf is $4\frac{1}{2}$ in. long, measured to the nearest $\frac{1}{2}$-inch.
- You can say the leaf is $4\frac{3}{8}$ in. long, measured to the nearest $\frac{1}{8}$-inch.

If the object you want to measure is longer than the ruler, you can use a longer ruler or a tape measure, or you can measure this way.

Notice where the end of the ruler is on the object. Then move the beginning of the ruler to that point. It is important not to leave gaps when you place the ruler down again. The rope is 2 feet 8 inches long.

Using a Compass

You can use a tool called a **compass** to make a circle.

ONE WAY You can use a safety compass.

MORE
HELP
See 316

1 Place the center of the large open circle where you want the center of your circle to be.

2 Move the inner part of the compass and place your pencil so that you have the radius that you want.

3 Hold the center point steady. Spin the pencil around to make the circle.

ANOTHER WAY You can use a compass that has a sharp point at one end and a pencil at the other end.

❶ Place the sharp point where you want the center of your circle to be.

❷ Open the compass to the radius you want.

❸ Hold the sharp end steady. Spin the pencil around to make the circle.

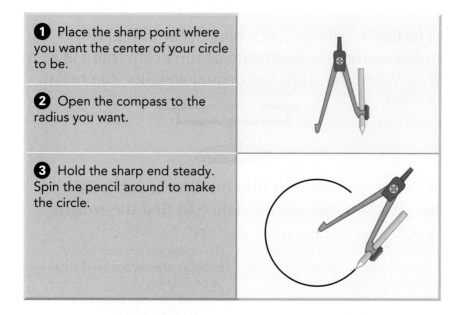

Using Balances and Scales

Balances and scales are tools used for weighing.

A **balance** usually has a beam that is supported in the center. On each side of the beam there is a tray. When the trays hold equal weights, the beam is level.

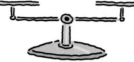

Suppose you want to find out how much a fish weighs. You can use a balance to find the weight.

If you place the fish on one side of the balance, the side with the fish will tip down. You try to balance the fish by putting weights on the other tray.	If the weights are not heavy enough, the balance will stay tipped down.
If the weights are too heavy, the side with the weights will tip down.	The beam will balance (or be straight) when the weights match the weight of the fish.

The fish weighs 1 pound 5 ounces.

A **scale** is also used for weighing.

You can read the weight of an object directly from the scale. The display can be **digital**, or it can be **graduated**, like a ruler.

The scale shows that the person weighs 89 pounds.

This person weighs 75 pounds.

Some people have smaller scales in their homes. They often use these scales to weigh items such as food. These scales can either be digital or graduated.

The pear weighs 5 ounces.

Drawing Solid Figures

Drawing Cubes

You can use squared paper to help you draw a cube.

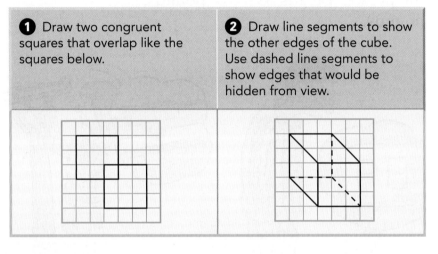

1 Draw two congruent squares that overlap like the squares below.

2 Draw line segments to show the other edges of the cube. Use dashed line segments to show edges that would be hidden from view.

Drawing Rectangular Prisms

You can use squared paper to help you draw a rectangular prism.

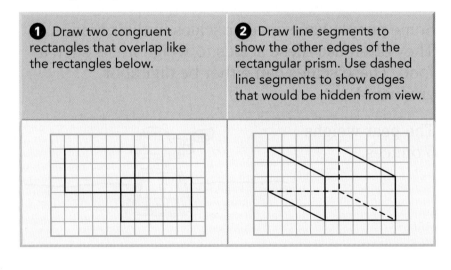

1 Draw two congruent rectangles that overlap like the rectangles below.

2 Draw line segments to show the other edges of the rectangular prism. Use dashed line segments to show edges that would be hidden from view.

MORE HELP
See 328

Drawing Pyramids

You can use squared paper to help you draw
a pyramid.

1 Draw a square and a point like the ones below.

2 Connect each corner of the square to the point above the square. Use dashed line segments for the edges that would be hidden from view.

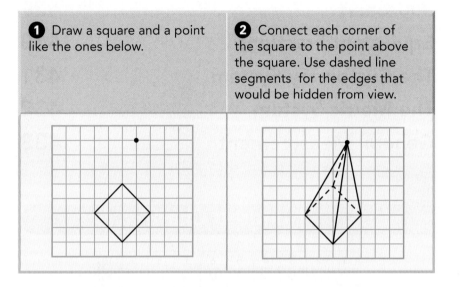

Drawing Cylinders

You can use squared paper to help you draw
a cylinder.

1 Draw two ovals like the ones below.

2 Connect the ovals. Use dashes to show the part of the oval that would be hidden from view.

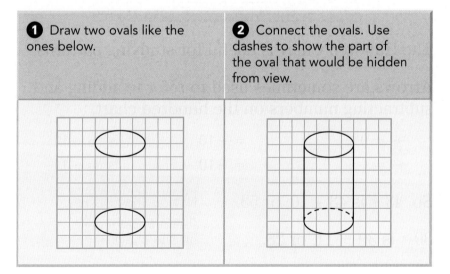

Handy Charts and Tables

Hundred Chart

1	2	3	4	5	6	7	8	9	10
11	12	13	14	15	16	17	18	19	20
21	22	23	24	25	26	27	28	29	30
31	32	33	34	35	36	37	38	39	40
41	42	43	44	45	46	47	48	49	50
51	52	53	54	55	56	57	58	59	60
61	62	63	64	65	66	67	68	69	70
71	72	73	74	75	76	77	78	79	80
81	82	83	84	85	86	87	88	89	90
91	92	93	94	95	96	97	98	99	100

The Hundred Chart is useful for studying patterns.

Arrows are sometimes used to refer to adding and subtracting numbers on the hundred chart.

$\rightarrow$ = +1 $\downarrow$ = +10 $\searrow$ = +11

$\leftarrow$ = −1 $\uparrow$ = −10 $\nwarrow$ = −11

So, 43 $\downarrow$ is 43 + 10, or 53.

39 $\nwarrow$ is 39 − 11, or 28.

Notice that 53 is directly below 43 on the chart.

300 Chart

1	2	3	4	5	6	7	8	9	10
11	12	13	14	15	16	17	18	19	20
21	22	23	24	25	26	27	28	29	30
31	32	33	34	35	36	37	38	39	40
41	42	43	44	45	46	47	48	49	50
51	52	53	54	55	56	57	58	59	60
61	62	63	64	65	66	67	68	69	70
71	72	73	74	75	76	77	78	79	80
81	82	83	84	85	86	87	88	89	90
91	92	93	94	95	96	97	98	99	100
101	102	103	104	105	106	107	108	109	110
111	112	113	114	115	116	117	118	119	120
121	122	123	124	125	126	127	128	129	130
131	132	133	134	135	136	137	138	139	140
141	142	143	144	145	146	147	148	149	150
151	152	153	154	155	156	157	158	159	160
161	162	163	164	165	166	167	168	169	170
171	172	173	174	175	176	177	178	179	180
181	182	183	184	185	186	187	188	189	190
191	192	193	194	195	196	197	198	199	200
201	202	203	204	205	206	207	208	209	210
211	212	213	214	215	216	217	218	219	220
221	222	223	224	225	226	227	228	229	230
231	232	233	234	235	236	237	238	239	240
241	242	243	244	245	246	247	248	249	250
251	252	253	254	255	256	257	258	259	260
261	262	263	264	265	266	267	268	269	270
271	272	273	274	275	276	277	278	279	280
281	282	283	284	285	286	287	288	289	290
291	292	293	294	295	296	297	298	299	300

Equivalent Fractions

You can use this chart to help find equivalent fractions. For example, to find an equivalent fraction for $\frac{4}{5}$, line up the edge of piece of paper with the end of the fourth $\frac{1}{5}$ bar.

The paper should also line up with the end of the eighth $\frac{1}{10}$ bar. So, $\frac{4}{5}$ is equivalent to $\frac{8}{10}$.

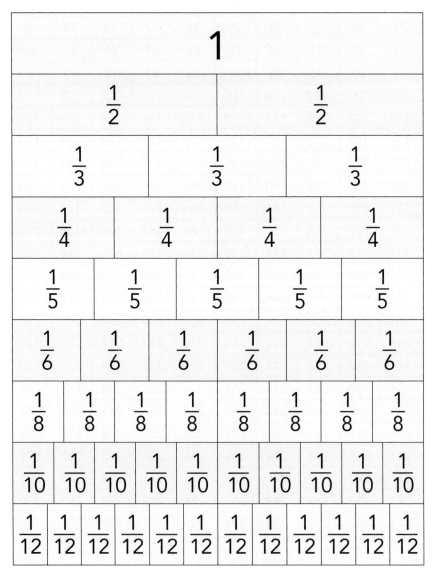

The Customary System

Linear Measure (length)

1 inch		2.54 centimeters
1 foot	12 inches	0.3048 meter
1 yard	3 feet	0.9144 meter
1 mile	5280 feet	1609.3 meters

Square Measure (area)

1 square ft	144 square in.	929.0304 square cm
1 square yd	9 square ft	0.837 square m
1 acre	43,560 square ft	4051.08 square m

Dry Measure (capacity, volume)

1 pint		33.60 cubic in.	0.5505 liter
1 quart	2 pints	67.20 cubic in.	1.1012 liters
1 peck	16 pints	537.61 cubic in.	8.8096 liters
1 bushel	64 pints	2150.42 cubic in.	35.2383 liters

Liquid Measure

1 cup	8 fluid ounces	14.438 cubic in.	0.2366 liter
1 pint	16 fluid ounces	28.875 cubic in.	0.4732 liter
1 quart	32 fluid ounces	57.75 cubic in.	0.9463 liter
1 gallon	128 fluid ounces	231 cubic in.	3.7853 liters

Weight (avoirdupois)

1 ounce	0.0625 pound	28.3495 grams
1 pound	16 ounces	453.59 grams
1 ton	2000 pounds	907.18 kilograms

Time

60 seconds	1 minute	168 hours	1 week
60 minutes	1 hour	12 months	1 year
24 hours	1 day	52 weeks	1 year
7 days	1 week	365.25 days	1 year

The Metric System

Linear Measure (length)

1 centimeter	0.01 meter	0.3937 inch
1 decimeter	0.1 meter	3.937 inches
1 meter		39.37 inches
1 dekameter	10 meters	32.8 feet
1 hectometer	100 meters	328 feet
1 kilometer	1000 meters	0.621 mile

Capacity Measure

1 centiliter	0.01 liter	0.338 fluid ounces
1 deciliter	0.1 liter	3.38 fluid ounces
1 liter		1.056 quarts
1 dekaliter	10 liters	2.642 gallons
1 hectoliter	100 liters	26.42 gallons
1 kiloliter	1000 liters	264.2 gallons

Volume Measure

1 cubic cm	1000 cubic mm	0.06102 cubic in.
1 cubic dm	1000 cubic cm	61.02 cubic in.
1 cubic m	1000 cubic dm	35.31 cubic ft

Mass

1 centigram	0.01 gram	0.0003527 ounce
1 decigram	0.1 gram	0.003527 ounce
1 gram	10 decigrams	0.03527 ounce
1 dekagram	10 grams	0.3527 ounce
1 hectogram	100 grams	3.527 ounces
1 kilogram	1000 grams	2.2046 pounds
1 metric ton	1,000,000 grams	2204.6 pounds

General Measurement

Benchmark Measures

1 inch	≈	distance from the tip of your thumb to the first joint
1 centimeter	≈	width of the tip of your index finger
1 foot	≈	length of your notebook
1 kilogram	≈	mass of your math textbook
1 minute	≈	time it takes to count to 60 saying *one thousand* between each number
1 pound	≈	weight of a loaf of bread
1 ounce	≈	weight of a slice of bread
1 gram	≈	mass of a paper clip

Common Abbreviations

c	cup	mg	milligram
cm	centimeter	mi	mile
d	day	min	minute
dm	decimeter	mL	milliliter
fl oz	fluid ounce	mm	millimeter
ft	foot	mo	month
gal	gallon	oz	ounce
g	gram	pt	pint
h	hour	qt	quart
in.	inch	s	second
kg	kilogram	t	ton
L	liter	wk	week
lb	pound	yd	yard
m	meter	y	year

Conversion Factors

to change	multiply by	to change	multiply by
cm to in.	0.3939	in. to cm	2.54
m to yd	1.0936	yd to m	0.9144
km to mi	0.6214	mi to km	1.6093
L to gal	0.2642	gal to L	3.7853
kg to lb	2.2046	lb to kg	0.4536

Maps

Latitude, Longitude, and Hemispheres

The **equator** divides the earth into two **hemispheres**, the northern hemisphere and the southern hemisphere.

The **prime meridian** extends from north to south and passes through Greenwich, England.

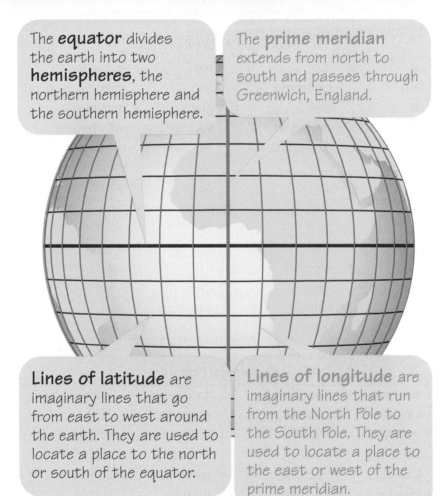

Lines of latitude are imaginary lines that go from east to west around the earth. They are used to locate a place to the north or south of the equator.

Lines of longitude are imaginary lines that run from the North Pole to the South Pole. They are used to locate a place to the east or west of the prime meridian.

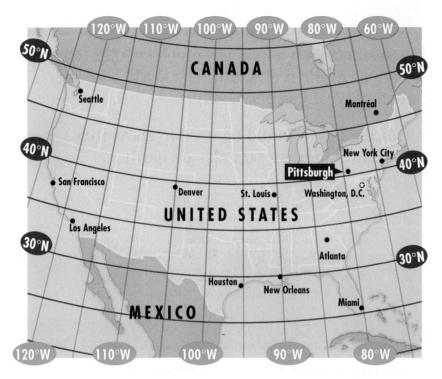

Both latitude and longitude are measured in degrees. Latitude numbers may be printed along the left- and right-hand sides of a map. Longitude numbers may be printed at the top and bottom of a map.

MORE
HELP
See
258–259

Two street names can be used to identify an intersection in a city. In a similar way, latitude and longitude can be used together to locate any point on earth.

EXAMPLE: Use the map above to locate Pittsburgh.

Pittsburg is near the east coast of the United States.

⭐ **ANSWER:** Pittsburgh lies near the 40° north line of latitude and the 80° west line of longitude.

Scale of Miles

The distances on a map are much smaller than the distances in the real world. The **scale** shows you how far it really is between places.

The scale below could be used to show that 1 inch on a map stands for 60 miles on earth.

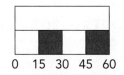

0   15   30   45   60

1 inch equals 60 miles.

Compass Rose

A **compass rose** shows you which way is north on the map. On most maps, north is at the top. When north is at the top, east is to the right, west is to the left, and south is to the bottom.

If a map does not show any compass rose, you can assume north is at the top.

Project Ideas

Math Fair Topics

- Explore Fibonacci numbers in nature.

- Investigate different types of knots.

- Investigate ancient number systems. Discuss advantages and disadvantages.

- Investigate ancient timekeeping devices. Make a sundial or a water clock.

- Investigate whether two different figures can be twisted, stretched, or squished to make the same shape.

- Find the perimeter and area of a local park.

- Conduct experiments about chance and compare probabilities.

- Make a scale model of a famous building.

- Make an abacus and explain how to use it.

- Identify common solid figures in the real world.

- Investigate different designs using patterns and geometric shapes.

- Make a compass rose and explain how to use it.

Collecting Data

Here are some ideas for topics you might use to collect data. You can make a graph to show your data.

Single Bar Graphs and Pictographs
- Favorite wild animal from a list of several
- Favorite types of books or movies

Double Bar Graphs
- The cost of several items at two grocery stores
- Video game scores of two players for several games

Line Graphs
- High or low daily temperatures
- Temperatures taken each hour during school time

Circle Graphs
- How you spent your day
- Favorite colors

Stem-and-Leaf Plots
- Number of students in each class in your school
- Number of minutes students spent on homework (or watching television) on a certain day

Line Plots
- Heights of students
- Number of letters in the first or last names of students
- Number of pets in a family

Venn Diagrams
- Number of students who are wearing red and/or blue
- Number of students with brothers and/or sisters

Number Systems

Roman Numerals

The Romans used numerals that are still used today. They are often used in movie credits or on clocks.

I	1	VIII	8	XXV	25	D	500
II	2	IX	9	XL	40	M	1000
III	3	X	10	XLV	45	$\overline{V}$	5000
IV	4	XI	11	L	50	$\overline{X}$	10,000
V	5	XII	12	LX	60	$\overline{L}$	50,000
VI	6	XIX	19	XC	90	$\overline{C}$	100,000
VII	7	XX	20	C	100	$\overline{D}$	500,000

The Romans didn't use place value. But they did use addition and subtraction in their number system.

The symbol for 26 is XXVI (10 + 10 + 5 + 1).

No letter is used more than three times. So, after a letter is repeated three times, use subtraction to write the next numeral. When a symbol for a smaller number is to the left of another symbol, it means to subtract.

XC = 100 − 10 = 90

Here's how to write our 1469.

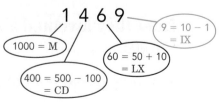

1469 = MCDLXIX

Babylonian Numerals

Over 5000 years ago, the Babylonians had a number system based on 60. It is called **Babylonian cuneiform**. They used these numerals.

∨ 1	∨∨∨∨ 4	∨∨∨∨ ∨∨∨ 7	< 10
∨∨ 2	∨∨∨ ∨∨ 5	∨∨∨∨ ∨∨∨∨ 8	∀ 60
∨∨∨ 3	∨∨∨ ∨∨∨ 6	∨ ∨∨∨∨ ∨∨∨∨ 9	

Like the Romans, the Babylonians did not use place value. So, the number we write as 82 would have been written like this: ∀ << ∨∨

Hindu Numerals

The Hindus in ancient India used nine number symbols. They could write any number using these symbols.

९ 1	୪ 4	ෙ 7
∠ 2	⅄ 5	Ζ 8
३ 3	ૐ 6	Ɛ 9

Early in their history the Hindus would write Ɛ ९ for 901.

Later they invented a zero and wrote Ɛ · ९ for 901.

You can see place value in these numerals! This is like the place value in our number system.

Yellow Pages

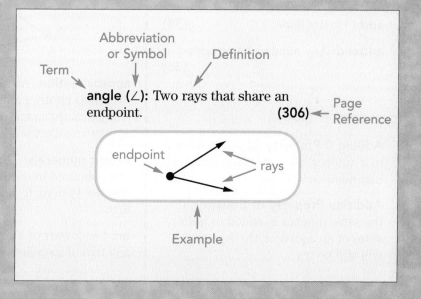

Term → **angle** (∠): Two rays that share an endpoint. **(306)**

Abbreviation or Symbol ↓

Definition

Page Reference

endpoint → • ⟨ rays

Example

A

acute angle: An angle with a measure less than 90°. **(308)**

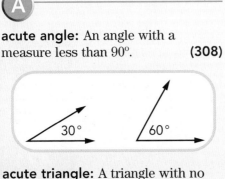

acute triangle: A triangle with no angle measuring 90° or greater. **(314)**

add (+): Combine. **(34)**

addend: Any number being added. **(36)**

$$5 + 3 + 2 = 10$$
addend   addend   addend

Adding 0 Property: If you add zero to a number, the sum is the same as that number. $5 + 0 = 5$ **(246)**

Addition Property of Equality: If the same number is added to both sides of an equation, the equation will still be true.

$5 + 2 = 7$

$5 + 2 + 3 = 7 + 3$

⦅10⦆   ⦅10⦆ **(248)**

addition sentence: An equation which shows a sum. $20 + 31 = 51$ **(36)**

algebra: A branch of mathematics that uses variables to express rules about numbers, number relationships, and operations. **(237)**

algebraic: Of or relating to algebra. **(237)**

algorithm: A step-by-step method for computing.

A.M.: Ante-meridian, which means before midday. Morning. 7:00 A.M. means 7 o'clock in the morning. **(337)**

angle (∠): Two rays that share an endpoint. **(306)**

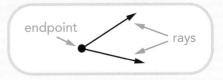

approximation: An amount that describes another amount without being exactly equal to it. 8 is an approximation for 8.2.

Arabic numerals: The number symbols used in our base-ten number system: 0, 1, 2, 3, 4, 5, 6, 7, 8, 9.

arc (⌒): Part of a curve between any two of its points.

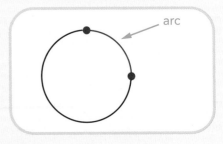

area (A): The measure, in square units, of the inside of a plane figure. The area of this rectangle is 6 square units. **(350)**

arithmetic: Calculation using addition, subtraction, multiplication, and division. **(33)**

array: An arrangement of objects in equal rows. **(61)**

Associative Property of Addition: *See Grouping Property of Addition*

Associative Property of Multiplication: *See Grouping Property of Multiplication*

average: A single number that gives an idea about all the numbers in a set. Usually, the average is the mean, but sometimes it is the median or the mode. *See also mean, median, mode* **(284)**

axes: Plural of *axis*. **(280)**

axis: A reference line from which distances or angles are measured in a coordinate grid. *See also horizontal axis, vertical axis* **(280)**

B

balance scale: A tool used for comparing the mass or weight of objects. **(424)**

bar graph: A graph that uses the height or length of rectangles to compare data. **(273)**

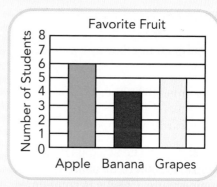

base of an exponent: The number to be raised to a power.
base $\rightarrow 5^2 \leftarrow$ exponent **(98)**

base of a solid figure: A special face of a solid figure. **(327)**

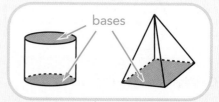

base ten: A number system in which each place has ten times the value of the next place to its right. **(5)**

billion: One thousand millions, written 1,000,000,000, or 10^9. *See thousand, million* **(11)**

C

calendar: A table showing a period of time organized into days, weeks, and months. **(341)**

capacity: The greatest amount that a container can hold. **(356)**

cardinal number: A whole number that names *how many objects* are in a group.

There are 6 cats in the house.
↑
cardinal number

Arthur is 6th in line.
↑
not a cardinal number

Celsius (C): The scale used in the metric system to measure temperature. Celsius is sometimes called Centigrade. **(361)**

center: A point that is the same distance from all points on a circle or a sphere. **(316)**

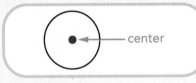

Centigrade: *See Celsius*

centimeter (cm): A metric unit of length equal to 0.01 ($\frac{1}{100}$) of a meter. **(347)**

certain event: Something that will *definitely* happen. An event with a probability of 1. If you have a bag filled with only green marbles, picking a green marble is a certain event. **(292)**

change: The amount of money returned when the amount paid for a purchase is greater than the total amount of the purchase. **(20)**

chord: A line segment that joins any two points on a circle.

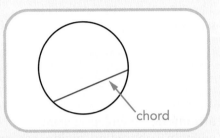

circle: A plane figure with all points the same distance from a fixed point called the *center*. **(316)**

circle graph: A graph that is used to show how parts make up a whole. **(282)**

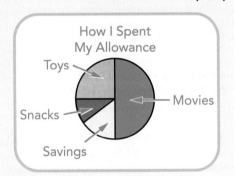

circumference (C): The distance around a circle.

clockwise: In the direction that the hands of a clock rotate. **(319)**

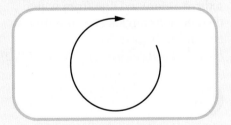

closed figure: A plane figure that completely surrounds an area. **(310)**

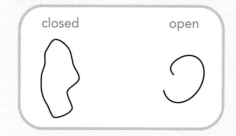

clustered: Grouped together. This data is clustered around 3 and 9. **(272)**

common: Shared; same. **(94)**

common denominator: For two or more fractions, a common denominator is a common multiple of the denominators. A common denominator for $\frac{2}{3}$ and $\frac{3}{4}$ is 12. **(222)**

common factor: A number that is a factor of two or more numbers. Common factors of 12 and 20 are 1, 2, and 4. *See also factor* **(94)**

common multiple: A number that is a multiple of two or more numbers. The numbers 12, 24, and 36 are some of the common multiples of 3 and 4. *See also multiple* **(95)**

Commutative Property of Addition: *See Order Property of Addition*

Commutative Property of Multiplication: *See Order Property of Multiplication*

compass: A tool used to draw a circle. **(422)**

compass rose: A mark on a map that shows direction, usually north. **(436)**

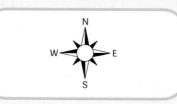

compatible numbers: A pair of numbers that are easy to work with mentally. Also called "friendly numbers." The numbers 150 and 5 are compatible numbers for estimating 148 ÷ 5. **(138)**

composite number: A number greater than 0 that has more than two different factors. The number 9 is a composite number because it has three factors: 1, 3, and 9. **(93)**

computation: The process of computing. **(145)**

compute: To find a numerical result, usually by adding, subtracting, multiplying, or dividing. **(145)**

cone: A 3-dimensional figure with one curved surface, one flat surface (usually circular), and one vertex. **(329)**

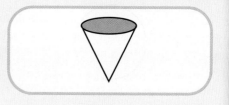

congruent: Having exactly the same size and shape. **(317)**

446

congruent figures: Figures with the same size and shape. These rectangles are congruent. **(317)**

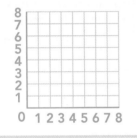

consecutive: In order, with none missing. 4, 5, 6 are consecutive whole numbers.

coordinate grid: A 2-dimensional system in which a location is described by its distance from two perpendicular lines called axes. **(258)**

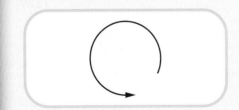

coordinate plane: *See coordinate grid*

counterclockwise: In a direction opposite to the direction that the hands of a clock rotate. **(319)**

counting numbers: 1, 2, 3, and so on.

cube (solid figure): A regular solid with six congruent square faces. **(330)**

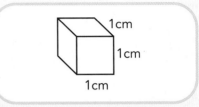

cube of a number: The third power of a number. 1000 is the cube of ten because $10 \times 10 \times 10 = 1000$. **(98)**

cubic unit: A unit, such as a cubic centimeter or cubic inch, used to measure volume. **(354)**

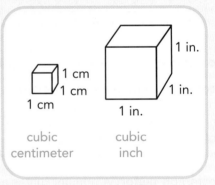

cubic centimeter   cubic inch

cup (c): A customary unit of capacity equal to 8 fluid ounces. **(356)**

currency: The official money issued by a government.

customary system: A system of measurement used in the U.S. The system includes units for measuring length, capacity, weight, and temperature. Feet, ounces, and gallons are examples of customary units of measure. **(431)**

cylinder: A 3-dimensional figure with two circular bases that are parallel and congruent. **(326)**

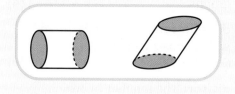

D

data: Information, especially numerical information. **(266)**

date: A way to refer to a specific day, week, and year. August 9, 2001 and 8/9/01 are dates. **(341)**

decagon: A polygon with ten sides. **(311)**

decimal number: A number containing a decimal point. **(22)**

decimal point: A dot separating the ones and tenths places in a decimal number. **(22)**

decimeter: A metric unit of length equal to 0.1 ($\frac{1}{10}$) of a meter. **(347)**

degree (angle measure): A unit for measuring angles. **(307)**

degree Celsius (°C): The metric unit of measurement for temperature. **(361)**

degree Centigrade (°C): *See degree Celsius*

degree Fahrenheit (°F): The customary unit of measurement for temperature. *See also Fahrenheit* **(360)**

denominator: The quantity below the line in a fraction. It tells how many equal parts are in the whole. In the fraction $\frac{3}{5}$, the denominator is 5. **(210)**

diagonal: A line segment that joins two vertices of a polygon but is not a side of the polygon. $\overline{AC}$ and $\overline{BD}$ are diagonals of rectangle *ABCD*. **(322)**

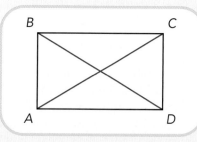

diagram: A drawing that shows a mathematical situation. **(269)**

diameter (d): A chord that goes through the center of a circle. **(316)**

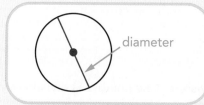

difference: The amount that remains after one quantity is subtracted from another. **(48)**

$$
\begin{array}{rl}
89 & \leftarrow \text{minuend} \\
-46 & \leftarrow \text{subtrahend} \\
\hline
43 & \leftarrow \text{difference}
\end{array}
$$

digit: Any one of these ten symbols: 0, 1, 2, 3, 4, 5, 6, 7, 8, or 9. **(2)**

dimension: Measurement in one direction. A figure with one dimension has a length, but no area or volume. A figure with two dimensions has length and area, but no volume. A figure with three dimensions has length, area, and volume. **(326)**

Distributive Property: When one of the factors of a product is a sum, multiplying each addend before adding does not change the product. **(244)**

$$6 \times (2 + 3) = (6 \times 2) + (6 \times 3)$$

$$6 \times 5 = 30 \qquad 12 + 18 = 30$$

divide (÷): To separate into equal groups and find the number in each group or the number of groups. **(76)**

dividend: A number that is divided by another number. **(76)**

$$6 \div 2 = 3$$

dividend   divisor   quotient

$$\begin{array}{r} 3 \leftarrow \text{quotient} \\ 2\overline{)6} \leftarrow \text{dividend} \end{array}$$

↑
divisor

divisible: One number is divisible by another if the remainder is zero when you divide. The number 8 is divisible by 2 but not by 3. **(206)**

divisibility rules: Patterns that make it easier to tell whether one number is divisible by another. **(206)**

division: The operation of making equal groups and finding the number in each group or the number of groups. **(74)**

division sentence: An equation which shows a quotient.
$60 \div 2 = 30$ **(76)**

divisor: The number by which another number is divided. **(76)**

$$6 \div 2 = 3$$

dividend   divisor   quotient

$$\begin{array}{r} 3 \leftarrow \text{quotient} \\ 2\overline{)6} \leftarrow \text{dividend} \end{array}$$

↑
divisor

dollar: The basic unit of U.S. currency. **(17)**

doubles: An addition fact that has two addends that are the same.
$6 + 6 = 12$ or $8 + 8 = 16$ **(42)**

E

edge: The line segment where two faces of a solid figure meet. A cube has 12 edges. **(327)**

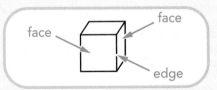

elapsed time: The amount of time that passes between two times. **(338)**

endpoint: A point at either end of a line segment or arc, or a point at one end of a ray. **(305)**

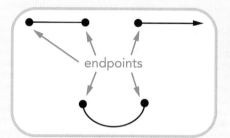

equal (=): Having the same value. **(36)**

Equality Properties of Equations: *See Addition Property of Equality and Multiplication Property of Equality*

equally likely: Having the same chance, or probability. For this spinner, landing on blue and landing on white are equally likely. **(294)**

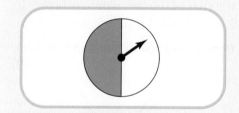

equation: A mathematical sentence with an equals sign. The amount on one side of the equals sign has the same value as the amount on the other side. $5 + 3 = 8$ and $x + 7 = 15$ are equations. **(36)**

equator: An imaginary line dividing the Northern and Southern hemispheres on the earth. The equator has a latitude of 0. **(434)**

equilateral triangle: A triangle with all sides the same length. **(315)**

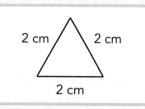

equivalent: Having the same value. Twelve inches and 1 foot are equivalent. **(26)**

equivalent fractions: Fractions that have the same value. $\frac{2}{3}$, $\frac{4}{6}$, and $\frac{10}{15}$ are equivalent fractions. **(220)**

estimate (es' ti mit): A number close to an exact amount; an estimate tells *about* how much or *about* how many. An estimate for the sum of 19 and 48 is 70. **(128)**

estimate (es' ti mate): To find a number close to an exact amount. You can estimate the sum of 19 and 48 by rounding each addend to the nearest ten and then adding the rounded numbers. **(128)**

evaluate: To find the value of a mathematical expression. When you evaluate $2 \times 3 + 4$, you get 10. **(253)**

even number: A whole number that has 2 as a factor. All even numbers end with 0, 2, 4, 6, or 8 and are divisible by 2. Some even numbers are 0, 6, 18, and 42. **(91)**

event: Something you can think of that must happen, may happen, or cannot happen. **(292)**

expanded form: A way to write numbers that shows the place value of each digit. $263 = 200 + 60 + 3$ **(5)**

exponent: The number that tells how many equal factors there are.

base → 10^3 ← exponent

$10^3 = 10 \times 10 \times 10$

10 is a factor 3 times. **(98)**

exponential form: A way of writing a number using exponents. $8 = 2^3$ **(98)**

expression: A variable or combination of variables, numbers, and operation symbols that represents a mathematical relationship. $6, 2 + 3, x, x + 4$, and $x + 2y$ are expressions. **(250)**

F

face: A flat surface on a solid figure. **(327)**

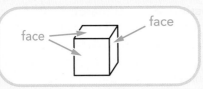

fact family: Number sentences that relate addition and subtraction or multiplication and division. Each number sentence in the fact family has the same numbers. **(54)**

Fact Family

$6 + 8 = 14$ $14 - 6 = 8$

$8 + 6 = 14$ $14 - 8 = 6$

factor: When you multiply two whole numbers to get a given number, then the two whole numbers are factors of the given number. 2 and 8 are factors of 16 because $2 \times 8 = 16$. **(89)**

factor tree: A method used to find the prime factorization of a number. **(96)**

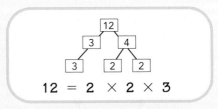

$12 = 2 \times 2 \times 3$

Fahrenheit (F): Temperature scale used in the customary system. **(360)**

favorable outcome: In probability, the outcome you are interested in measuring. It is not necessarily the most likely outcome. Suppose you are tossing a coin. If you want to know the probability of the coin landing heads-up, then heads is the favorable outcome. **(294)**

Fibonacci sequence: A special series of numbers in which each number is the sum of the two numbers before it. 1, 1, 2, 3, 5, 8, 13, ...

figure: A shape in 2 or 3 dimensions. **(310)**

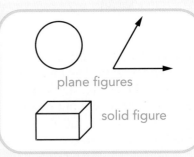

plane figures

solid figure

finite: Countable or measurable. There is a finite number of students enrolled in the school.

flip: A mirror image of a figure on the opposite side of a line. A flip is also called a reflection. (318)

flip

fluid ounce (fl oz): A customary unit of capacity equal to 2 tablespoons. (356)

foot (ft): A customary unit of length equal to 12 inches. (346)

feet (ft): Plural of foot. (346)

formula: A rule that is written as an equation. To find the area of any rectangle, you can multiply its length by its width. You can write this rule as an equation, $A = lw$. (262)

fraction: A way to describe a part of a whole or a part of a group by using equal parts. (210)

$\dfrac{4}{5}$ ← numerator (number of equal parts being described)

← denominator (total number of equal parts in the whole or group)

frequency: The number of times a value occurs in a set of data. (272)

front-end estimate: An estimate made by computing with the digits in the greatest place.

$$\begin{array}{r} 26 \to 20 \\ +37 \to +30 \\ \hline 50 \end{array}$$ ← front-end estimate

(134)

function: A set of ordered pairs such that for any first number (the input) there is only one possible second number (the output). The set of ordered pairs (2, 4), (4, 8) and (6, 12) are a function.

The set of ordered pairs (2, 4), (2, 8), (4, 8) and (4, 16) are *not* a function. (260)

function table: A table that lists pairs of numbers that show a function. *See function* (261)

Input	Output
3	11
6	14
9	17
10	18

G

gallon (gal): A customary unit of capacity equal to 4 quarts. (356)

geometry: The mathematics of the properties and relationships of points, lines, angles, surfaces, and solids. (300)

googol: A number that is written with a 1 followed by 100 zeros.

graduated: Divided into equal intervals. (425)

gram (g): The standard unit of mass in the metric system. The mass of a large paperclip is about 1 gram. (359)

graph: A drawing that shows a relationship between sets of data. *See bar graph, circle graph, line graph, pictograph* (264)

greatest common divisor (GCD):
See greatest common factor

greatest common factor (GCF):
The greatest number that is a factor
of every number in a set of numbers.
3 is the greatest common factor of 9
and 15. **(94)**

grid: A pattern of horizontal and
vertical lines, usually forming squares.

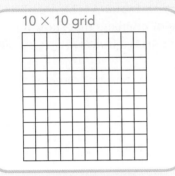

10 × 10 grid

Grouping Property of Addition:
Changing the grouping of three or
more addends does not change
the sum.

$(3 + 4) + 8 = 3 + (4 + 8)$

15   15

(242)

**Grouping Property of
Multiplication:** Changing the
grouping of three or more factors
does not change the product.

$(2 \times 3) \times 4 = 2 \times (3 \times 4)$

24   24

(243)

H

half gallon: A customary unit of
capacity equal to 2 quarts. **(356)**

half hour: 30 minutes. **(335)**

half past: 30 minutes after the hour.
(335)

half turn: A rotation of 180° (or half
of one revolution). **(319)**

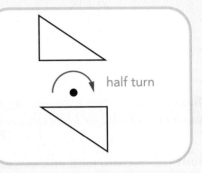

half turn

heptagon: A polygon with
seven sides. **(311)**

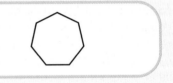

hexagon: A polygon with six sides.
(311)

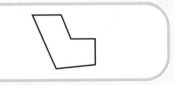

hexagonal prism: A prism with
six-sided bases.

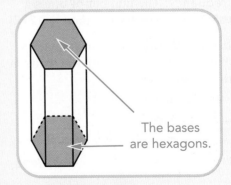

The bases
are hexagons.

highest common factor: *See greatest common factor*

horizontal: Parallel to the horizon. A horizontal line is straight across. **(303)**

horizontal line

horizontal axis: In a coordinate grid, the *x*-axis is the horizontal axis.**(274)**

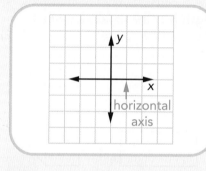

identity element for addition: Zero. *See Identity Property of Addition* **(246)**

identity element for multiplication: One. *See Identity Property of Multiplication* **(246)**

Identity Property of Addition: If you add zero to a number, the sum is the same as that number. $8 + 0 = 8$ **(246)**

Identity Property of Multiplication: If you multiply a number by one, the product is the same as that number. $18 \times 1 = 18$ **(246)**

impossible event: An event with a probability of 0. If you have a bag filled with red and blue marbles, picking a green marble is an impossible event. **(292)**

improper fraction: A fraction with a value greater than 1 that is not written as a mixed number. The numerator of an improper fraction is greater than the denominator. $\frac{8}{2}$ and $\frac{4}{3}$ are improper fractions.

inch (in.): A customary unit of length equal to $\frac{1}{12}$ foot. **(346)**

inequality: A mathematical sentence that compares two amounts using the symbols $<$ or $>$. The sentence $4 + 2 > 4$ is an inequality. **(12)**

infinite: Not countable or measurable. There are an infinite number of whole numbers.

integers: Positive numbers, their opposites, and zero.

$... \ ^{-}3, ^{-}2, ^{-}1, 0, 1, 2, 3 ...$ **(238)**

intersect: To meet or cross. **(303)**

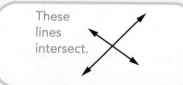

These lines intersect.

irregular polygon: A polygon whose sides are not all the same length or whose angles do not all have the same measure **(311)**

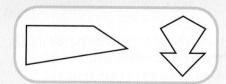

isosceles triangle: A triangle that has exactly two congruent sides. **(315)**

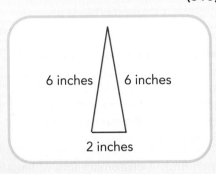

kilogram (kg): A metric unit of mass equal to 1000 grams. **(359)**

kiloliter (kl): A metric unit of capacity equal to 1000 liters. **(357)**

kilometer (km): A metric unit of length equal to 1000 meters. **(347)**

latitude: Distance north or south of the equator. Measured in degrees from 0° at the equator to 90° at each pole. **(434)**

leap year: A year which has 366 days; usually occurs every 4 years. Leap years are years which are multiples of 4, unless the year is a multiple of 100. Then the year must be a multiple of 400. The years 1984 and 2000 are leap years. The years 1999 and 3000 are not leap years. **(344)**

least common denominator (LCD): The least common multiple of the denominators of two or more fractions. The LCD of $\frac{1}{3}$ and $\frac{2}{5}$ is 15.

least common multiple (LCM): The least common multiple of a set of two or more numbers. The LCM of 3 and 5 is 15. **(95)**

length: The distance along a line or figure from one point to another. The length of the line segment is 5 feet. **(345)**

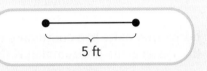

length (l): One dimension of a 2- or 3-dimensional figure. **(262)**

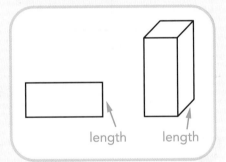

like denominators: *See common denominator*

like fractions: Fractions with a common denominator. $\frac{3}{8}$ and $\frac{7}{8}$ are like fractions. **(222)**

likely event: An event with a probability that is close to 1. If you roll a number cube labeled 1, 2, 3, 4, 5, and 6, rolling a number greater than 1 is a likely event. **(293)**

line: A set of connected points continuing without end in both directions. **(303)**

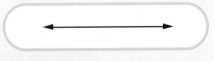

line graph: A graph used to show change over time with points connected by line segments. **(280)**

Plant Growth

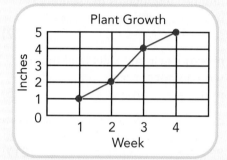

line of symmetry: A line that divides a figure into two congruent parts that are mirror images of each other. **(322)**

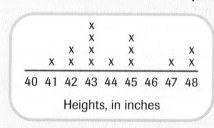

line of symmetry

line plot: A graph showing frequency of data on a number line. **(272)**

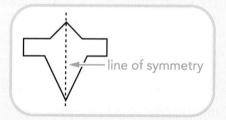

Heights, in inches

line segment: A part of a line with two endpoints. **(305)**

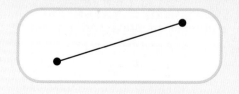

line symmetry: If a figure can be folded along a line so that the two halves match exactly, then the figure has line symmetry. *See line of symmetry* **(322)**

logic: The study of mathematical reasoning. **(396)**

longitude: Distance east or west of a reference circle which goes through Greenwich, England, and the North and South Poles. Measured in degrees from 0° at Greenwich to 180° east or 180° west. **(434)**

lowest terms: *See simplest form*

mass: The amount of matter in an object. Usually measured by comparing with an object of known mass. While gravity influences weight, it does not affect mass. **(358)**

mean: A number found by dividing the sum of two or more numbers by the number of addends. The mean is often referred to as the average. The mean of 6, 4, and 11 is 21 ÷ 3, or 7. **(285)**

measure: A comparison to some other known unit, or to find the measure of something. **(332)**

median: The middle number when numbers are arranged from least to greatest. The median of 3, 4, 7, 9, and 10 is 7. When the set has two middle numbers, the median is the mean of the two middle numbers. The median of 38, 44, 46, 49 is (44 + 46) ÷ 2, or 45. **(286)**

mental math: The process of computing an exact answer in your head. **(102)**

meter (m): The standard unit of length in the metric system. **(347)**

metric system: A system of measurement based on tens. The basic unit of length is the meter. The basic unit of mass is the gram. The basic unit of capacity is the liter. **(432)**

metric ton: A metric unit of mass equal to 1000 kilograms. **(359)**

millimeter (mm): A metric unit of length equal to 0.001 $(\frac{1}{1000})$ of a meter. **(347)**

million: One thousand thousands written as 1,000,000, or 10^6. *See thousand* **(8)**

minuend: In subtraction, the minuend is the number you subtract from. **(48)**

$$\begin{array}{rl} 56 & \leftarrow \text{minuend} \\ -30 & \leftarrow \text{subtrahend} \\ \hline 26 & \leftarrow \text{difference} \end{array}$$

minute (min): One sixtieth of an hour or 60 seconds. **(336)**

mirror image (reflection): The reverse image of a figure. *See flip* **(319)**

missing addend: In an addition sentence in which one addend is not given, the missing addend is the number that makes the sentence true. In $3 + \blacksquare = 7$, the missing addend is 4. **(47)**

missing factor: In a multiplication sentence in which one factor is not given, the missing factor is the number that makes the sentence true. In $5 \times \blacksquare = 45$, the missing factor is 9. **(77)**

mixed decimal: A decimal number with an integer part and a decimal part. 7.4 is a mixed decimal. **(25)**

mixed number: A number that has a whole number (not 0) and a fraction. $2\frac{1}{3}$ is a mixed number. **(217)**

mode: The number that appears most frequently in a set of numbers. There may be one, more than one, or no mode.
The set of numbers 2, 2, 2, 3, 3, and 5 has one mode, 2.
The set of numbers 10, 10, 15, 15, and 29 has two modes, 10 and 15.
The set of numbers 4, 18, 22, and 96 has no mode. **(288)**

month: One of the 12 divisions in a year. **(342)**

multiple: The product of a given whole number and any other whole number. 12 is a multiple of 3 (and of 4) because $4 \times 3 = 12$. **(90)**

multiplicand: In multiplication, the multiplicand is the factor being multiplied. **(62)**

$$\begin{array}{rl} 6 & \leftarrow \text{multiplicand} \\ \times 3 & \leftarrow \text{multiplier} \\ \hline 18 & \leftarrow \text{product} \end{array}$$

$$3 \times 6 = 18$$

multiplier   multiplicand   product

multiplication: The operation of repeated addition of the same number. 3×6 is the same as $6 + 6 + 6$. **(60)**

Multiplication Property of Equality: If both sides of an equation are multiplied by the same number, the equation will still be true. **(249)**

$$5 + 2 = 7$$
$$3\,(5 + 2) = 3 \times 7$$

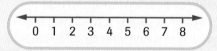

multiplication sentence: An equation which shows a product. $2 \times 46 = 92$ **(62)**

multiplier: In multiplication, the multiplier is the factor being multiplied by. **(62)**

$$\begin{array}{rl} 5 & \leftarrow \text{multiplicand} \\ \times 9 & \leftarrow \text{multiplier} \\ \hline 45 & \leftarrow \text{product} \end{array}$$

$$9 \times 5 = 45$$
multiplier multiplicand product

multiply ($\times$): *See multiplication*

Multiplying by 1 Property: If you multiply a number by 1, the product is the same as that number. $1 \times 3 = 3$ **(246)**

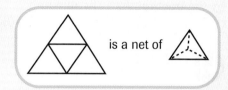

natural numbers: The counting numbers: 1, 2, 3, 4, 5, ...

negative numbers: Numbers less than zero. Negative numbers are to the left of zero on a number line. Some examples of negative numbers are $^-2$, $^-3\frac{1}{2}$, and $^-9.2$. **(238)**

net: A 2-dimensional shape that can be folded into a 3-dimensional figure. **(330)**

is a net of

nonagon: A polygon with nine sides. **(311)**

nonstandard units: Units other than customary or metric units used for measurement. A paper clip might be used as a nonstandard unit of length. **(345)**

numeral: A symbol used to represent a number. 4 is the numeral for four in our decimal system and IV is the Roman numeral for four.

number line: A diagram that represents numbers as points on a line. **(26)**

0 1 2 3 4 5 6 7 8

number sentence: An equation or inequality with numbers. $7 + 8 = 15$ or $6 + 2 > 5$ **(36)**

458

numerator: The number written above the line in a fraction. It tells how many equal parts are described by the fraction. In $\frac{5}{8}$, the numerator is 5. **(210)**

obtuse angle: An angle with a measure greater than 90° and less than 180°. **(308)**

98°   120°

obtuse triangle: A triangle with one obtuse angle. **(314)**

octagon: A polygon with eight sides. **(311)**

odd number: A whole number that ends in 1, 3, 5, 7, or 9. An odd number does *not* have 2 as a factor, so it is not divisible by 2. Some odd numbers are 3, 13, 57, and 99. **(91)**

open figure: A plane figure that does not completely enclose an area. **(310)**

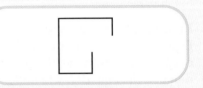

operation: Addition $(3 + 2 = 5)$, subtraction $(7 - 3 = 4)$, multiplication $(2 \times 8 = 16)$, division $(12 \div 3 = 4)$, and raising a number to a power $(3^2 = 9)$ are some mathematical operations. **(32)**

opposite of a number: A number that is the same distance from 0 on the number line as another number. $^-8$ is the opposite of $^+8$. **(238)**

opposite sides: Sides of a figure that are directly across from each other.

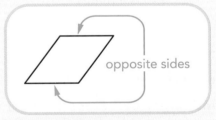

opposite sides

Order Property of Addition: Changing the order of the addends does not change the sum. $7 + 3 = 3 + 7$ **(240)**

Order Property of Multiplication: Changing the order of the factors does not change the product. $9 \times 4 = 4 \times 9$ **(241)**

ordered pair: A pair of numbers used to name a location on a grid. The first number tells the distance from the vertical axis. The second number tells the distance from the horizontal axis. (4, 3) is the ordered pair for point *A*. **(258)**

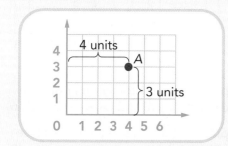

ordinal number: A number that tells you the position of people or things that are in order. First, second, third, and fourth are the first four ordinal numbers. **(16)**

origin: The intersection of the horizontal and vertical axes in a coordinate plane. It is described by the ordered pair (0, 0).

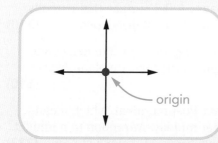

ounce (oz): A customary unit of weight equal to $\frac{1}{16}$ of a pound. **(358)**

outcome: One of the possible things that can happen in a probability experiment. **(293)**

overestimate (over es' ti mit): A number greater than an actual amount. **(132)**

overestimate (over es' ti mate): To find a number greater than an actual amount. **(132)**

P

parallel lines: Lines that are always the same distance apart. **(304)**

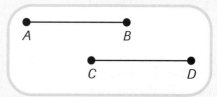

parallel segments: Line segments which lie on parallel lines. **(304)**

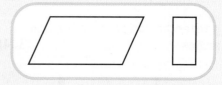

parallelogram: A quadrilateral with two pairs of parallel and congruent sides. **(312)**

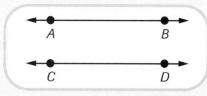

pentagon: A polygon that has five sides. **(311)**

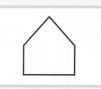

per: For each. The gasoline cost $1.25 per gallon. **(31)**

460

percent (%): Per hundred. If 20 out of 100 marbles are red, 20 percent (or 20%) of the marbles are red. **(31)**

perfect square: The product of an integer multiplied by itself. 16 is a perfect square because $4 \times 4 = 16$. **(99)**

perimeter (P): The distance around a figure. The perimeter of this figure is 5 inches. **(348)**

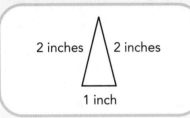

period: A group of three places used for the digits in large numbers. Periods are usually separated by commas. **(9)**

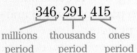

perpendicular(⊥): Forming right angles. **(304)**

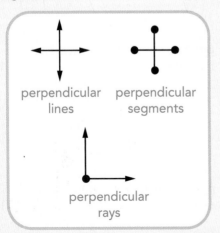

pictograph: A graph that uses pictures or symbols to show data. **(270)**

After School Activities	
Art	🚶 🚶 🚶 🚶
Soccer	🚶 🚶 🚶 🚶 🚶
Chess	🚶 🚶 🚶
Key: Each 🚶 stands for 5 students.	

pint (pt): A customary unit of capacity equal to 2 cups. **(356)**

place value: The value of the place of a digit in a number. **(2)**

place-value chart: A chart that shows the place value of each digit in a number. **(5)**

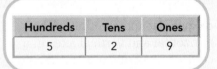

Hundreds	Tens	Ones
5	2	9

plane: A flat surface that extends infinitely in all directions. **(310)**

plane figure: Any 2-dimensional figure. Polygons are plane figures. **(310)**

P.M.: Post-meridian, which means after midday. Afternoon to midnight. 11:00 P.M. is 11 o'clock at night. **(337)**

point: An exact location in space represented by a dot. **(302)**

point symmetry: A figure that can be turned exactly 180° about a point and fit exactly on itself has point symmetry. A parallelogram has point symmetry.

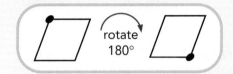

polygon: A closed plane figure made by line segments. **(311)**

polyhedron: A solid figure in which all the faces are polygons.

positive numbers: Numbers that are greater than zero. Positive numbers are to the right of zero on a number line. **(238)**

pound (lb): A customary unit of weight equal to 16 ounces. **(358)**

power: The number of times a number is repeated as a factor. 3 to the fourth power is 3^4, or $3 \times 3 \times 3 \times 3$. **(98)**

power of 10: A number with 10 as a base and a whole number exponent. 10^2 and 10^3 are powers of 10. **(98)**

prime factorization: A way to show a number as the product of prime factors. The prime factorization of 12 is $2 \times 2 \times 3$. **(96)**

prime meridian: An imaginary line around the earth that passes through Greenwich, England, and the North and South Poles dividing the globe into eastern and western sections. **(434)**

prime number: A whole number greater than 0 that has exactly two different factors, 1 and itself. 5 is a prime number because the only factors are 1 and 5. **(92)**

prism: A 3-dimensional figure that has two congruent and parallel faces that are polygons. The rest of the faces are parallelograms. **(328)**

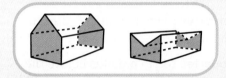

probability: The chance of an event happening. **(291)**

product: The result of multiplication. **(62)**

$$\begin{array}{r} 5 \\ \times 3 \\ \hline 15 \end{array} \begin{array}{l} \leftarrow \text{factor} \\ \leftarrow \text{factor} \\ \leftarrow \text{product} \end{array}$$

$$\nearrow \overset{3 \times 5 = 15}{\underset{\text{factor} \quad \text{factor} \quad \text{product}}{\uparrow \quad \nwarrow}}$$

proper fraction: A fraction less than 1. $\frac{2}{3}$ is a proper fraction. $\frac{3}{2}$ is not. (It is an improper fraction.)

property: A rule about numbers that is always true when you compute no matter which numbers you use. **(240)**

pyramid: A polyhedron whose base is a polygon and whose other faces are triangles that share a common vertex. **(327)**

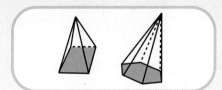

Q

quadrilateral: A four-sided polygon. (311)

quantity: An amount.

quart (qt): A customary unit of capacity equal to 2 pints. (356)

quarter hour: 15 minutes. (335)

quarter past: 15 minutes after the hour. Quarter past 2 is 2:15. (335)

quarter to: 15 minutes before the hour. Quarter to 4 is 3:45. (335)

quarter turn: One-fourth of a revolution. (319)

quotient: The result of division. (76)

R

radii: Plural of *radius*. (316)

radius (r): A line segment from the center of a circle to any point on the circle. (316)

ragged: Not lined up evenly. When decimal points of numbers are lined up vertically, the right side of the numbers may look uneven. (158)

3.250
11.4
0.65

range: The difference between the greatest number and the least number in a set of numbers. The range of the numbers 5, 9, 8, 2, and 6 is 7 (9 − 2). (290)

ray: A part of a line that has one endpoint and goes on forever in one direction. (305)

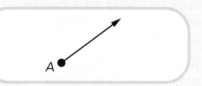

rectangle: A quadrilateral with two pairs of congruent, parallel sides and four right angles. (313)

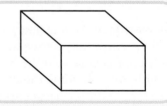

rectangular prism: A prism with six rectangular faces. (426)

reflection: *See flip*

reflex angle: An angle that measures more than 180°. Angle *J* is a reflex angle.

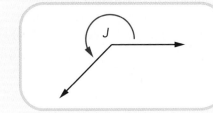

region: A part of a plane.

regroup: Use place value to think of a number in a different way to make arithmetic easier. You can think of

$$
\begin{array}{r}
31 \\
-15 \\
\hline
16
\end{array}
\quad \text{as} \quad
\begin{array}{r}
20 + 11 \\
-(10 + 5) \\
\hline
10 + 6
\end{array}
$$

In both cases, the difference is 16.

(148)

regular polygon: A polygon with all sides the same length and all angles the same measure. **(311)**

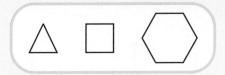

remainder: In whole number division, when you have divided as far as you can without using decimals, what has not been divided yet is called the remainder. In the following example, the remainder is 2. **(75)**

rename: *See regroup*

revolution: One turn of 360° about a point. **(319)**

rhombi: Plural of *rhombus*. **(313)**

rhombus: A parallelogram with all four sides equal in length. **(313)**

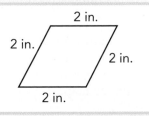

right angle (∟): An angle that measures exactly 90°. **(308)**

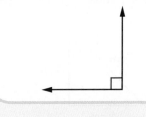

right triangle: A triangle that has one 90° angle. **(314)**

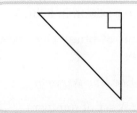

Roman numerals: The symbols used in the ancient Roman number system. Some examples of Roman numerals are I (1), V (5), and X (10). **(439)**

rotation: *See turn*

round a whole number: To find the nearest ten, hundred, thousand (and so on.) 39 rounds up to 40; 33 rounds down to 30. **(128)**

scale: An instrument used for weighing. **(425)**

scale (on a map): A statement or diagram that tells the actual distance represented by a distance on the map. **(436)**

scale (on a graph): The numbers along the axes of a graph. **(275)**

scalene triangle: A triangle that has no congruent sides. **(315)**

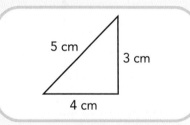

second (ordinal number): The number two position in a line. **(16)**

second (unit of time): One sixtieth of a minute. **(337)**

segment: *See line segment*

sequence: A set of numbers arranged in a special order or pattern.

set: A group of numbers or other things.

short division: A method for dividing by a 1-digit number in which only the quotients and the remainders are written down. The example below shows how to divide 741 by 3 using short division. **(204)**

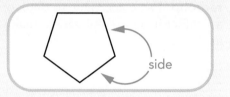

side of a polygon: Any of the line segments that form a polygon. **(311)**

signed number: Positive or negative number. ⁺4 and ⁻6 are signed numbers. **(238)**

similar figures: Figures that have the same shape, but not necessarily the same size. **(320)**

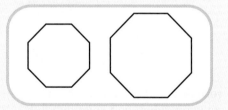

simplest form: A fraction whose numerator and denominator have no common factors other than 1. The simplest form of $\frac{10}{25}$ is $\frac{2}{5}$. **(221)**

simplify a fraction: To divide the numerator and denominator of a fraction by a common factor. Simplifying a fraction decreases both the numerator and the denominator, but the value of the fraction stays the same. *See also simplest form* **(221)**

slide: A transformation that slides a figure a given distance in a given direction. A slide is also called a translation. **(318)**

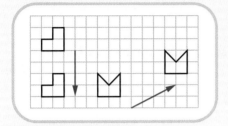

solid: *See solid figure*

solid figure: A figure with three-dimensions. *See dimension* **(326)**

solution of an equation: The number or numbers that can be substituted for a variable to make an equation true. The solution of $x + 6 = 8$ is $x = 2$. **(256)**

solution of a problem: The answer to a problem, sometimes including the method used to solve it. **(367)**

space figure: *See solid figure*

sphere: A solid figure made up of points that are all the same distance from a point called the center. **(329)**

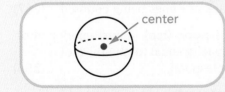

square: A parallelogram with four congruent sides and four right angles. **(313)**

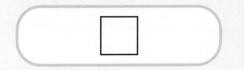

square corner: A corner that forms a right angle. **(308)**

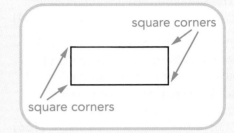

square number: A number that is the result of multiplying an integer by itself. Any square number of dots can be arranged in a square array. *See perfect square* **(99)**

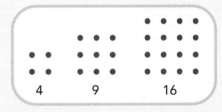

square pyramid: A pyramid with a square base. **(331)**

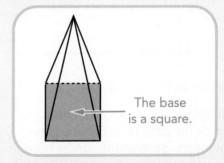

square root ($\sqrt{}$): The number that when multiplied by itself results in a given number. The square root of 36 is 6 ($\sqrt{36} = 6$) because $6 \times 6 = 36$.

square unit: A unit, such as a square centimeter or square inch, used to measure area. **(350)**

standard form: A number written with one digit for each place value. The standard form for the number two hundred six is 206. **(4)**

statistics: The mathematics used when collecting, organizing, and studying data, or the numbers used to describe a set of data. Mean, mode, and range are examples of statistics. **(266)**

stem-and-leaf plot: A graph used to organize data by grouping the values of their digits. **(278)**

Ages of Garden
Club Members

```
3 | 0 0 1 5 6
4 | 1 2 2 8 6
5 |
6 | 2 3 9 9    Key:
7 | 0 2        3|0 represents 30
```

straight angle: An angle with a measure of 180°. **(308)**

subtract (−): *See subtraction*

subtraction: An operation that gives the difference between two numbers. Subtraction can be used to compare two numbers, or to find out how much is left after some is taken away. **(46)**

subtraction sentence: An equation which shows a difference.
$64 - 23 = 41$ **(48)**

subtrahend: In subtraction, the subtrahend is the number you subtract. **(48)**

$$
\begin{array}{rl}
53 & \leftarrow \text{minuend} \\
-22 & \leftarrow \text{subtrahend} \\
\hline
31 & \leftarrow \text{difference}
\end{array}
$$

sum: Total. The result of addition. **(36)**

$$16 + 14 = 30$$
addend   addend   sum

survey: The process of asking a group of people the same question. **(266)**

symmetry: *See line, point, and turn symmetry*

T

table: An organized way to list data. Tables usually have rows and columns of data. **(268)**

tablespoon (tbsp): A customary unit of capacity equal to $\frac{1}{2}$ of a fluid ounce, or $\frac{1}{16}$ of a cup, or 3 teaspoons. **(356)**

tally marks: Marks made to keep track of things being counted. **(267)**

teaspoon (tsp): A customary unit of capacity equal to one-third of a tablespoon. **(356)**

temperature: A measure of hotness or coldness. **(360)**

tessellation: A covering of a plane without overlaps or gaps using combinations of congruent figures. **(324)**

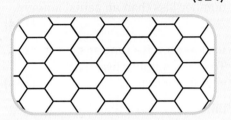

thousand: Ten hundreds written as 1000, or 10^3. **(6)**

three-dimensional: Having length, width, and height. Having volume. You are three-dimensional. Your shadow is two-dimensional. **(326)**

three quarters of an hour: 45 minutes. **(335)**

time line: A number line with points that show years or dates. **(344)**

time zones: A region on the earth ($\frac{1}{24}$ of the way around) where clock time is the same throughout. The clock time in one time zone is one hour earlier than the zone immediately to the east. **(340)**

ton (t): A customary unit of weight equal to 2000 pounds. **(358)**

transformation: A rule for moving every point in a plane figure to a new location. Slides, flips, and turns are transformations. **(318)**

translation: *See slide*

trapezoid: A quadrilateral with one pair of parallel sides and one pair of sides that are not parallel. **(312)**

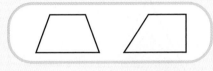

triangle: A polygon with three sides and three angles. **(311)**

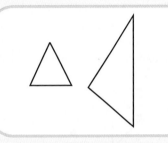

triangular numbers: The numbers 1, 3, 6, 10, ... They are called triangular numbers because they can represent the number of dots used in making the pattern below.

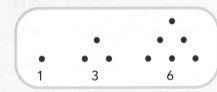

triangular prism: A prism with triangular bases. **(330)**

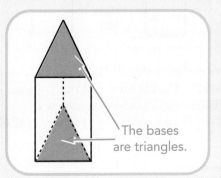

The bases are triangles.

triangular pyramid: A pyramid with a triangular base. **(331)**

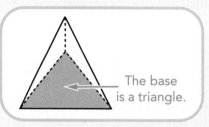

The base is a triangle.

turn: The transformation that occurs when a figure is turned a certain angle and direction around a point. A turn is also called a rotation. **(319)**

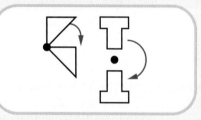

turn center: The point around which a figure is turned or rotated. **(319)**

turn symmetry: A figure that can be turned less than 360° about a point and fit exactly on itself has turn (or rotational) symmetry. A square has turn symmetry. **(323)**

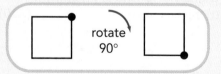

rotate 90°

two-dimensional: Having length and width. Having area, but not volume. The image on a movie screen is two-dimensional. **(326)**

 U

underestimate (under es' ti mit): A number less than an actual amount. **(134)**

underestimate (under es' ti mate): To find a number less than an actual amount. **(134)**

unit: A precisely fixed quantity used for measure.

unit fraction: A fraction that has 1 as its numerator. $\frac{1}{2}$, $\frac{1}{3}$, and $\frac{1}{4}$ are all unit fractions. **(226)**

unlike fractions: Fractions with different denominators. $\frac{2}{5}$ and $\frac{2}{6}$ are unlike fractions.

unlikely event: An event with a probability that is close to zero. If you spin this spinner, landing on blue is an unlikely event. **(292)**

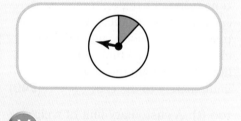

V

variable: A symbol that can be replaced by a number in an expression, equation, or formula. Variables are often letters of the alphabet. In $y + 3$, the variable is y. **(250)**

Venn diagram: A drawing that shows in which categories numbers or objects in a set belong. (269)

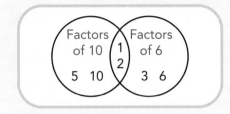

vertex of an angle: The point at which two line segments, lines, or rays meet to form an angle. (306)

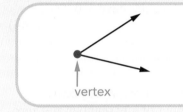

vertex of a polyhedron: A point on a polyhedron where three or more faces intersect. (327)

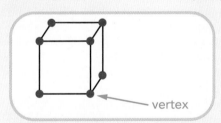

vertex of a cone: The point at the tip of a cone. (327)

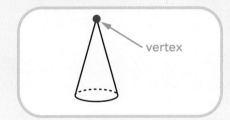

vertical: At right angles to the horizon. A vertical line is straight up and down. (303)

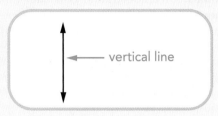

vertical axis: In a coordinate grid, the y-axis is the vertical axis. (274)

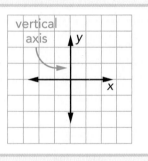

vertices: Plural of *vertex*. (306)

volume (V): The number of cubic units of space a solid figure takes up. (354)

W

weight: A measure of how heavy an object is. (358)

whole number: Any of the numbers 0, 1, 2, 3, 4, 5, and so on. (2)

width (w): One dimension of a 2- or 3-dimensional figure. (262)

x-axis: On a coordinate grid, the horizontal axis.

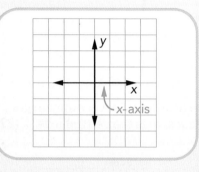

x-coordinate: In an ordered pair, the value that is written first. It tells the distance of a point from the *y*-axis. In (4, 1), 4 is the *x*-coordinate. **(258)**

y-axis: On a coordinate grid, the vertical axis.

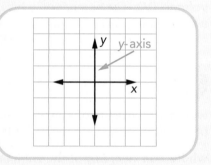

y-coordinate: In an ordered pair, the value that is written second. It tells the distance of a point from the *x*-axis. In (4, 1), 1 is the *y*-coordinate. **(258)**

yard (yd): A customary unit of length equal to 3 feet. **(346)**

year: The amount of time it takes for the earth to make one complete revolution around the sun, 365.25 days. Since it is more convenient to have a whole number of days each year, each year has 365 days except leap years which have 366. *See leap year* **(344)**

Z

Zero Property of Multiplication: The product of any number and zero is zero. $8 \times 0 = 0$ **(247)**

Glossary of Mathematical Symbols

Symbol	Meaning	Example
+	plus (addition)	$8 + 6 = 14$
+	positive	$^{+}2$: the number 2 units to the right of zero on a number line
−	minus (subtraction)	$12 − 5 = 7$
−	negative	$^{-}3$: the number 3 units to the left of zero on a number line
×	multiplied by, or times	$3 × 6 = 18$
÷ or ⟌	divided by	$12 ÷ 4 = 3 \quad 4\overline{)12}^{\,3}$
=	is equal to	$4 + 3 = 7$
≠	is not equal to	$6 − 2 ≠ 5$
≅	is congruent to	Rectangle $ABCD \cong$ Rectangle $WXYZ$
~	is similar to	$\triangle JKL \sim \triangle QRS$
≈	is approximately equal to	$78 − 24 ≈ 80 − 25$
<	is less than	$8 + 1 < 10$
≤	is less than or equal to	$5 ≤ 5$

Symbol	Meaning	Example
$>$	is greater than	$9 > 7$
$\geq$	is greater than or equal to	$4 \geq 2$
$(\ )$	parentheses: used as grouping symbols	$(2 + 7) - (6 - 3) =$ $9 - 3 = 6$
$\%$	percent	30%: 30 percent
¢	cents	41¢: 41 cents
$	dollars	$2.70: 2 dollars and 70 cents
°	degree	90° is the total number of degrees in a right angle.
°F	degrees Fahrenheit	82°F
°C	degrees Celsius, or Centigrade	25 °C
'	foot (or feet)	6': 6 feet
"	inch (or inches)	4": 4 inches
$\sqrt{\ }$	square root	$\sqrt{25} = 5$
$\angle$	angle	$\angle A$
$\triangle$	triangle	$\triangle JKL$

Symbol	Meaning	Example
$\overleftrightarrow{ST}$	line ST	S ———— T
$\overline{XY}$	line segment XY	X ———— Y
$\overrightarrow{AB}$	ray AB	A ———— B
$\overset{\frown}{CD}$	arc CD	D C
⌐	right angle	$\angle ABC$ is a right angle. A B C
$\perp$	is perpendicular to	$\overleftrightarrow{AB} \perp \overleftrightarrow{CD}$ A C D B
$\parallel$	is parallel to	$\overleftrightarrow{MN} \parallel \overleftrightarrow{OP}$ M N O P

Index

482

Illustration Credits

Estelle Carol: pp. 3, 9–10, 12–13, 15, 17–18, 19–21, 23, 25, 29, 38–40, 42, 54–55, 57, 64, 66, 71, 83, 86, 88, 92–93, 102–103, 114, 119, 123, 133, 137, 141, 147, 150, 165, 171, 179, 196–197, 211–212, 217, 226, 232, 238, 245, 247–249, 252, 258–259, 262–263, 268, 276, 278, 284, 288–289, 292–298, 302–305, 307–309, 323–324, 328–331, 334, 337, 346–347, 351, 356–357, 359, 372–374, 378, 384, 387, 392–393, 407, 412, 421, 436

Scott Ritchie: pp. 6, 7, 8, 12, 16, 20–21, 24–25, 28, 31, 34–35, 38, 41–42, 46–49, 59–61, 69, 72–78, 80, 85, 87, 106, 108, 111, 114, 116, 124–125, 128, 138–139, 141, 143, 146, 152, 159, 165, 168, 172, 174, 178, 180, 184–185, 190, 194–195, 199, 204, 206, 210–211, 213–214, 216, 225, 227–228, 239, 242, 246, 250, 254, 260, 266–267, 270, 278, 282, 284, 287, 290–291, 297, 299, 306, 310–311, 314–321, 326, 343, 345, 348–349, 352, 356–361, 366–367, 370, 376, 380, 382, 386, 389–390, 392, 394–396, 398–400, 405–406, 408, 411, 422–425, 437

Joe Spooner: pp. 1, 33, 101, 145, 209, 237, 265, 301, 333, 365

Map Art/Joe Lemonnier: pp. 434–435

Robot Characters: Terry Taylor

Technical Art: Nesbitt Graphics Inc.

Cover Design and Illustration: Bill SMITH STUDIO